THE SMALL BUSINESS GUIDE

THE Small Business GUIDE

SOURCES OF INFORMATION FOR NEW AND SMALL BUSINESSES

COLIN BARROW

BRITISH BROADCASTING CORPORATION

First published in conjunction with
the BBC Television series *Business Club*

The series is produced by John Twitchin

The illustration on the front cover of
the book is by Stuart Hughes

The author would like to thank the following people and
organisations for their help in compiling and checking material in
this guide:

Lucinda Dean, David Hibbs, Rosemarie McLavy, Thames
Polytechnic, The Thames Enterprise Agency Limited, Shell UK PLC
and the London Borough of Greenwich;

Chris Miller of Birmingham University for the use of her Local
Authority survey;

Peter Saunders of Thames Polytechnic for his bookkeeping survey;

Philip Beresford of *The Sunday Telegraph* for use of his Enterprise
Zone table;

The National Westminster Bank PLC for permission to reproduce
their business checklist.

This book is set in Century
by Input Typesetting Limited, London
Printed and bound in England by
Pitman Press Limited, Bath

CONTENTS

5

SECTION 8 Training for business   226

SECTION 9 Glossary of key business terms   244

SECTION 10 Gazeteer   250

Geographic listing of key local organisations referred to in the text.

Great care has been taken in the compilation of information given in this book. All prices were correct at the time of going to press. However, the author and publisher cannot be held responsible for any inaccuracies.

We recommend that before taking any action, appropriate professional advice is sought.

THE NEED FOR INFORMATION

To launch successfully a small business or expand an existing one is not a simple task. Good ideas, hard work, enthusiasm, skills and knowledge about your product, and how to make it, though essential, are not enough. Evidence for this is the ever-increasing volume of business failures and liquidations: in 1982 firms have been folding at the rate of three hundred per week, the highest figure on record. Nearly half of those failures are small businesses. In fact, 70 per cent of new businesses do not last even one year. These facts have made it increasingly clear that small businesses need special help, particularly in their formative period. For example, owners and managers often need help in acquiring business skills in such areas as basic bookkeeping and accounting. Most failing businesses simply do not know their financial position. The order book is very often full when the cash runs out.

Then they need information with which to make realistic assessments of the size and possibilities of their chosen market. Over-optimism about the size and ease with which a market can be reached is an all too common mistake.

Owners and managers also need to know what sorts of finance are available and how to put themselves in the best possible position to raise it. Surprisingly, there is no shortage of funds. Problems lie, rather, in the business proposition itself or, more often, in the way in which the proposition is made to the financier. This calls for a 'business plan', a statement of business purpose, with the consequences spelt out in financial terms. For example, you must describe what you want your business to do, who its customers will be, how much they will spend, who will supply you, how much their supplies will cost. Then you must translate those plans and projections into cash: how much your business will need; how much you already have; how much you expect 'outsiders' to put in. For most people this calls for new knowledge. They have never prepared a business plan before, and they do not know how to start. Very often the same is true of the bank manager they are talking to, so they too may need help or education in this important area.

This plan will also help them to escape the 'pneumonia' of small businesses – underestimation of the amount of start-up capital they will need. It is difficult, if not impossible, to go back to a bank and ask for another 30 per cent of funding six months after opening the doors, and retain any credibility at all. And yet this is what happens. New businesses consistently underestimate their capital requirements. Small businesses consistently underestimate how much they will need to finance growth. Both end up struggling where they need not have struggled, or failing where there was no 'market' reason for failure. Inventors and technologists have special problems of communication and security when they try to translate their ideas into businesses. All too often their inventions have been left for other countries to exploit, or else they feel unhappy about discussing the ideas, believing that a patent is their only protection. But more often than not they simply do not know who to talk to, little realising that sophisticated help is often close at hand. Thus a path from the laboratory to the market-place has to be illuminated so that small firms and inventors can see a clear route.

New technologies have to be made available to new business. The microcomputer that has revolutionised big business has now begun to knock on the doors of smaller businesses. For this reason these firms have to know how to exploit this technology and so remain competitive – or they may join the ranks of the failures.

New and revived business opportunities are springing up to meet the needs and aspirations of would-be 'entrepreneurs'. Franchising, workers' co-operatives and management buy-outs are just three such areas. These have grown from relative obscurity in the late 1970s to being major business opportunities in the 1980s. Grants and incentives to start up in rural areas, or in declining city areas are also a new feature of the small business scene.

There is inevitably a spate of paperwork, red tape and legislation surrounding every business venture. The registration for VAT, pensions for the self-employed and employees' rights very often deter people either from launching into business or expanding in it. They believe, incorrectly, that it is possible to stand still and survive. They also overestimate the problems and underestimate the skills of the army of inexpensive professional advisers on hand to educate the novice.

All this implies that in order to keep out of the failure statistics it is vital for the owner or manager of a new or small business to be *better informed*.

There are now hundreds of organisations and even more publications that can provide the much-needed information for small business. Many of these organisations have only recently come into being. Indeed, 1980–1982 saw the birth of the great majority of the specialist small-business advisory services. So 'entrepreneurs' have plenty of help to turn to. They very often do not know where that help is, or just how much it can do for them. This book is a guide to these organisations and their services, and the important directories, books and periodicals that will provide up-to-date information on each main topic. Enough information is generally included to allow a choice of service or organisation, or of publications to find and read.

The decision to include or exclude an entry is based on two criteria. Does the organisation (or directory) provide either a service or information of specific help to a new or small business? Would the entry simply extend the reader's choice without necessarily extending the possible reward?

This is a reference book and is not intended to be read in its entirety. The reader will need to use the contents pages to focus attention on the areas of greatest interest (or importance) to him or her. Time spent in planning and preparation is rarely wasted. Unfortunately, there is much evidence that suggests that many new and small businesses do little of either.

SOURCES OF DIRECT HELP AND ADVICE

There are now some two hundred organisations specifically concerned with providing help, advice and resources (including finance) for small businesses and those starting them. For the most part, these services are provided free or at a very low cost. In order to give a better understanding of their nature and purpose it will help to look at them in six groups: National Agencies, Local Enterprise Agencies, Local Councils, Property Services, Enterprise Zones and Independent Business Associations.

NATIONAL AGENCIES

Although all the agencies and advisory services have their roots in the local community, the direct initiative for starting them often came from a central body. Five such bodies are in the forefront of these initiatives:

Small Firms Service This service is provided by the Department of Industry and operates through a nationwide network of Small Firms Centres. It provides information and counselling services to help owners and managers of small businesses with their plans and problems. It also helps those thinking of starting up, and there is no limit to the sorts of business the service will help. The range of advice available is wide, covering such fields as finance, training, marketing, exporting, diversification and new technology.

The service can also put you in contact with the right people in government departments, local authorities, chambers of commerce, the professions or any other body that can play a part in solving your problems. It can also find national and international sources of information. The centres are manned by experienced businessmen who can probably answer your questions on the spot or tell you who to speak to.

If your problem cannot be settled on the telephone you will be invited to meet your local counsellor. There are some fifty Area Counselling Offices around the country, so you will not have to travel far. Each centre is backed by the full resource of the Department of Industry, whose aim is to help you get the right answers. In the end, however, the decisions you make on the basis of advice given are your responsibility and yours alone, so you must also consult your own professional advisers before acting on that advice.

To contact your nearest Small Firms Centre dial 100 and ask the operator for the national Freephone number 2444, or you can make contact direct. They provide a range of free leaflets both on their services and on various aspects of running a business.

Small Firms Centres

Birmingham: Small Firms Centre, 6th Floor, Ladywood House, Stephenson Street, Birmingham B2 4DT. (021 643 3344) Contact: Mr J. Colclough

Bristol: Small Firms Centre, 5th Floor The Pithay, Bristol BS1 2NB. (0272 294546) Contact: Mr A. S. W. Corbridge

Cambridge: Small Firms Centre, 24 Brooklands Avenue, Cambridge CB2 2BU. (0223 63312) Contact: R. Fenley

Cardiff: Small Firms Centre, 16 St David's House, Wood Street, Cardiff CF1 1ER. (022 396116) Contact: Mr D. Pendlebury

Glasgow: Small Firms Centre, 57 Bothwell Street, Glasgow G2 6TU. (041 248 6014) Contact: Mr L. Baston

Leeds: Small Firms Centre, 1 Park Row, City Square, Leeds LS1 5NR. (0532 445151) Contact: Mr R. Mawhinney

Liverpool: Small Firms Centre, 1 Old Hall Street, Liverpool L3 9HJ. (051 236 5756) Contact: Mr A. Monk

London: Small Firms Centre, 8–10 Bulstrode Street, London W1M 5DQ. (01 487 4342) Contact: Mr N. J. Turner

Manchester: Small Firms Centre, 3rd Floor, 320–325 Royal Exchange Buildings, St Ann's Square, Manchester M2 7AH. (061 832 5282) Contact: R. Curry

Newcastle: Small Firms Centre, 22 Newgate Shopping Centre, Newcastle upon Tyne NE1 1ZP. (0632 325353) Contact: Mr C. J. Mather

Nottingham: Small Firms Centre, 48–50 Maid Marion Way, Nottingham NG1 6GF. (0602 49791) Contact: J. T. Gibbon

Wales The Welsh Development Agency (Small Business Section), Treforest Industrial Estate, Pontypridd, Mid Glamorgan CF37 5UT. (044 385 2666) Contact: John Collins

Scotland, The Scottish Development Agency (Small Business Division), 102 Telford Road, Edinburgh EN4 2NP. (031 343 1911/6) Contact: Campbell-Russell

Northern Ireland, The Local Enterprise Development Unit, Lamont House, Purdys Lane, Mewtownbreda, Belfast BT8 4AR. (0232 691031) Contact: K Gilbert and G Briggs

Council for small industries in rural areas (CoSIRA) is the main agent of the Development Commission, whose aim is to encourage small rural business in England.* They define rural areas as anywhere with a central population under 10,000. Most small manufacturing and service businesses employing fewer than twenty people

* Services in Scotland, Wales and Northern Ireland, are located at Small Firms centres, listed above.

13

are eligible to use CoSIRA's services, as are small tourism businesses that provide overnight accommodation, but in certain areas only. There are a few limitations and exceptions. Agriculture, horticulture and the professions are not eligible, but retail businesses such as village shops, post offices and so on can use the advisory service but are not eligible for financial aid.

CoSIRA concentrates on providing consultancy advice, training and finance.

Consultancy advice is co-ordinated by local Small Industries organisers. It covers the areas common to all businesses such as finance, accountancy and marketing, and it extends to specialist areas such as engineering, woodworking and plastics.

Training courses are provided in a wide range of skills either locally or in CoSIRA's own workshops. They cater for everyone from experienced craftsmen to the absolute beginner.

Finance and funding propositions can be drawn up for presentation to the banks, ICFC (Industrial & Commercial Finance Corporation) or another lender. CoSIRA has some funds of its own. These are used in certain cases to 'top up' the money needed to get a new business started or to help a business through the first year or two of its life. This money will be provided in the form of a loan over a maximum of twenty years for buildings; and five years for plant and equipment. Loans can range from a minimum of £250 to a maximum of £50,000.

No charge is made for a preliminary discussion with an organiser. A modest charge is usually made if further advisory services are called in.

To make contact with CoSIRA, select your nearest organiser from the list below. If there is no one near you, or you simply want more information on CoSIRA services, contact the head office in Wiltshire.

CoSIRA Organisations
Avon *See* Gloucester & North Avon.
Beds & Herts CoSIRA, Agriculture House, 55 Goldington Road, Bedford
    MK40 3LU. (0234 61381) Contact: E. D. Dunning
Berks *See* Oxon.
Bucks *see* Oxon.
Cambs CoSIRA, 24 Brooklands Avenue, Cambridge CB2 2BU. (0223
    354505) Contact: R. B. L. Dunn
Cheshire Shropshire and Staffs CoSIRA, Strickland House, The Lawns,
    Park Street, Wellington, Telford, Shropshire TF1 3BX. (0952 47161/2/3)
    Contacts: J. C. Stannert, J. Edwards, R. H. Adams
Cleveland *See* Durham.
Cornwall CoSIRA, 2nd Floor, Highshore House, New Bridge Street, Truro,
    Cornwall TR1 1AA. (0872 3531 or 3281) Contacts: M. A. Jennings, P. M.
    Wharton, A. Waldron
Cumbria CoSIRA, Ullswater Road, Penrith, CA11 7EH. (0768 65752) Contacts: R. J. D. Dodgson, D. Heritage, Miss E. C. Habron

Derby CoSIRA, 43 Kedleston Road, Derby DE3 1FP. (0332 42909) Contact: R. Hollingsworth

Devon CoSIRA, Matford Lane, Exeter EX2 4PS. (0392 52616) Contacts: D. J. Rees, R. A. Hatt

Dorset CoSIRA, Room 12/13, Wing D, Government Buildings, Prince of Wales Road, Dorchester Dorset. (0305 68558) Contact: J. S. Hamriding

Durham, Cleveland, Tyne & Wear CoSIRA, Morton Road, Darlington, Co. Durham DL1 4PT. (0325 487123/4/5) Contacts: R. P. Smith, R. L. Kevern

Essex CoSIRA, Bees Small Business Centre, Hay Lane, Braintree, Essex CM7 6ST. (0376 47623) Contact: P. Williams

Gloucester & North Avon CoSIRA, 24 Belle Vue Terrace, Malvern, Worcs. WR14 4PZ. (06845 64506) Contact: G. D. Thomas

Hants & Isle of Wight CoSIRA, Northgate Place, Staple Gardens, Winchester SO23 8SR. (0962 4747) Contacts: J. G. Fraser, A. S. Finch

Hereford & Worcester CoSIRA, 24 Belle Vue Terrace, Malvern, Worcs WR14 4PZ. (06845 64506) Contacts: A. H. Fraser, R. S. Hesbrook

Herts *See* Beds.

Humberside CoSIRA, 14 Market Place, Howden, Goole, N. Humberside DN14 7RT. (0430 31138) Contacts: M. G. Oliver, R. E. Jones

Isle of Wight *See* Hants or part time office, Isle of Wight CoSIRA, 6–7 Town Lane, Newport, Isle of Wight. (0983 528019)

Kent CoSIRA, Gresham Chambers, 40 High Street, Maidstone ME14 1JH. (0622 65222) Contact: P. Graham

Lancs CoSIRA, 15 Victoria Road, Fulwood, Preston PR2 4PS. (0772 717461) Contact: H. Shaw

Leics CoSIRA, Box 6, East Street, Bingham, Notts NG13 8DS. (0949 39222/3) Contacts: W. A. Dale, M. P. Bell, N. Timm

Lincs CoSIRA, Council Offices, Eastgate, Sleaford, Lincs (0529 303241) Contacts: N. Hutton-Jamieson, J. Taylor

Norfolk CoSIRA, Augustine Steward House, 14 Tombland, Norwich NR3 1HF. (0603 24498) Contacts: G. G. Morgan, G. B. Giles

Northants CoSIRA, Hunsbury Hill Farm, Hunsbury Hill Road, Northampton NN4 9QX. (0604 65874) Contact: M. J. Morris

Northumberland CoSIRA, Sanderson House, Bridge Street, Morpeth, Northumberland NE61 1NT. (0670 58807) Contacts: J. Buxton, R. Kerben

Notts CoSIRA, Box 6, East Street, Bingham, NG13 8DS. (0949 39222/3) Contact: P. J. Thomas

Oxon, Berks & Bucks CoSIRA, The Maltings, St Johns Road, Wallingford, Oxon. (0491 35523) Contacts: G. H. N. Clissold, J. B. C. Balkwill

Shropshire *See* Cheshire.

Somerset & South Avon CoSIRA, 1 The Crescent, Taunton TA1 4EA. (0823 76905) Contacts: G. P. Ginno, D. R. Patten

Staffs *See* Cheshire.

Suffolk CoSIRA, 28A High Street, Hadley, Ipswich, Suffolk

Surrey CoSIRA, 2 Jenner Road, Guildford GU1 3PN. (0483 38385) Contact: G. F. Carter

Sussex CoSIRA, Sussex House, 212 High Street, Lewes BN7 2NH. (07916 3422) Contact: M. Harding

15

Tyne & Wear *see* Durham.
Warwicks CoSIRA, The Abbotsford, 10 Market Place, Warwick CV4 4SL.
(0926 499593) Contact: J. Harbidge
*Wilts CoSIRA, 141 Castle Street, Salisbury SP1 3TP. (0722 6255) Contact: P.
Curbishley
North Yorkshire CoSIRA, The Lodge, 21 Front Street, Acomb, York YO2
3BW. (0904 793228) Contacts: J. C. McKinney, T. Hope, W. H. Silcock
West and South Yorks CoSIRA, Council Offices, York Street, Barnsley,
South Yorks S70 1BD. (0226 86141, ext. 481 or 484) Contact: K. G. Dutton, B. Lister

---

Action Resource Centre (ARC) This was set up in 1973 by a group
of businessmen to research and demonstrate how business skills
could best be used for the community. Since 1976 ARC has concentrated on helping to create employment opportunities, using people
seconded from industry and business to work on selected projects.
Each ARC project is chosen with specific local needs and conditions
in mind. For example, in the London Borough of Islington they run
a Small Business Counselling Service; in Dundee, their company,
Goodwill Enterprise Ltd, takes in old furniture, refurbishes it and
sells it to the public, thus creating work for more than thirty people;
in Nottingham, ARC has introduced a financial advisory service for
community organisations in the area. With financial and other support for several hundred major companies, and with 100 professional
business advisers seconded from those companies working on projects up and down the country, their local impact is significant.

To find out what ARC is doing near you, contact your nearest
regional manager.

Action Resource Centre regional managers
Greater London, Henrietta House, 9 Henrietta Place, London W1M 9AG.
(01 629 3826) Contacts: Cecilia Allen
Islington, 201/202 Upper Street, Islington, London N1. (01 359 3924) Contacts: Norman Humphrey, Dorothy Pearce
Leics, The Business Advice Centre, 30 New Walk, Leicester LE1 6TF.
(0533 554464) Contacts: Ian Sothcott, Rachel Phipps
Merseyside – Liverpool Craft Centre, 20–22 Matthew Street, Liverpool
L2 6RT. (051 236 2046) Contact: Noreen Taylor
Notts, 13/15 Bridlesmith Gate, Nottingham NG1 2GR. (0602 51822/599741)
Contacts: John Pike, Anne Pollard
South Wales, c/o ICI Fibres, Pontypool, Gwent NP4 8YD (04955 2420, ext.
319)
South Yorks, c/o Sheffield City Poly, Dyson House, Pond Street, Sheffield
S1 1WB. (0742 750036, direct line 0742 738261, ext 74) Contact: John J.
Patton
Tyne & Wear, 28 Exchange Buildings, Quayside, Newcastle upon Tyne,
NE99 2AN. (0632 614073) Contacts: Kieran Hosty, Ann Moss

*Also address of Headquarters

West Midlands, 118/120 Clifton Road, Birmingham B12 8SH. (021 449 5614/ 3705) Contacts: Geraint Prichard-Jones, Pearlita Sheckleford
West Yorks, c/o ICI Fibres, Hookstone Road, Harrogate HG2 8QN. (0423 68021, ext. 1295) Contact: Michael Kelly
Northern Regions
Management co-ordinator, Charles Hossell, ICI Hyde Products Ltd PO Box No 15, Newton Works, Hyde, Cheshire SK1 44EJ (061 368 400)
Consultant, Ruth I. Johns, 4 Castle Close, Warwick CV34 4DB. (0926 499497)
Scottish Action Resource Centre
Director, Frank Bishop, 54 Shandwick Place, Edinburgh EH2 4RT. (031 226 3669)
Clydeside, 4 Blythswood Square, Glasgow G2 4AB. (041 226 3639) Contact: Andy Cleland

---

BSC (Industry) Ltd British Steel, through this subsidiary set up expressly for the purpose, is embarking on a process of industrial regeneration. They concentrate on steel closure areas (Cardiff, Clyde valley, Corby, Deeside, Derwentside, Garnock valley, Hartlepool, Newport, Port Talbot, Scunthorpe and Teesside), and their objective is to put back sound jobs in those areas where the British Steel Corporation carried out substantial closures.

To date, activity has centred on providing small industrial workshops and offices. These range in size from a few hundred to a few thousand square feet, and are priced at about £2 per square feet. Perhaps the most important part of their package of help is their consultancy service. From examining the market viability of any business proposition, their team of consultants can work right through to preparing a detailed business plan. They have access to special EEC funds and detailed knowledge of UK grants and assistance, and can put together a most attractive financial package for the would-be entrepreneur. This help is available to anyone thinking of setting up in one of the designated areas. To date they have provided such help to over 1,000 businesses.

At present BSC Industry, although working closely with the local community, is an independent company responding to its own initiatives. Over the next two years they plan to help create ten enterprise trusts using their existing local facilities as a foundation. These trusts will have a wider ownership, bringing in local government, local industries, communities and chambers of commerce into a formal group. This will make this initiative more akin to the local enterprise agencies described later.

Contact points for further information on BSC Industry service are:

LONDON OFFICE
British Steel Corporation (Industry) Ltd, NLA Tower, 12 Addiscombe Road, Croydon CR9 3JH. (01 686 0366) Contacts: John Northcott, John Partridge

SCOTLAND (Cambuslang, Motherwell, Monksland, Hamilton & Glengarnock)

British Steel Corporation (Industry) Ltd, British Steel House, 31 Oswald Street, Glasgow G1 4PQ (041 248 2560) Contacts: Peter Agnew, Stewart Morrison

Motherwell Industrial Executive, 43 Civic Square, Motherwell ML1 1TP. (0698 59443/66166) Contact: Terry Currie

Garnock Valley Task Force, Clydesdale Bank Chambers, 44 Main Street, Kilbirnie, Ayrshire KA25 7BY. (050 582 5455/5447/2439) Contact: Bill Dunn

Clyde Workshops, Fullarton Road, Tollcross, Glasgow G32 8YL. (041 641 4972/3) Contact: Stuart Morrison

NORTH-EAST ENGLAND (Derwentside and Hartlepool/Teesside)

British Steel Corporation (Industry) Ltd, Berry Edge Road, Consett, Co. Durham DH8 5EU. (0207 509124) Contacts: Laurie Haveron, Eddie Hutchinson, Bill Robinson, John Sudworth

British Steel Corporation (Industry) Ltd, Church House, Grange Road, Middlesbrough, Cleveland TS1 2LR. (0642 243252/244737) Contacts: Alan Humble, Bill Heaviside

Hartlepool Workshops, Usworth Road Industrial Estate, Usworth Road, Hartlepool, Cleveland TS25 1PD. (0429 65128/35648) Contact: George Barnes, Barbara Elsdon

WEST CUMBRIA (Workington)

Moss Bay Enterprise Trust Ltd, MOBET Trading Estate, Workington, Cumbria CA14 5AE. (0900 65656/4321) Contacts: Max de Redder, John Roonan

SCUNTHORPE

British Steel Corporation (Industry) Ltd, Normanby Park Works, PO Box 1, Scunthorpe, South Humberside DN16 1BP. (0724 843411 Ext 3130) Contacts: David Mann, Derek Marshall, Jim Parker

CORBY

Corby Workshops, Central Works Site, Corby, Northants NN17 1YB. (05366 64215/3) Contact: Geoff Bent

NORTH WALES (Deeside)

British Steel Corporation (Industry) Ltd, Park House, Deeside Industrial Park, Deeside, Clwyd CH5 2NZ. (0244 815262/815783) Contacts: Peter Summers, Norman Sturt, Felicity Agar

SOUTH WALES (Port Talbot, Blaenau, Gwent, Cardiff and Newport)

British Steel Corporation (Industry) Ltd, Gabalfa, Cardiff CF4 1XS. (0222 615031) Contacts: Brian Magrett, David Taylor, Bob Yorke, Owen Evans, Tony Warrilow

Cardiff Workshops, Unit A, Lewis Road, East Morris, Cardiff CF1 5EG. (0222 486661/486686) Contacts: Graham Blackburn, Joe Orr, Nigel Milton

Blaenau Gwent Workshops, Unit 6, Pond Road, Brynmawr, Gwent NP3 4BL. (0495 311625) Contact: Ray Davies

---

URBED (Urban and Economic Development) Ltd, 359 The Strand, London WC2 0HS (01 378 7525). This was established in 1976 with a grant from one of the Sainsbury Charitable Trusts in order to 'find practical solutions to the economic problems of rundown urban areas'.

It has carried out a series of research studies in a cross-section of inner city areas, which have enabled URBED to develop a unique understanding of local economies, the needs of small firms, and the problems of under-utilised resources in inner city areas. Its surveys have formed the basis of a number of reports, including *Industrial Estates and the Small Firm*, published in 1977, and *Local Authorities and Economic Development*, in 1978.

The company contributes to many conferences and working parties on employment and inner city regeneration, and has initiated or helped to popularise a number of basic ideas and solutions to the problems of local economic development. These include the establishment of workshops, working communities, small enterprise centres, industrial associations, small business clubs and local enterprise trusts. Through research into demand, case studies of successful conversions, feasibility studies and promotional material, the company has encouraged the conversion of redundant buildings into premises for small firms.

It provides consultancy services for a range of clients, including local and public authorities and government departments.

URBED's education initiatives include: creating a business idea (an eight-week part-time course); assessing your prospects (a weekend course); getting your business going (a three-month course).

Their New Enterprise Network (NET) meets on the last Tuesday of each month. It is intended for anyone who has recently set up a business and is looking for support.

LOCAL ENTERPRISE AGENCIES

Local Enterprise Agencies or Trusts have been formed in about a hundred places up and down the UK. Some have been in existence for a decade, but the great majority were formed in the last two or three years. They have in common the objectives of encouraging new and small businesses to start up in a particular area, and of helping businesses in their area to survive and prosper.

These agencies are usually run by a small staff who can call on the wealth of expertise within the organisations sponsoring the agency. It can be very useful to know in what particular field agencies' sponsors have experience and expertise. Many hundreds of organisations have sponsored one or more Enterprise Agencies. Sponsors include local government; chambers of commerce; universities, polytechnics and colleges; industrial and commercial companies both large and not so large; banks and merchant banks; accountancy firms; newspapers and television companies; insurance companies and building societies. Moreover, organisations such as HM Dockyards, the Port of London Authority and the General and Municipal Workers' Union have played significant roles in the launching of Local Enterprise Agencies.

It is hard to think of any major sector of the business and financial world that is not represented as a sponsor, but a careful study of the agency sponsors listed below may reveal some notable gaps. The services provided by sponsoring bodies to the agencies include: financial support towards running costs; office and workshop space; secretarial and administrative services; management and commercial advice; training facilities and resources; literature production and dissemination (including the use of advertising media); desk or field research; and board representation and help with forming and developing policy.

A rather smaller number of organisations second staff to help in the day-to-day running of the Enterprise Agency. These are very often specialists from banking or the property world, or experienced managers within big companies. There are even a few academics returning a step closer to the commercial world. These advisers are an important resource within the agency, but the sponsoring company is amply rewarded. For example, a secondee from a major clearing bank will see more new business proposals in a week at an Enterprise Agency than he may see in a year at a small local branch. At the end of his year's secondment he will be a seasoned campaigner and probably a better judge of a good proposal.

Some organisations, such as BSC and ARC, who operate nationally, carry out much of their work through a local organisation similar to an Enterprise Agency in broad concept. Indeed, BSC Industry is currently converting its regional initiative into Enterprise Trusts, taking local councils, chambers of commerce and others into partnership to ensure the continuity of their initiative.

The scope of activities of each agency varies considerably. Some have focused their attention on providing small workshops and office premises; others run business advice clinics to help people to find money and other resources.

Courses and workshops on exporting, bookkeeping, tax and employing people are run by some agencies, usually through their links with local colleges. Still others run 'marriage bureaux', putting people with ideas in touch with people with resources.

If you are actively considering starting up a business or are experiencing problems with you existing business then you would certainly be well advised to contact your nearest Enterprise Agency. If they cannot help or answer your questions they will almost certainly know who can.

Here is a brief guide to the agencies and their services:

	Manage premises	Register of premises	Advice centre	Counselling service	Education	Commercial funds	Computer advice	Full-time staff

ALDERSHOT

Blackwater Valley Enterprise Trust Limited, 6
Gordon Road, Aldershot, Hampshire.
Contact: William Talbot
Founded: 1982
Sponsors: (Trustees) Johnson Wax Ltd., local
banks, local chambers of commerce and Rotary
Clubs.

(row: Manage premises ●, Register of premises ●, Advice centre ●, Full-time staff ●)

ASHFORD, Kent

Enterprise Ashford Ltd, 28 North Street, Ash-
ford, Kent, TN24 8JR. (0233 30307 and 29255)
Contact: A. J. Duncan
Founded: 1982
Sponsors: Unilever PLC Charter Consolidated Ltd,
Zambia Engineering Services Ltd, Ashford
Chamber of Trade and Industry, Ashford Bor-
ough Council, Finn-Kelley and Chapman, Ash-
ford Trades Council

(row: Manage premises ●, Register of premises ●, Advice centre ●, Full-time staff ●)

BARNSLEY

**Employment Promotion and Development
Unit,** South Yorkshire County Council, County
Hall, Barnsley S70 2TN. (0226 86141 ext. 552)
Contact: R. L. Briant
Founded: 1979
Sponsors: South Yorkshire County Council

(row: Manage premises ●, Register of premises ●, Advice centre ●, Counselling service ●, Education ●, Commercial funds ●, Full-time staff ●)

BARNSTAPLE

Dartington North Devon Trust, Bridge Chambers, Barnstaple, North Devon EX31 1HB. (0271
76365)
Founded: 1980

(row: Manage premises ●, Advice centre ●, Computer advice ●, Full-time staff ●)

	Manage premises	Register of premises	Advice centre	Counselling service	Education	Commercial funds	Computer advice	Full-time staff

BASINGSTOKE and ANDOVER

Basingstoke Enterprise Centre, c/o Civic Offices, London Road, Basingstoke, Hampshire RG21 2AT. (0256 56222)
Contact: D. W. Pilkington
Founded: 1982 (October)
Sponsors: Local authority, High Street Banks, Local employers.
Seconded from: High Street Banks.

| Basingstoke Enterprise Centre | ● | ● | ● | | | | ● | |

BATH

Mendip and Wansdyke Local Enterprise Group, Ammerdown, Radstock, Bath BA3 5SN. (0761 35321)

| Mendip and Wansdyke | ● | ● | ● | ● | | | ● | |

BIRKENHEAD

In Business Ltd, Small Business Centre, Claughton Road, Birkenhead L41 6ES. (051 647 7574)
Contact: Paul Farrow.
Founded: 1980
Sponsors: Unilever UK Holdings PLC, UML Ltd, Wirral Metropolitan Borough Council, Wirral Chamber of Commerce
Staff seconded from: Unilever UK Holdings PLC, Banks

| In Business Ltd | ● | ● | ● | ● | | ● | | ● |

BIRMINGHAM

Birmingham Venture, Chamber of Commerce House, PO Box 360, 75 Harborne Road, Edgbaston, Birmingham B15 3DH. (021 454 6171 Ext 269 or 281) Contact: Graham Ashmore
Founded: 1980

| Birmingham Venture | ● | ● | ● | ● | ● | | ● | |

Sponsors: Barclays Bank PLC, Bass Mitchells and Butlers Ltd, Birmingham Post and Mail Ltd, Bryant Construction PLC, Cadbury Ltd, Delta Rod Holdings Ltd, Robert M. Douglas Holdings Ltd, Esso Petroleum Company PLC, GKN Fasteners Ltd, Kalamazoo Ltd, Lloyds Bank PLC, Lucas Industries PLC, Midland Bank PLC, National Westminster Bank PLC, Shell (UK) PLC, Thorn-EMI PLC

Staff seconded from: Arthur Young McClelland Moore & Co., Lucas Airling

	Manage premises	Register of premises	Advice centre	Counselling service	Education	Commercial funds	Computer advice	Full-time staff
Small Business Centre, Aston University, 200 Aston Brook Street, Birmingham B6 4SA.(021 359 3011) Founded: 1967 Sponsors: University of Aston	●		●	●	●		●	●

BRAINTREE

	Manage premises	Register of premises	Advice centre	Counselling service	Education	Commercial funds	Computer advice	Full-time staff
B.E.E.S., Braintree Encourages Enterprise, Causeway House, Bocking End, Braintree, Essex, CM7 6HB (0376 23131 or 43140) Contact: Stuart Beckwith			●	●			●	

BRIDGWATER

	Manage premises	Register of premises	Advice centre	Counselling service	Education	Commercial funds	Computer advice	Full-time staff
Small Industries Group, Dunwear Bungalow, River Lane, Dunwear, Bridgwater, Somerset TA7 0AA. (0278 424456) Contact: Fred Wedlake Founded: 1976	●	●	●	●			●	●

BRISTOL

	Manage premises	Register of premises	Advice centre	Counselling service	Education	Commercial funds	Computer advice	Full-time staff
Aid to Bristol Enterprise, 16 Clifton Park, Bristol BS8 3BY. (0272 741518) Contacts: P. S. Cotterill and D. A. Weaks	●	●	●	●	●		●	●

	Manage premises	Register of premises	Advice centre	Counselling service	Education	Commercial funds	Computer advice	Full-time staff

Founded: 1979
Sponsors: British Aerospace (Aircraft), British Aerospace (Dynamics), Dickinson Robinson Group, Harvey's of Bristol, Imperial Group, Bain Dawes PLC, Mardon Packaging International, Rolls Royce, Barclays Bank PLC, Bristol Chamber of Commerce and Industry, Bristol Corporation, Midland Bank PLC, National Westminster Bank PLC, Sun Life Assurance, Lloyds Bank PLC, Western British Road Services Ltd, Marks and Spencer PLC

	Manage premises	Register of premises	Advice centre	Counselling service	Education	Commercial funds	Computer advice	Full-time staff
New Work Trust Co. Ltd, Avondale Workshops, Woodland Way, Kingswood, Bristol BS15 1QH. (0272 603871) Contact: Michael Winwood Sponsors: more than 210 public and private institutions	●	●	●				●	●
Small Business Centre, Bristol Polytechnic, Coldharbour Lane, Frenchay, Bristol BS16 1QY. (0272 656261) Contact: John M. Howdle Founded: 1968				●		●	●	

BURY

	Manage premises	Register of premises	Advice centre	Counselling service	Education	Commercial funds	Computer advice	Full-time staff
Bury Enterprise Centre, 12 Tithebarn Street, Bury BL9 0JR. (061 797 5864) Contact: D. Gough Founded: 1982 Sponsors: Bury Enterprise Committee Staff seconded from: private industry, MSC	●	●	●	●	●		●	●

CHATHAM

	Manage premises	Register of premises	Advice centre	Counselling service	Education	Commercial funds	Computer advice	Full-time staff
Medway Enterprise Agency Ltd, Railway Street, Chatham, Kent ME4 4RR. (0634 45228) Contact: Guy Sibley Founded: 1982 Sponsors: Babcock Construction Equipment Co Ltd, Barclays Bank PLC, Berry Wiggins Ltd,		●	●	●	●		●	●

24

British Petroleum PLC, Gillingham Borough
Council, HM Dockyard, Chatham, Lloyds Bank
PLC, Marconi Avionics Ltd, Medway and Gil-
lingham Chamber of Commerce, Midland Bank
PLC, National Westminster Bank PLC,
Rochester-upon-Medway City Council, The Cor-
poration of Lloyds
Staff seconded from: major clearing banks

CONSETT

	Manage premises	Register of premises	Advice centre	Counselling service	Education	Commercial funds	Computer advice	Full-time staff
Derwentside Industrial Development Agency	●	●	●	●	●			●
Corby Business Advisory Bureau	●	●	●	●			●	●
Restormell Local Enterprise Trust Ltd	●	●	●					●

Derwentside Industrial Development Agency,
Derwentside Industrial Centre, Berry Edge
Road, Consett, Co. Durham DHB 5EU. (0207
509124/5) Contacts: L. Maveron, J. Carney
Founded: 1979
Sponsors: British Steel Corporation (broader in-
dustrial support within next few months)
Staff seconded from: Barclays Bank PLC, National
Westminster Bank PLC

CORBY

Corby Business Advisory Bureau, Douglas
House, Queen's Square, Corby, Northants NN17
1PL. (05366 62571) Contact: L. C. Howard
Founded: 1978
Sponsors: Dept. of Environment, Commission for
New Towns, Northamptonshire County Council,
Corby District Council
Staff seconded from: Corby Industrial Development
Centre, British Steel Corporation (Industry) Ltd

CORNWALL

Restormell Local Enterprise Trust Ltd, Lower
Penarwyn, St Blazey, Par, Cornwall PL24 2DF.
(072 6813079) Contact: Alf Tourell

	Manage premises	Register of premises	Advice centre	Counselling service	Education	Commercial funds	Computer advice	Full-time staff
Founded: 1981. Sponsors: ECLP, TAWU, St Austell Chamber of Commerce								
West Cornwall Enterprise Trust Ltd, Wesley Street, Camborne TR14 8DR. (0209 714914) Contact: Philip Staton	●	●	●					●
Enterprise Carrickfergus Ltd., Courtaulds Industry Centre, 75 Belfast Road, Carrickfergus, Co. Antrim BT38 8PH. (09603 68005) Contact: P. J. Conway			●	●				●
Coventry Business Centre Ltd, Spire House, New Union Street, Coventry CV1 2PS. (0203 552781) Contact: A. E. Kimberley			●	●	●			
Coventry City Council, Development Division, Dept. of Homes and Property Services, Coventry. (0203 25555) Contact: M. Bullock.	●	●			●	●		

Founded: 1981
Sponsors: ECLP, TAWU, St Austell Chamber of
  Commerce

West Cornwall Enterprise Trust Ltd, Wesley
  Street, Camborne TR14 8DR. (0209 714914) Contact: Philip Staton
Founded: 1982
Sponsors: CompAir Ltd, Cornwall County Council,
  Deverish Redruth Brewery Ltd, Falmouth Shiprepair Ltd, Kerrier District Council, Lloyds
  Bank PLC, Marks and Spencer PLC, Penryn
  Aranite Ltd, Phar-o-Plant Ltd, Port of Falmouth Chamber of Commerce, The Rank
  Organisation PLC, E. Thomas & Company Ltd,
  Shell UK PLC, Carrick District Council

CO. ANTRIM

Enterprise Carrickfergus Ltd., Courtaulds Industry Centre, 75 Belfast Road, Carrickfergus,
  Co. Antrim BT38 8PH. (09603 68005)
Contact: P. J. Conway

COVENTRY

Coventry Business Centre Ltd, Spire House,
  New Union Street, Coventry CV1 2PS. (0203
  552781) Contact: A. E. Kimberley
Founded: 1982
Sponsors: Coventry City Council, Coventry Chamber of Commerce and Industry, Confederation of
  Shipbuilding and Engineering Unions
Staff seconded from: Lloyds Bank PLC

Coventry City Council, Development Division,
  Dept. of Homes and Property Services, Coventry. (0203 25555) Contact: M. Bullock.

CRANFIELD

Interwork Business Development Centre, Cranfield Institute of Technology, Cranfield, Bedfordshire MK43 0AL. (0234 752767) Contact: Brian Wilson, Director
Staff seconded from: ICI

DARLINGTON

Darlington Enterprise Association Ltd, Town Hall, Darlington, Co. Durham DL1 5SR. (Darlington 60651) Contact: Clive Owen
Founded: 1982
Sponsors: Darlington Borough Council
Staff seconded from: Enterprise North

DEVON

East Devon Small Industries Group, 115 Heathpark, Honiton, Devon, EX14 8BR- Tel: 0404 41806
Contact: A. D. Johnson
Founded: 1981
Sponsors: Local authority, local businesses.

DURHAM

Association for Business and Commerce (0385 62421) Contact: Ian Thorpe

Enterprise North, Durham University Business School, Mill Hill Lane, Durham DH1 3LB. (0385 41919) Contact: Derek L. Craven
Founded: 1973
Enterprise North is an integral part of the Small Business Centre at Durham University Business School

Organisation	Manage premises	Register of premises	Advice centre	Counselling service	Education	Commercial funds	Computer advice	Full-time staff
Interwork Business Development Centre	●	●						●
Darlington Enterprise Association Ltd	●	●	●	●	●			●
East Devon Small Industries Group	●	●	●					●
Enterprise North		●	●	●				●

	Manage premises	Register of premises	Advice centre	Counselling service	Education	Commercial funds	Computer advice	Full-time staff

GLASGOW

Bridgeton Business Club, c/o Milroy Engineering Company Ltd, 23 McPhail Street, Glasgow G40 1EL. (041 554 2344) Contact: Mr W Hibberd
Founded: 1961

Services: Manage premises, Register of premises, Advice centre, Full-time staff

GRAVESEND

Gravesham Industry, Gravesham Borough Council, Civic Centre, Windmill Street, Gravesend DA12 1AU. (0474 64422) Contact: Mr Dewar.
Founded: 1981

Services: Advice centre, Counselling service, Education, Computer advice

HALIFAX

Calderdale Information Service for Business and Industry (CALDIS), Library Centre, Percival Whitely College of Further Education, Francis Street, Halifax, West Yorkshire HX1 3UZ. (0422 58221) Contact: D. Marley
Founded: 1966
Sponsors: Business and industrial organisations in Calderdale
Staff seconded from: local business and industry

Services: Manage premises, Register of premises, Advice centre, Counselling service, Computer advice, Full-time staff

HARLOW

Harlow Enterprise Agency, c/o Town Hall, Harlow, Essex CM20 1HJ. Tel 0279 39880
Contact: David Ross
Founded: 1982
Sponsors: Harlow Council, Harlow Chamber of Trade, Harlow and District Employers Group, Banks.

Services: Manage premises, Register of premises, Advice centre, Counselling service, Computer advice, Full-time staff

	Manage premises	Register of premises	Advice centre	Counselling service	Education	Commercial funds	Computer advice	Full-time staff

HARTLEPOOL

Hartlepool New Development Services (HANDS), Hartlepool Borough Council, Civic Centre, Hartlepool, Cleveland TS24 8AY. (0429 66522) Contact: Ron Preece, Eddie Morley
Founded: 1980
Sponsors: Hartlepool College of Further Education
Staff seconded from: BSC, local authority, industry, banks, etc.

Services: Manage premises • Register of premises • Advice centre • Counselling service • Education • Full-time staff •

ISLE OF WIGHT

Isle of Wight Enterprise Agency, 6/7 Town Lane, Newport, Isle of Wight. (0983 529120) Contact: R. C. Neve, Director
Founded: 1981
Sponsors: Isle of Wight County Council together with local industry

Services: Register of premises • Advice centre • Counselling service • Computer advice • Full-time staff •

KIDDERMINSTER

Kidderminster Small Firms Club, Kidderminster College, Hoo Road, Kidderminster, Worcs DY10 1LX. (0562 66311) Contact: John Moyle

Services: Counselling service • Commercial funds • Full-time staff •

LANCASHIRE

Rossendale Enterprise Trust Ltd, Holme Spring Mill, Grane Road, Haslingden, Rossendale, Lancs BB4 4PN. (0706 217709) Contact: R. H. Pearson
Founded: 1981
Sponsors: Rossendale Borough Council
Staff seconded from: National Westminster Bank PLC

Services: Manage premises • Advice centre • Counselling service • Computer advice • Full-time staff •

	Manage premises	Register of premises	Advice centre	Counselling service	Education	Commercial funds	Computer advice	Full-time staff

LANCASTER

Enterprise Lancaster, Town Hall, Lancaster LA1 1PJ. (0524 65272) Contact: R. H. Kelsall Founded: 1968

Manage premises	Register of premises	Advice centre	Counselling service	Education	Commercial funds	Computer advice	Full-time staff
●	●	●	●	●	●		

LEEDS

Leeds Business Venture, 9th Floor, Marrion House, The Marion Centre, Leeds LS2 8LY (0532 446474)
Contact: M. R. Walker
Founded: 1980
Sponsors: E. J. Arnold & Son Ltd, Burton Group Manufacturing, Bain Dawes Kirkstall Forge Engineering Ltd, Lewis's Ltd, Peat Marwick, Mitchell & Co, Graham Poulter Group Ltd, Town Centre Securities Ltd, Vickers Ltd, Howson Algraphy Group, John Waddington Ltd, Yorkshire Bank PLC, Yorkshire Post Newspapers Ltd
Staff seconded from: Marks & Spencer PLC, Lloyds Bank PLC

Manage premises	Register of premises	Advice centre	Counselling service	Education	Commercial funds	Computer advice	Full-time staff
●	●	●	●				●

LCVS Enterprises Ltd, 31–34 Aire Street, Leeds LS6 4HT. (0532 435897) Contact: W. Shott
Founded: 1980
Staff seconded from: ICI Fibres, Harrogate via Action Resource Centre

Manage premises	Register of premises	Advice centre	Counselling service	Education	Commercial funds	Computer advice	Full-time staff
●	●	●					●

LEICESTER

Leicestershire Business Venture, 30 New Walk, Leicester A1 6JS. (0533 554464 ext. 34/35) Contacts: Mr T. Connor and Ms S. Beech
Founded: 1981
Sponsors: Bain Dawes PLC, Barclay Bank PLC, Bonfield Hirst Turner, Bovis Construction Ltd,

Manage premises	Register of premises	Advice centre	Counselling service	Education	Commercial funds	Computer advice	Full-time staff
		●	●				●

	Manage premises	Register of premises	Advice centre	Counselling service	Education	Commercial funds	Computer advice	Full-time staff

British Shoe Corporation Ltd, British United Shoes Machinery Co Ltd, Coral PLC, Dunlop Ltd, Everards Brewery Ltd, Fisons PLC, GEC Power Engineering Ltd, Harvey Ingram, Industrial and Commercial Finance Corporation Ltd, T. W. Kempton Ltd, Leicester Building Society, Lloyds Bank PLC, Marks & Spencer PLC, Metal Box PLC, Midland Bank PLC, National Westminster Bank PLC, Peat, Marwick Mitchell & Co, HTN Peck (Holdings) Ltd, Pedigree Petfoods, Pork Farms Ltd, Riker Laboratories, R. Rowley & Co, Sears Engineering Ltd, Sketchley PLC, Stead & Simpson PLC, United Biscuits (Holdings) PLC, Walker's Crisps Ltd, Leicester City Council, Leicester County Council
Staff seconded from: the private sector

LEICESTER

Leicestershire Small Firms Centre, 8 St Martins, Leicester. Tel: 0533 29684
Contact: Cliff Britt
Founded: 1979
Sponsors: Leicester Polytechnic, Leicestershire County Council, Leicester City Council.
Seconded from: Leicester Polytechnic, freelance consultants and advisers.

	Manage premises	Register of premises	Advice centre	Counselling service	Education	Commercial funds	Computer advice	Full-time staff
Leicestershire Small Firms Centre	●	●	●	●	●		●	●

LIVERPOOL

Action Resource Centre, Merseyside, c/o Liverpool Craft Centre, 20/22 Matthews Street, Liverpool L2 6RE. (051 236 0263) Contact: Donald Stuart
Founded: 1976
Staff seconded from: Tate and Lyle, and Unilever

	Manage premises	Register of premises	Advice centre	Counselling service	Education	Commercial funds	Computer advice	Full-time staff
Action Resource Centre				●				

	Manage premises	Register of premises	Advice centre	Counselling service	Education	Commercial funds	Computer advice	Full-time staff

LONDON

London Enterprise Agency (LENTA), 69 Cannon Street, London EC4 N5AB. (01 236 2676 or 01 248 4444) Contact: Brian Wright
Founded: 1979
Sponsor: Barclays Bank PLC, BP PLC, BOC PLC, General Electric Company PLC, IBM PLC, ICFC Ltd, Marks & Spencer PLC, Midland Bank PLC, Shell (UK) PLC, United Biscuits (UK) PLC, Whitbread & Co PLC
Staff seconded from: Barclays Bank PLC, Midland Bank PLC, Shell (UK) PLC, IBM PLC, BP PLC, Department of the Environment, LCCI and Marks & Spencer PLC

●	●	●	●	●	●		●

Hackney Business Promotions Centre, 1–11 Hoxton Street, Hackney, London N1 6NL. (01 739 9606) Contact: Dennis Statham
Founded: 1978
Staff seconded from: Barclays Bank PLC, Marks & Spencer PLC, London Polytechnic, City University Business School

●	●	●	●	●	●		●

Hammersmith and Fulham Business Resources Ltd, c/o Economic Development Unit, Hammersmith Town Hall, King Street, London W6. (01 748 3020) Contact: Anthony Lloyd
Founded: 1981
Sponsors: London Borough of Hammersmith and Fulham, London Enterprise Agency, Barclays Bank PLC
Staff seconded from: London Enterprise Agency, London Borough of Hammersmith and Fulham Economic Development Unit

●	●	●	●	●	●	●	●

Islington Small Business Counselling Service, 201-202 Upper Street, London N1 1RQ Tel: 01 359 3924
Contact: Norman Humphrey
Founded: 1979
Seconded from: High street banks

		●	●				●

	Manage premises	Register of premises	Advice centre	Counselling service	Education	Commercial funds	Computer advice	Full-time staff
Kensington and Chelsea Resources Centre, 1 Thorpe Close, London W10 (01 969 9455) Contact: John Horgan Sponsors: Kensington and Chelsea Council	●	●	●	●				●
Lambeth Business Advisory Service, Lambeth Town Hall, Brixton, London SW2 1RW. (01 274 7722 ext. 2424) Contact: Keith Lewis Sponsors: Lambeth Borough Council Staff seconded from: British Petroleum Ltd, National Westminster Bank PLC, LENTA	●	●	●	●				●
New Ventures Ltd, Old Loom House, Backchurch Lane, London E1 1LU. (01 788 1067) Contact: A. J. B. Scholefield or Mrs M Scholefield Founded: 1981	●	●	●	●			●	●
Spitalfields Small Business Association, 170 Brick Lane, London E1. (01 247 1892) Contact: John Friend	●		●	●				●
Thames Enterprise Agency Ltd, 19 Penhall Road, Charlton, London SE7 8RX. (01 858 8611) Contact: Colin Barrow Founded: 1980 Sponsors: Barclays Bank PLC, British Oxygen Company PLC, Morgan Grampian Ltd, Greenwich Chamber of Commerce, Industrial & Commercial Finance Corporation, Lloyds Bank PLC, London Borough of Greenwich, Midland Bank PLC, Sykes Pumps Ltd, Standard Telephones & Cables Ltd, Thames Polytechnic, Keyswitch Varley Ltd, Woolwich Equitable Building Society	●	●	●	●	●		●	●
Tower Hamlets Centre for Small Businesses Ltd, 99 Leman Street, London E1. (01 283 1030 ext. 448) Contact: B Kennon Founded: 1978 Sponsors: City of London Polytechnic, London Enterprise Agency, Tower Hamlets Council, Truman Ltd, National Westminster Bank PLC,		●	●				●	●

	Manage premises	Register of premises	Advice centre	Counselling service	Education	Commercial funds	Computer advice	Full-time staff

Port of London Authority, International Timber, World Trade Centre, Ian Raitt PR, Tower Hamlets Group of London Chamber of Commerce, Hackney and Tower Hamlets Chamber of Commerce, GLC, Docklands Dev. Corp.
Staff seconded from: BP, Barclays Bank PLC

Wandsworth Business Resource Service, 140 Battersea Park Road, London, sw11 Tel: 01 720 7053
Contact: K. G. Perks
Sponsors: London Enterprise Agency, Wandsworth Borough Council and the GLC
Staff seconded from: LENTA

Manage premises	Register of premises	Advice centre	Counselling service	Education	Commercial funds	Computer advice	Full-time staff
●	●	●			●		●

Wandsworth Enterprise Development Agency Ltd, Unity House, 50-60 Wandsworth High Street, London, sw18 4LN Tel: 01 870 1910
Contact: Douglas Jack
Founded: 1980
Sponsors: Council of London Borough of Wandsworth, Industrial Common Ownership Finance Ltd., London Chamber of Commerce & Industry

Manage premises	Register of premises	Advice centre	Counselling service	Education	Commercial funds	Computer advice	Full-time staff
							●

LOWESTOFT

Lowestoft Enterprise Trust, Oulton Works, School Road, Lowestoft, Suffolk NR33 9NA. (0502 63286) Contact: C. J. Barnes
Founded: 1981
Sponsors: Philips Electronics Ltd, Shell (UK) PLC, Waveney District Council

Manage premises	Register of premises	Advice centre	Counselling service	Education	Commercial funds	Computer advice	Full-time staff
●		●	●	●			●

LUTON

Bedfordshire & Chiltern Enterprise Agency (BECENTA), Enterprise House, 7 Gordon Street, Luton LU1 2QP. (0582 452288) Contact: D. J. Upcott

Manage premises	Register of premises	Advice centre	Counselling service	Education	Commercial funds	Computer advice	Full-time staff
●	●	●	●	●		●	●

Founded: 1981
Sponsors: Bedfordshire C. C., Barclays Bank, National Westminster Bank, Midland Bank, Lloyds Bank, Vauxhall, Whitbread, Electrolux
Staff seconded from: High street banks as above.

MAIDSTONE

Maidstone Enterprise Agency Limited, 25a Pudding Lane, Maidstone, Kent ME14 1PA Tel: 0622 675547
Contact: John Lee
Founded: 1982
Sponsors: Barclays Bank, Maidstone Chamber of Commerce, R. Corben & Son (Maidstone) Ltd., Courage Eastern Ltd., ICI Plant Protection Div., Kent C. C., Kimberley Clarke Ltd., Maidstone Borough Council, National Westminster Bank, Reed Group Ltd., Trebor Ltd., Whatman Reeve, Angel Ltd., Whitbread Fremlins Ltd.,
Staff seconded from: National Westminster Bank

MANCHESTER

Manchester Business Venture, c/o Tootal Group PLC, 56 Oxford Street, Manchester M60 1HJ. (061 228 1144) Contact: Mr J. MacDonald
Founded: 1982
Sponsors: Barclays Bank, BOC, Co-op Bank, Courtaulds, Ferranti Ltd, John Laing Construction Ltd, Lloyds Bank, Manchester Evening News, Marks & Spencer, Maydella Manufacturing Co Ltd, Midland Bank, Nat. West. Bank, Readson Ltd, Refuge Assurance Co Ltd, James Seddon UK, Tootal Group, Trustee Savings Bank, United Biscuits, William & Glyn's Bank, Arthur Young McClelland Moores & Co
Staff seconded from: Marks & Spencer

	Manage premises	Register of premises	Advice centre	Counselling service	Education	Commercial funds	Computer advice	Full-time staff
Maidstone Enterprise Agency Limited	•	•	•					•
Manchester Business Venture	•	•	•	•			•	•

	Manage premises	Register of premises	Advice centre	Counselling service	Education	Commercial funds	Computer advice	Full-time staff
Greater Manchester Economic Development Corp Ltd	●	●				●		
North West Industrial Development Association			●					●
Melton Industrial Development Aid Scheme (Midas)	●	●						●
New Enterprise Centre	●	●	●				●	●

Greater Manchester Economic Development Corp Ltd, Bernard House, Piccadilly Gardens, Manchester M1 4DD. (061 247 3878) Contact: ME. E. Morton
Founded: 1979
Sponsors: Greater Manchester County Council, district authorities within Greater Manchester, local industry and commerce
Staff seconded from: Greater Manchester County Council

North West Industrial Development Association, Brazennose House, Brazennose Street, Manchester M2 5AZ Tel: 061 834 6778
Contact: Chris Koral
Founded: 1931
Sponsors: local authorities, chambers of commerce, trade unions, CBI, Members of Parliament, local financial commercial and industrial concerns, public bodies.

MELTON MOWBRAY

Melton Industrial Development Aid Scheme (Midas), Melton Mowbray, Leicester, LE14 2BR. Tel: 0664 0006
Contract: D.F. Hodgson
Founded: 1981
Sponsors: Pedigree Petfoods (Division of Mars Ltd), Leicestershire County Council, Melton Borough Council.
Seconded from: Pedigree Petfoods.

MIDDLESBROUGH

New Enterprise Centre, Silver Street, St Hilda's, Middlesbrough TS2 1NF. (0642 224839) Contact: K. C. Sharp

	Manage premises	Register of premises	Advice centre	Counselling service	Education	Commercial funds	Computer advice	Full-time staff

Founded: 1981
Sponsors: Middlesbrough Borough Council

Teesside Small Business Club Ltd, Thornaby Old Town Hall, Mandale Road, Thornaby-on-Tees, Cleveland TS17 6AP. (0642 607699) Contact: S. Newton
Founded: 1972

Manage premises	Register of premises	Advice centre	Counselling service	Education	Commercial funds	Computer advice	Full-time staff
●	●						●

NORTHAMPTON

'Input' Northamptonshire Industrial Promotion Unit, 65 The Avenue, Cliftonville, Northampton NN1 5B6. (0604 37401) Contact: A. G. McKay
Founded: 1980
Sponsors: Northamptonshire Chamber of Commerce and Industry, Northamptonshire County Council, Northamptonshire Development Corporation

Manage premises	Register of premises	Advice centre	Counselling service	Education	Commercial funds	Computer advice	Full-time staff
●	●	●				●	●

NORTHWICH

Vale Royal Small Firms Ltd. (Business back-up), Mid Cheshire Business Centre, Winnington Avenue, Winnington, Northwich, Cheshire, CW8 4EE.
Tel: 0606 77711
Contact: John Bone, General Manager Kathleen Pass, Administrative Assistant.
Founded: 1981
Sponsors: Cheshire County Newspapers, Cheshire County Council, County Glass, ICI Mond Division, Iveco (UK) Ltd, Lloyds Bank PLC, Manpower Services Commission, National Westminster Bank, Frank Roberts & Sons Ltd., Trustee Savings Bank, Vale Royal District Council.
Seconded from: ICI Mond Division, Trustee Savings Bank.

Manage premises	Register of premises	Advice centre	Counselling service	Education	Commercial funds	Computer advice	Full-time staff
●	●						●

	Manage premises	Register of premises	Advice centre	Counselling service	Education	Commercial funds	Computer advice	Full-time staff

NORWICH

Norwich Enterprise Agency Trust (NEAT), 112 Barrack Street, Norwich NR3 1TX. (0603 613023) Contact: Bill Page
Founded: 1981
Sponsors: Anglia Television Ltd, Bally Group (UK) Ltd, Barclays Bank PLC, Boulton & Paul Ltd, Eastern Counties Newspapers Ltd, ICFC Ltd, Industrial Commission, Jarrold & Sons Ltd, Lloyds Bank PLC, Marks & Spencer PLC, Midland Bank PLC, National Westminster Bank PLC, Norwich & Norfolk Chamber of Commerce and Industry, Norwich City Council, Norwich Union Insurance Group, Reckitt & Colman Ltd, Rowntree-Mackintosh Ltd, University of East Anglia
Staff seconded from: National Westminster Bank PLC

(NEAT: Advice centre ●, Counselling service ●, Education ●, Full-time staff ●)

NOTTINGHAM

Nottingham Community Project, Baker Gate House, Belward Street, Nottingham NG1 1JZ. (0602 581933) Contact: C. Collinge

(Register of premises ●, Advice centre ●, Counselling service ●, Education ●)

Small Business Centre, Trent Polytechnic, Burton Street, Nottingham NG1 4BU. (0602 48248 Rxt 2488) Contact: Terry Faulkner
Founded: 1975

(Counselling service ●, Education ●, Computer advice ●, Full-time staff ●)

Trent Small Business Club, 13–15 Bridlesmith Gate, Nottingham. Contact: Mr S Swann
Founded: 1980
Staff seconded from: SFIC, ARC, Trent Polytechnic

(Counselling service ●, Computer advice ●)

OXFORD

Oxford Enterprise Trust, c/o 125 London Road, Headington, Oxford. Tel: 0865 63092

(Manage premises ●, Advice centre ●, Counselling service ●, Full-time staff ●)

Contact: J. W. C. Burrough
Founded: 1982
Sponsors: local investment companies

PETERBOROUGH

Peterborough Enterprise Program (PEP), c/o Peterborough Development Corporation, Touthill Close, PO Box 3, City Road, Peterborough PE1 1UJ. (0733 63931) Contact: David Bath Staff seconded from: Barclays Bank PLC

PLYMOUTH

South Hams Small Industries Grioup, The Croft, Brixton, Plymouth, Devon. Tel: 0752 880210
Contact: Alan Lovering
Founded: 1979
Sponsors: Business people, entrepreneurs, local supporters.
Staff seconded from: local firms

PORTSMOUTH

Portsmouth Area Enterprise First Floor Offices, 27 Guildhall Walk, Portsmouth PL1 2RY. (0705 833321) Contact: W. Summer
Founded: 1982
Sponsors: Barclays Bank PLC, BAT Industries PLC, Dunham Bush Ltd, East Hampshire District Council, Fareham Borough Council, FPT Industries Ltd, Gosport Borough Council, Havant Borough Council, Hedley Greentree Partnership, HM Dockyard, IBM (UK) PLC, Lloyds Bank PLC, Marconi Space and Defence Systems, Marks & Spencer PLC, Midland Bank PLC, National Westminster Bank PLC, Pall Europe, Portsmouth Building Society, Ports-

	Manage premises	Register of premises	Advice centre	Counselling service	Education	Commercial funds	Computer advice	Full-time staff
Peterborough Enterprise Program (PEP)	●	●	●	●				
South Hams Small Industries Grioup	●	●	●	●			●	●
Portsmouth Area Enterprise	●	●					●	●

mouth City Council, Plessey Co PLC, South East Hampshire Chamber of Commerce, L. S. Vail & Sons, Whitbread and Company PLC, Williams & Glyn's Bank Ltd, Zurich Insurance Group
Staff seconded from: Whitbread and Co PLC

READING

	Manage premises	Register of premises	Advice centre	Counselling service	Education	Commercial funds	Computer advice	Full-time staff
Berkshire Enterprise Agency, Old Shire Hall, The Forbury, Reading, Berks RG1 3EJ. (0734 585715) Contact: Ansel Harris. Founded: 1982. Sponsors: Berkshire County Council. Staff seconded from: Marks & Spencer PLC		●	●					

ROCHDALE

METRA, c/o TBA Industrial Products Ltd., PO Box 40, Rochdale, OL12 7EQ. Tel: 0706 7356250 Contact: B. McCormack

---

RUNCORN

	Manage premises	Register of premises	Advice centre	Counselling service	Education	Commercial funds	Computer advice	Full-time staff
Business Links Ltd, 62 Church Street, Runcorn, Cheshire WA7 1LD. (092 85 63037) Contact: I. M. Jones or A. B. Griffiths. Founded: 1979. Sponsors: Halton Borough Council, ICI, Cheshire County Council, Grosvenor Estates Ltd, Runcorn & Warrington Development Corporation, National Westminster Bank PLC. Staff seconded from: ICI		●	●		●	●		

SCUNTHORPE

	Manage premises	Register of premises	Advice centre	Counselling service	Education	Commercial funds	Computer advice	Full-time staff
Industrial Development Enterprise Agency, Civic Centre, Ashbey Road, Scunthorpe, South Humberside DN16 1AB. (0724 862141) Contact: Ian Hutchinson		●	●		●	●		

Founded: 1979
Sponsors: Scunthorpe County Council

SITTINGBOURNE

Swale Work Initiation Measure (SWIM), Dolphin House, Church Road, Sittingbourne, Kent. NE10 3RT(0795 79665/6) Contact: W. A. Penney
Founded: 1981
Sponsors: Manpower Services Commission, Kent County Council Careers Service, Committee of Secondary School Headmasters, Kent County Council Social Services, Swale Borough Council, Swale Area Committee of Kent Association of Parish Councils, local chambers of commerce, VOICE, the Industrial Employers Association

---

SOUTHAMPTON

Southampton Enterprise Agency Ltd, 57a Winchester Road, Southampton, Hants. SO1 5RL (0703 788088) Contact: John Townesend
Founded: 1981
Sponsors: BAT Industries PLC

SOUTHPORT

Southport Enterprise, 54 West Street, Southport PR8 1QS. (0704 38511 Ext 30) Contact: J. D. Anderson
Founded: 1981
Sponsors: Sefton Metropolitan Borough Council, Southport Trades Council, Manpower Services Commission

---

ST HELENS

Community Centre of St Helen's Trust Ltd, PO Box 36, St Helens, Merseyside. (0744 692570)

	Manage premises	Register of premises	Advice centre	Counselling service	Education	Commercial funds	Computer advice	Full-time staff
SWIM	●	●						●
Southampton Enterprise Agency Ltd			●	●	●			●
Southport Enterprise			●	●	●			●
Community Centre of St Helen's Trust Ltd	●	●	●	●				●

Contact: W. E. G. Humphry
Founded: 1978
Sponsors: General and Municipal Workers' Union,
National Westminster Bank PLC, Pilkington
PLC, Rockware Glass PLC, St Helen's Borough
Council, St Helen's Chamber of Commerce, Eric
B. Miller PLC, Merseyside County Council,
Midland Bank PLC, EETPU

	Manage premises	Register of premises	Advice centre	Counselling service	Education	Commercial funds	Computer advice	Full-time staff
STAFFORD								
Staffordshire Development Association, PO Box 11, County Buildings, Martin Street, Stafford ST16 2LH. (0785 3121 ext. 7370) Contact: Michael Cox — Founded: 1974	●	●		●				●
STIRLING								
Venture Forth, Central Regional Council, Viewforth, Stirling FK8 2ET. (0786 3111 ext. 216) Contact: J. T. Cameron — Founded: 1979	●	●	●					●
STOKE-ON-TRENT								
Business Initiative, North Staffs & District, Gordon Chambers, 36 Cheapside, Marley, Stoke-on-Trent ST1 1HE. (0782 279013) Contact: Christopher Stokoe, Director — Founded: 1981	●	●	●			●	●	

STAFFORD

Staffordshire Development Association, PO
Box 11, County Buildings, Martin Street, Stafford ST16 2LH. (0785 3121 ext. 7370) Contact:
Michael Cox
Founded: 1974

STIRLING

Venture Forth, Central Regional Council, Viewforth, Stirling FK8 2ET. (0786 3111 ext. 216)
Contact: J. T. Cameron
Founded: 1979
Sponsors: Ratepayers of the Central Region
Staff seconded from: Weir Pumps Ltd, ICI Ltd,
Cape Insulation Ltd

STOKE-ON-TRENT

Business Initiative, North Staffs & District, Gordon Chambers, 36 Cheapside, Marley, Stoke-on-Trent ST1 1HE. (0782 279013) Contact: Christopher Stokoe, Director
Founded: 1981
Sponsors: Barclays Bank PLC, Blythe Colours Ltd,
Borough of Newcastle-under-Lyme, Britannia
Building Society, Century Oils PLC, G. H.
Downing Co Ltd, H. & R. Johnson Tiles Ltd,

Lloyds Bank PLC, Mathey Printed Products Ltd, Michelin Tyre PLC, Midland Bank PLC, National Westminster Bank PLC, North Staffs Chamber of Commerce, North Staffs Trustee Savings Bank, Peat, Marwick, Mitchell & Co, Royal Doulton Tableware Ltd, The Small Back Room, Wade Potteries Ltd, Wedgwood PLC, Wood, Mitchell & Co Ltd
Staff seconded from: National Westminster Bank PLC, Peat, Marwick, Mitchell & Co.
(Accountants)

	Manage premises	Register of premises	Advice centre	Counselling service	Education	Commercial funds	Computer advice	Full-time staff
SUNDERLAND								
New Enterprise Advisory Service, Citizens Advice Bureau, 48 John Street, Sunderland, Tyne & Wear SR1 1QH. Tel: 0783 44027 — Contact: Ivor Saville — Founded: 1978 — Seconded from: Delloite, Haskins & Sells, Chartered Accountants	●	●	●					●
SWINDON								
Swindon Enterprise Trust Ltd, 1 Commercial Road, Swindon, Wilts SN1 5NE. (0793 487793) — Contact: R. H. D. Hardy — Founded: 1982 — Sponsors: Thamesdown Borough Council plus local industry	●	●	●	●			●	●
TELFORD								
Telford Development Corporation, Priorslee Hall, Telford, Shropshire TF2 9NT. (0952 613131) — Contact: W. D. J. Macrell, Industrial Director — Founded: 1963 — Sponsors: New Town Development Corporation	●	●	●	●	●		●	●

43

TYNE & WEAR

Business Opportunities Research Unit, Town Centre Library, Washington, Tyne & Wear NE38 7RZ. Tel: 0632 470823
Contact: Sue Final
Founded: 1981
Sponsors: Sunderland Borough Council, Sunderland Polytechnic, Wearside College of Further Education, Minkwermouth College of Further Education.

WAKEFIELD

Kirklees and Wakefield Venture Trust, Walker House, 12 Rishworth Street, Wakefield WF1 2QP. (0924 381343) Contact: L. Mullins
Founded: 1981
Sponsors: Kirklees and Wakefield Chamber of Commerce and Industry, Wakefield Metropolitan District Council, Kirklees Metropolitan Council

WALSALL

Walsall Small Firm Advice Unit, Jerome Chamber, Lower Bridge Street, Walsall WJ1 1EX. (0922 646614) Contact: Frank Cookson
Founded: 1980
Staff Seconded from: National Westminster Bank PLC

WASHINGTON

Tyne and Wear Small Business Club, Usworth Hall, Stephenson District 12, Washington NE37

Organisation	Manage premises	Register of premises	Advice centre	Counselling service	Education	Commercial funds	Computer advice	Full-time staff
Business Opportunities Research Unit			●	●				●
Kirklees and Wakefield Venture Trust			●	●	●	●		●
Walsall Small Firm Advice Unit	●	●	●	●	●		●	●
Tyne and Wear Small Business Club	●		●	●	●		●	●

3HS, Tyne and Wear. (0632 475555) Contact: Hugh McQuillon
Founded: 1978
Staff seconded from: ICI Ltd via Action Resource Centre (Tyne and Wear), Manpower Services Commission

---

WOLVERHAMPTON

	Manage premises	Register of premises	Advice centre	Counselling service	Education	Commercial funds	Computer advice	Full-time staff
Wolverhampton Enterprise Ltd, Lich Chambers, 44 Queen Square, Wolverhampton WV1 1TS. (0902 23104) Contact: Mrs Jane Gilbert. Founded: 1982. Sponsors: Wolverhampton Borough Council, Wolverhampton Chamber of Commerce, Wolverhampton and Bilston Trades Council. Staff seconded from: Coopers and Lybrand	●	●	●	●		●		●

WORCESTER

	Manage premises	Register of premises	Advice centre	Counselling service	Education	Commercial funds	Computer advice	Full-time staff
Hereford & Worcester Business Promotion Centre, Taylors Lane, Worcester WR1 1PN. Tel: 0905 21312. Contact: John Chidlow. Founded: 1978. Sponsors: Hereford & Worcester County Council	●	●		●				●

WORKINGTON

	Manage premises	Register of premises	Advice centre	Counselling service	Education	Commercial funds	Computer advice	Full-time staff
Moss Bay Enterprise Trust (MOBET), Mobet Trading Estate, Workington, Cumbria CA14 5AE. (0900 65056) Contact: John J. Roonan. Founded: 1981. Sponsors: British Steel (Industry) Ltd, Cumbria County Council, Allerdale District Council, Copeland Borough Council. Staff seconded from: British Steel Corporation, Cumbria County Council, Allerdale District Council, National Westminster Bank PLC	●	●	●	●		●		●

You may not have a local Enterprise Agency but feel that there are local problems that such an agency could help solve. In this case, to make contact with your local council's Industrial Development Officer or the chamber of commerce would be a good starting point. Recently a private initiative, 'Business in the Community', has been formed to encourage and help industry and commerce with local economic and social development. It will give advice on setting up local Enterprise Agencies: *Business in the Community,* 91 Waterloo Road, London SE1 8XP. (01 928 6423) Contact Mr D. G. Milne, Director.

From April 1982 contributions to approved Enterprise Agencies, in cash or kind, from companies, partnerships and sale traders, should be eligible for tax relief. The essential requirement for approval is that the agency is not a profit-making body.

The Department of the Environment and the Department of Industry, through their regional offices (listed below), will offer advice to individuals or firms who are thinking about establishing an agency.

Department of the Environment and Department of Industry Regional Offices

NORTH-WEST

DoE, Room 1122, Sunley Building, Piccadilly Plaza, Manchester M1 4BE. (061 832 9111) Contact: Mr D J Morrison

DI, Sunley Building, Piccadilly Plaza, Manchester M1 4BE. (061 236 2171)

NORTH

DoE, Room 704, Wellbar House, Gallowgate, Newcastle-upon-Tyne NE1 4TX. (0632 327575 ext. 307) Contact: Mr R Bell

DI, Stanegate House, 2 Groat Market, Newcastle-upon-Tyne NE1 1YN. (0632 324722)

YORKSHIRE & HUMBERSIDE

DoE, Room 1108, City House, New Station Street, Leeds LS1 4JH. (0532 438232 ext. 402) Contact: Mr K Beaumont

DI, Priestley House, Park Row, Leeds LS1 5LF. (0532 443171)

WEST MIDLANDS

DoE, Room 815, Five Ways Tower, Frederick Road, Edgbaston, Birmingham B15 1SJ. (021 643 8191 ext. 2542) Contact: Mr N. H. Perry

DI, Ladywood House, Stephenson Street, Birmingham B2 4DT. (021 632 4111)

EAST MIDLANDS

DoE, Room 609, Cranbrook House, Cranbrook Street, Nottingham NG1 1EY. (0602 46121 ext. 261) Contact: Mr N. H. Perry

DI, Severns House, 20 Middle Pavement, Nottingham NG1 7DW. (0602 56181)

EASTERN

DoE, Room 402, Charles House, 375 Kensington High Street, London W14 8QH. (01 603 3444 ext. 413) Contact: Miss K. B. Pailling
DI, Charles House, 375 Kensington High Street, London W14 8QH. (01 603 2060)

SOUTH-EASTERN

DoE, Room 535, Charles House, 375 Kensington High Street, London W14 8QH. (01 603 3444 ext. 4) Contact: Mr N. Thompson
DI, Charles House, 375 Kensington High Street, London W14 8QH. (01 603 2060)

LONDON

DoE, Room C8/10, 2 Marsham Street, London SW1P 3EB. (01 212 3186) Contact: Mr R. Williams

SOUTH-WEST

DoE, Room 10A/03, Froomsgate House, Rupert Street, Bristol BS1 2QB. (0272 297201 ext. 342)
DI, The Pithay, Bristol BS1 2PB. (0272 291071)

LOCAL COUNCILS

The worsening economic climate, with ever-increasing closure of firms and rising unemployment, has stimulated local authorities to add their encouragement to that of other organisations in helping new and small businesses.

Some useful facts have emerged from a study completed in March 1982 by Chris Miller of Birmingham University's Centre for Urban and Regional Studies. This shows that some local authorities are doing much more than others. The only way to check what is happening in your area is to talk to your council's Industrial Development Officer. The following facts might be useful as background information when talking with him. Chris Miller's stratified survey of eighty-six local authorities in England and Wales showed that only three were not providing some kind of specific assistance to small firms. The main ways in which local authorities seem to be helping are described below.

Policies Complaints that past policies had frequently harmed or restricted the development of many small businesses have been taken seriously. For example seventy-five of the local authorities in this sample were making provision for small enterprise developments. They were, for example, identifying disused buildings and converting them into 'nursery units' for use by small firms; sixty-six were relaxing controls on industry and, for example, allowing light industry into residential areas; sixty-four were giving priority to indus-

47

trial and commercial planning applications; and forty-one of the authorities were operating a policy of local 'bias' in their own purchasing of goods and services. A smaller number were trying to link this policy with their efforts to encourage small firms by themselves providing a ready market for some products. Others run local business-to-business exhibitions so that people can see what is available locally.

Advice and Information Local authorities are also aware of the difficulties experienced by many small businessmen in dealing with the 'Bureaucracy'. Many have tried to improve the co-ordination and adminstration of their services that relate to business. This is often through the employment of an Industrial Development Officer (72 per cent of the sample had one) or through a small firms advice/information service (67 per cent).

Here are some examples of local authority activities in this area. Northamptonshire County Council has set up INPUT to encourage the development of new firms. It runs small business exhibitions: it is establishing small marketing clubs with the aim of encouraging more inter-trade amongst local companies (these consist of six one-hour sessions when the principal of five small industries will discuss small industry problems); and it has also held 'Search for the Entrepreneur' campaigns.

Berkshire County Council runs a Business Advisory Service, a joint public/private-sector service providing general management advice to small firms.

The GLC runs training courses for would-be as well as existing small businessmen throughout the year in conjunction with the London Enterprise Agency. The London Borough of Bexley operate a Small Business Development Centre providing information on premises and advice and counselling for would-be and existing small businessmen. Similarly, Brent runs a Business Information Centre; Hackney a Business Promotions Centre; and Tower Hamlets, a Small Business Centre.

Tamworth District Council runs a small business workshops approximately every twelve months, and these provide advice on how to set up and/or develop new enterprises.

Rhymney Valley District Council runs seminar forums to discuss problems experienced by local industrialists.

St Helen's Metropolitan District Council has set up, in conjunction with other local bodies such as banks, firms and unions, the St Helen's Trust to help small businesses. It is an Enterprise Trust which acts as a kind of switchboard, helping new businesses to make contact with local sources of facilities available in the major firms and institutions. It also provides advice on how to raise funds commercially, and in some cases provides 'seed capital'. It works alongside new businesses through all the formative stages, providing information or advice on such matters, as business management, opportunities and markets.

Norwich City Council, Wakefield Metropolitan District Council, and Bedfordshire County Council have also been involved in setting up Enterprise or Venture Trusts to assist small businesses through activities similar to those of the St Helen's Trust.

Kensington Council runs a Resource Centre, providing advice on setting up a business and has run local education workshops on 'How to Start a Business'. It has also provided a workshop/retail project, where people can work during the week and open the units up as shops at the weekends.

The London Borough of Greenwich has played a major role in forming a local Enterprise Agency, a Co-operative Development Agency and a local counselling service for local small businesses.

Somerset County Council's Economic Development Unit published a 71-page booklet entitled Help for the Small Firm, a guide to sources of assistance for the small firm. As well as giving information on local authorities, the guide gives a good overview of national resources and sources of finance.

Loans and Grants. Some local authorities also provide loans and grants to certain types of new and small businesses. This activity tends to be limited to metropolitan, county, district councils and London boroughs, although a few shire county councils do provide some financial assistance. (See table overleaf)

Many of the local authorities offered their loans and/or grants specifically for small firms.* There are also some new initiatives being developed. For example, Scunthorpe District Council considers the financing of business development plans for small companies and the payment of grants to cover part of a small firm's bank loan interest. North Yorkshire County Council launched a Small Business Grant Scheme in April 1982, under which companies employing fewer than twenty skilled workers will be eligible for grants up to £1,000 per annum for three years. In exceptional circumstances this could be raised to £2,000.

In June 1982 the West Yorkshire Metropolitan County Council and the Midland Bank formed a partnership to invest within the County boundaries. Up to £10 million a year will be available for joint equity investments in unquoted companies. This is the first link of this nature between a British clearing bank and a county council.

* Merseyside County Council has run a number of schemes to assist small firms – e.g., CHASE (County Help for Active Small Enterprises), which provides interest-relief grants for construction works, plant and machinery, and working capital.

Loans and Grants by Local authorities (%)

Contributions	Metropolitan counties	Metropolitan districts	Shire counties	Shire districts	London boroughs	% of total authorities surveyed
Land acquisition	100	58	9	24	18	27
Construction of industrial premises	100	75	27	18	45	34
Purchase of industrial buildings	100	75	18	13	36	28
Provision or improvement of services to industrial land	100	67	18	13	27	26
Provision or improvement of services to industrial buildings	100	67	18	13	27	26
Plant & machinery	100	67	27	11	27	27
Relocation from outside authority's area	33	33	5	5	18	12
Relocation within authority's area	33	67	5	5	18	16
Provision of rent-free periods for new or relocated firms on council land property	–	75	23	53	45	30

Finance for Co-operatives A more recent area of local authority activity is the provision of finance for co-operatives. Of the authorities surveyed 28 per cent were providing financial assistance to co-operatives (all the metropolitan counties, 58 per cent of metropolitan districts, 5 per cent of shire counties, 21 per cent of shire districts, and 45 per cent of London boroughs). Cleveland County Council and the London Borough of Greenwich have set up Co-operative Development Agencies to encourage the development of co-operatives. (See section on Co-operatives for more information on CDAs.)

Analysis Studies A number of local authorities now undertake analyses of particular relevance to small firms. Of the authorities surveyed 74 per cent had carried out studies of the particular needs of small firms; and 23 per cent of authorities had instigated investigations of gaps in the market for certain products. (This latter activity is mainly undertaken by the county councils – 67 per cent of the metropolitan counties and 41 per cent of the shire counties.)

As examples, Leicester City investigates new product availability such as through the availability of licences or franchises. Sunderland Metropolitan District has a Business Opportunities Research Unit which provides technical and market research support to small firms. The London Borough of Hackney runs the City Technology Centre, which offers information and advice on developments in new technology.

Enterprise Competitions Many local authorities have sponsored or co-sponsored competitions for new or existing small businesses with substantial prizes in cash or kind.

You may find it profitable, therefore, to get in touch with your local council's Chief Executive's department. Ask to speak to the Industrial Development Officer, and find out what your local authority can do to help you.

More information
A useful book and two new information services, on economic activities in local authorities are listed below.

The UK Business Relocation Handbook, published by Parrish Rogers, Jubilee House, Weston Favel, Northampton NW3 4WW. (0604 407288) £17.00 including p&p. Gives details of local authority officers responsible for industrial and economic development. Also gives details of local professional advisers.

Financial Resources for Economic Development (FRED) is a service for those who need immediate, reliable and up-to-date information on the help available to develop new enterprises and to maintain and expand those that exist. A loose-leaf reference manual brings together full details of the wide range of financial and other assistance available for business development. It is available from the Institute of Local Government, University of Birmingham, PO Box 363, Birmingham B15 2TT.

Local Economic Development Information Service (LEDIS) was launched in April 1982 to provide concise and factual information on local economic employment initiatives being implemented throughout the UK. The service sets out to show how much each initiative costs, how long it took to develop, what the aim of the initiative was and, finally, how successful it was. The Planning Exchange, 186

Bath Street, Glasgow G2 4HL (041 332 8541) can provide further details of the service.

PROPERTY SERVICES

Finding suitable premises is one of the main problems that many people starting up a new business encounter. However, apart from the Enterprise Agencies and local councils, a growing number of organisations are helping to provide suitable premises for new and small businesses.

The Government has recently made a number of important tax provisions with the aim of encouraging developers and others to build or renovate small industrial premises. For example, until April 1985, small workshops of less than 1,250 sq. ft. will be eligible for 100 per cent accelerated tax allowance, an extremely attractive proposition to most businesses. A property development company to be called Inner City Enterprises (ICE), blessed by the Government and backed by the financial institutions, is under active consideration. This company (if it is formed) will take the initiative in finding suitable sites to be developed for new firms in the cities.

Government or National Property Services There are a number of government or national organisations which can help and advise on the availability of premises:

English Industrial Estates Corporation, Team Valley Trading Estate, Gateshead, Tyne & Wear NE11 0WA. (0632 878941)

CoSIRA, 141 Castle Street, Salisbury SP1 3TP. (0722 6255)

Beehive Workshops Ltd are developing small workshops of 500–1,000 sq. ft. in many parts of the country. The rents, which start from £30.00 per week, cover all structural and external repairs and normal user insurance. All mains services – electricity, water, telephone and gas (where available) – are provided and brought to the unit. A toilet, hand basin and electric water heater are also provided in each unit. Tenancy agreements can be terminated at three months' notice. Larger units of 1,500–2,500 sq. ft. are also available on some locations on leases from 6 to 12 years.
Contact the Estate Manager at:

Salterbeck Industrial Estate, Workington, Cumbria CA14 5DX. (0946 830469);
53 Fore Street, Bodmin, Cornwall PL31 2JB. (0208 3631);
Sandon House, 157 Regent Road, Liverpool L5 9TF. (051 933 2020);

Forster House, Allensway, Thornaby-on-Tees, Cleveland TS17 9HA. (0642 604911);
Hallgate House, 19 Hallgate, Doncaster, South Yorkshire DN1 3NN. (0302 66865);
Methven House, Kingswear, Team Valley, Gateshead, Tyne and Wear NE11 OLN. (0632 874711).

The Department of Industry has sections responsible for helping business people to find small industrial and office premises. They very often maintain registers, and will certainly be able to put you in contact with estate agents who are concerned with industrial/office premises in their region.

ENGLAND

Eastern Region/South-eastern Region, Charles House, 375 Kensington High Street, London W14 8QH. (01 603 2060)

East Midlands Region, Severns House, 20 Middle Pavement, Nottingham NG1 7DW. (0602 56181)

West Midlands Region, Ladywood House, Stephenson Street, Birmingham B2 4DT. (021 632 4111)

North-eastern Region, Stangate House, 2 Groat Market, Newcastle upon Tyne NC1 1YN. (0632 324722)

North-west Region, Sunley Building, Piccadilly Plaza, Manchester M1 4BA. (061 236 2171)

South-western Region, The Pithay, Bristol BS1 2PB. (0272 291 071); Phoenix House, Notte Street, Plymouth. (0752 21891)

Yorkshire & Humberside, Priestly House, 1 Park Row, Leeds LS1 5LF. (0532 443171)

NORTHERN IRELAND

Department of Commerce, Chichester House, 64 Chichester Street, Belfast BT1 4JX. (0232 34488)

Local Enterprise Development Unit, Lamant House, Purdy's Lane, Newton Breda, Belfast BT8 4TB. (0232 691 031)

SCOTLAND

Scottish Office, Alhambra House, 45 Waterloo Street, Glasgow G2 6AT. (041 248 2855)

Scottish Development Agency, Small Business Division, 102 Telford Road, Edinburgh EH4 2NP. (031 343 1911)

Highlands and Islands Development Board, Bridge House, 26 Bank Street, Inverness IV1 1QR. (0463 34171)

WALES

Welsh Office Industry Department, Government Buildings, Gabilfa, Cardiff CF4 4YL. (0222 62131)

British Steel (Industries) Ltd, NLA Tower, 12 Addiscombe Road, Croydon CR9 3JH. (01 686 0366); they have small industrial and office premises available in the areas in which they operate, see page 17.

Some Local Property Services A growing number of organisations specialise in providing small office and workshop facilities at modest prices.
Some of these are listed below:

BIRMINGHAM
Birmingham New Enterprise Workshop, Clifton Road, Balsall Heath, Birmingham. (021 449 8125) Contact: Mr Isherwood

CARDIFF
Cardiff Workshops, Unit A, Lewis Road, East Moors, Cardiff. (0222 48661) Contact: G. R. Blackburn

COUNTY DURHAM
British Steel Corporation (Industry) Ltd, Berry Edge Road, Consett, Co. Durham. (0207 509124) Contact: E. Hutchinson

CUMBRIA
Moss Bay Enterprise Trust, Mobat Trading Estate, Workington, Cumbria. (0900 2197) Contact: M. Redder

DUNDEE
Dundee Enterprise Workshop, Logie Avenue, Dundee DD2 2ER. (0382 67951) Contact: Mrs Finnan

GLASGOW
Clyde Workshops, Fullarton Road, Tollcross, Glasgow G32 8YL. (041 641 4972) Contact: S. Morrisson

HAMILTON
Hamilton New Enterprise Workshops, Portland Place (Behind Brown's Car Wash), Hamilton. (0698 283082) Contact: John Murray

LONDON
Barley Mow Workspace Ltd, 10 Barley Mow Passage, Chiswick, London W4 (01 994 6477) Contact: P. G. Shearmur
Clerkenwell Workshops, 31 Clerkenwell Close, London EC1. (01 271 4821) Contact: T. Haines
Hope Sufferance Wharf, 61 St Mary Church Street, London SE16. (01 237 5299) Contact: Ron Perfield
The Old Nichol, 19 Old Nichol Street, London E2 7HR. (01 729 4243) Contact: Mrs Phillipa Ashton
Panther House, 38 Mount Pleasant, London WC1X 0AP. (01 278 8011) Contact: A. S. Perloff
Thames Enterprise Agency, 19 Penhall Road, Charlton, London SE7 8RX. (01 858 8611) Contact: Colin Barrow

NEWCASTLE UPON TYNE
Newcastle upon Tyne New Enterprise Workshop, Albion Row, Byker, Newcastle upon Tyne NE6 1LQ. (0632 764244) Contact: R. Dolman

NOTTINGHAM
Sharespace, 13/15 Bridlesmith Gate, Nottingham NG1 2GR. (0602 583851)
Contact: Virginia Sturt

PAISLEY
Paisley New Enterprise Workshop, Storey Street, Paisley. (889 0688)
Contact: John Murray

TYNE AND WEAR
Tyne and Wear Innovation and Development Co Ltd, Unit 3, Innovation Centre, Tyne and Wear NE10 0UW. (0632 382468) Contact: Dr J. A. Hedley

WEST YORKSHIRE
Pennine Heritage Ltd, The Birchplace Centre, Hebden Bridge, West Yorkshire HX7 8GD. (042 284 3626) Contact: Jennifer Holt

Some important new London initiatives

These are recorded in part because they are new and important and also as they may be indicative of trends elsewhere in the country.

London Industrial Centre, Greater London Council, Island Block, County Hall, London SE1 7PB. (01 633 7494) This provides a wide range of free advisory services to help businessmen to locate, relocate and expand in London. These include:

- a register of available sites and buildings for rent or sale throughout Greater London, whether in public or private ownership;
- advice on administrative and statutory requirements, such as building, planning and fire regulations – aimed at saving time and cutting through all unnecessary red tape, so that delays and frustrations in implementing development plans are minimised;
- assistance and advice on all matters concerned directly or indirectly with the development or redevelopment of industrial/commercial land and buildings, whether privately or publicly owned;
- help with the recruitment of staff by operating a scheme to find homes for essential workers;
- immediate access to a network of contacts in industry, the thirty-two London boroughs, and government departments concerned with trade, and industry and land use;
- contacts with banks and finance houses to help firms resolve their financial problems;
- information on eligibility for grants or loans in support of schemes to protect and create jobs in certain designated areas of London under the Inner Urban Areas Act, 1978.

(Other major cities probably have similar centres; ring your town hall for details.)

LENTA Properties Ltd, 69 Cannon Street, London EC4 5AB. (01 248 4444 ext. 226 or 222, or 01 236 2676/7). Formed in 1981 to act as a catalyst in the supply of premises and an adviser to those look-

55

ing for premises in and around London. It has also bought and developed property itself. One site completed in 1982 has forty-five small workshops and stores ranging from 200 to 1,300 sq. ft.

Small Business Property Investment (London) Ltd, 1 Buckingham Place, London sw1e 6hs. (01 834 3279). Set up a Unit Trust in 1982 to invest in small business property in the Greater London area. Using some £7 million of local authority pension fund money, it can provide finance to help the development of suitable premises for small firms. The Trust is promoted by an associate company of the Chartered Institute of Public Finance and Accountancy, Granby Hunter and URBED (Urban & Economic Development Ltd).

Conventional Methods

Do not forget the more obvious ways of finding premises. These still account for the great majority of satisfied customers.

Dalton's Weekly specialises in a wide range of business areas, including both vacant property and going concerns.

Local newspapers often have a special day each week for business premises; see Section 3 (page 68) for more details.

Business transfer agents are analogous to estate agents and are listed in the Yellow Pages.

Local authorities frequently have lists; contact your Industrial Development Officer for advice on local agencies.

Estate agents specialising in business premises are listed in the *Yearbook of the Royal Institute of British Architects*, available in the commercial section of larger public libraries.

ENTERPRISE ZONES

Eleven Enterprise Zones have been defined within some inner cities and other neglected urban black spots. The zones can give new businesses substantial financial benefits as well as freedom from control. In this way business both inside and on the perimeter of the zones will be strengthened. The zones are not aimed exclusively at small or new firms, but nevertheless they provide an attractive commercial inducement to locate in them. The first zone to become operational was in the lower Swansea Valley in June 1981.

The facilities, grants and other assistance available within each zone are comprehensively described in *Zoning in on Enterprise* by David Rodrigues and Pete Bruinvels (Kogan Page Ltd, 120 Pentonville Road, London n1). The zones are:

Belfast Enterprise Zone Office, Clarendon House, 9/21 Adelade Street, Belfast BT2 8DJ. (0232 248449)

Clydebank Enterprise Zone, Clydebank District Council, Clydebank District Council Offices, Clydebank G81 1GG. (041 941 1331)

Corby Enterprise Zone, Corby District Council, Civic Centre, George Street, Corby, Northants NM17 1TB. (05366 2551)

Dudley Enterprise Zone, Industrial Development Unit, Dudley Metropolitan Borough, Council House, Dudley, West Midlands DY1 18F. (0384 55433)

Hartlepool Enterprise Zone, Hartlepool Borough Council, Civic Centre, Hartlepool, Cleveland FS24 8AY. (0429 66522)

Isle of Dogs Enterprise Zone, London Docklands Development Corporation, West India House, Millwall Dock, London E14. (01 515 3000)

Trafford Park Enterprise Zone, Borough Council, Birch House, Talbot Road, Old Trafford, Lancershire. (061 872 6133)

Speke Enterprise Zone, Liverpool Development Agency, 11 Dale Street, Municipal Buildings, Liverpool L2 2ET. (051 227 3296)

Swansea Enterprise Zone, 63–75 Samlet Road, Llanlet, Swansea SA7 9AG. (0792 795777)

Tyneside Enterprise Zone, Gateshead MBC, Town Hall, West Street, Gateshead MA8 1B. (0632 771011)
and
Newcastle City Council, Civic Centre, Newcastle. (0632 328520)

Wakefield Enterprise Zone, City of Wakefield MDC, Newton Bar, Wakefield. (0924 370211)

The table overleaf gives some appreciation of each enterprize zone's record for first year of operation.

Zone	Date set up	Size (acres)	No of new jobs promised or created	No of new firms moving in	New factory space built or under construction (sq. feet)
Belfast	Oct 1981	523	275	15	250,000
Clydebank	Aug 1981	570	1,500	117	1,100,000
Corby	June 1981	280	2,300	32	1,200,000
Dudley	July 1981	538	400	26	250,000
Hartlepool	Oct 1981	265	550	17	255,000
Isle of Dogs	April 1982	482	3,000	10	790,000
Newcastle	Aug 1981	1,114	1,500	36	600,000
Trafford	Aug 1981	790	800	45	1,200,000
Speke	Aug 1981	328	263	10	1,400,000
Swansea	June 1981	735	951	40	520,000
Wakefield	July 1981	140	100	3	60,000

Source: Sunday Telegraph, August 1982, Philip Beresford

The government clearly is pleased with the scheme as plans were announced in August 1982 to double the number of zones.

INDEPENDENT BUSINESS ASSOCIATIONS

Alliance of Small Firms & Self-employed People Ltd, 42 Vine Road, East Molesey, Surrey KT8 9LF. (01 979 2293)

The alliance aims to represent and publicise the interests of its members at both national and local level. Membership costs £15.00 per annum, and a legal expenses insurance cover is available for a further £10.00. Members can use the Alliance's Enquiry Services, which give advice and information on a wide range of tax, legal and employment matters. If they cannot give you an answer they will put you in touch with a consultant who can. The first consultation is free, and thereafter you agree a price with the consultant direct.

Association of Independent Businesses, Trowbray House, 108 Weston Street, London SE1 3QB. (01 403 4066). This was established in 1968 to promote the cause of the smaller business. The aim of the association is to remove discrimination against independent businesses in existing and proposed legislation, and so it maintains close contact with both Whitehall and Westminster.

Its small national office staff has a limited capacity to answer members' queries on typical problems that face independent businesses. They can also signpost enquirers to other useful sources of advice.

Black Business Development Unit, Polytechnic of the South Bank, Manor House, 58 Clapham Common Northside, London SW4 9RZ. (01 223 8977/8)

The Business Management Association, St Marks Hall, Balderton Street, London W1Y 1TG. (01 493 1001).

The association is an independent body that is representative of small businesses operating on an international basis. Annual subscriptions start at £25, with a registration fee of £15. The principal benefits are set out below.

- Consultancy facilities and services: This is a problem-solving service covering a variety of business topics, including management, finance, sales and marketing, public relations, education and training.
- Business contacts: through a network of agents throughout the free trading world the association can provide on-the-spot market information and business contacts.
- International trade: The association have a specialist team who can advise on all matters of international trade, including market feasibility and product analysis.
- The Legal Advisory Service: This is available only to corporate and fellow members. It offers advice on many business legal matters.

Chambers of Industry and Commerce Apart from playing an important role in providing information and help for existing businesses, chambers of commerce have been a major force in the launching of many of the most prominent and effective Enterprise Agencies. They have also sponsored many local new business competitions. They are a very important source of information, advice and help for new and small businesses.

Confederation of British Industry (CBI), Centre Point, 103 New Oxford Street, London WC1A 1DU. Their Smaller Firms Council carries out research and publishes papers concerning the needs of smaller firms. Through this work they set out to influence government policy towards small business and government-sponsored activity in this field.

The Forum of Private Business Ltd, Ruskin Room, Drury Lane, Knutsford, Cheshire WA16 0ED. (0565 4467). This is a non-profit-making organisation with the objectives of promoting and preserving a system of free competitive enterprise in the UK, and also of giving private people a greater voice in the legislation that affects their business. The forum researches and distributes a *Referendum* nine times a year, keeping members informed and asking their views on a number of topical and important business issues. It makes government aware of these views both directly and by various public relations activities. The Forum also plays a role by initiating training programmes in schools and colleges to show the importance of free enterprise in our society. Voting membership rises to a maximum of £250.00 per annum.

The Institute of Directors, 116 Pall Mall, London SW1Y 5ED. (01 839 1233). The institute represents the interests both of the directors of large companies and owner directors of smaller ones. In particular, it has a service for putting those looking for funds or other resources in touch with those with funds to invest.

Institute of Small Business, 13 Golden Square, London W1R 4AL. (01 437 4923)

The institute publishes a range of periodicals aimed at the self-employed and those in small businesses, available by subscription only.

International Labour Office, Small Enterprise Development Section, CH-1221 Geneva 22 Switzerland. Contact: A. C. J. Albregts. The ILO was created under the Treaty of Versailles in 1919 together with the League of Nations. It is concerned with the conditions of work, pay and employment opportunities amongst other subjects. The main thrust of their small enterprise work is aimed at the developing countries though they do have publications and training materials focusing on the needs of small businesses in developed countries.

Job Creation Limited, 17/18 Old Bond Street, London, w1x 3da. (01 409 2229) Executive Director – Guy Halliwell. Established in June 1980 to take responsibility for job creation programmes in specific locations. They set out to create new job opportunities in three related ways:

- by establishing and managing the physical and psychological environment in which new businesses can start up and prosper, often by the conversion of old buildings into new business centres;
- by helping existing local businesses to take opportunities for expansion or diversification;
- by attracting mobile projects to areas of concern.

They offer this service throughout the UK to government agencies and local authorities facing high unemployment; and to industry facing the problems of closures and major redundancies. The profitability of Job Creation Limited in this work is directly linked to the actual number of long term jobs created. Evolving from the core activity of creating jobs, Job Creation Limited operates in four other areas:

- through consultancy by conducting feasibility studies for job creation programmes, and also by undertaking major strategic studies;
- by developing, setting up and managing Advanced Business Centres and Science Parks, an area in which Job Creation Ltd and its associates are exceptionally qualified;
- in the field of property by disposing of or converting redundant industrial sites often combining job creation with turning a property liability into a valuable asset;
- by European Community Representation, through their Brussels office, working on behalf of UK companies, and assisting them to obtain maximum grants and loans from EEC funds.

They already have an impressive client list of major companies and councils, and a very high powered team of executives and associates. Regional offices are:

Job Creation Limited, Belfast Enterprise Zone Office, Clarendon House, 9–21 Adelaide Street, Belfast, bt2 8dj (02322 48449)
Contact: Denis Myles
Gosport Job Creation Project, 15 Lees Lane, Gosport, Hampshire, po12 3ul (07017 80711/24331)
Contact: David Morgan
Southwark Job Creation, 226 Tower Bridge Road, London, se1 2ll (01 403 5222)
Contact: Rob Maidment/Colin Fricker/Jill Boggiss

Lochaber Job Creation Project, High Street, West End, Fort William, Invernessshire, PH33 6EB (0397 5623/5668)
Contact: Donald Skinner
Wirral Job Creation Project (from 1st October 1982), Odyssey Works, Birkenhead. Tel. to be advised.
Brussels Job Creation Limited, Avenue du General de Gaulle, 27c, 1050 Brussels, Belgium (010 322 648 9154)
Contact: Brigette Deconinck
Job Creation Limited, Korte Poten 7, 2511 EB The Hague, Netherlands. (010 31 70 65 3338)
Contact: Roger Thurman

The National Federation of Self-Employed and Small Businesses Ltd,

32 St Annes Road, West Lytham St Annes, Lancashire FY8 1NY. (0253 720911) Press and Parliamentary office: 45 Russell Square, London WC1. (01 636 3828) The federation is a campaigning pressure group in business to promote and protect the interests of all who are either self-employed or who own or are directors of small businesses. Formed in 1974, it now has some 50,000 members in 300 branches throughout the UK. The federation has the funds to take major test cases of importance to small business through the expensive legal process leading to the House of Lords (or European Court of Human Rights). They have been particularly effective in taxation and VAT matters.

Amongst other benefits, members are covered by a legal expenses and compensation cover scheme. The cover includes:

- *VAT tribunal representation*, and costs up to £10,000 per case to appeal in VAT disputes;
- *defence of health and safety prosecutions,* covering costs of prosecution under the Health and Safety at Work Act, 1974;
- *in-depth investigation cover,* to meet accountants' fees in helping to deal with Inland Revenue investigation;
- *Industrial Tribunal Compensation Awards*, to meet unfair dismissal awards. (This is supported by a telephone legal advice service.)

Full membership costs £18.00 per annum.

New World Business Consultancy,

28 Camberwell Green, London SE5 7AA. (01 708 0130).

This is an advisory service focusing on the business development potential of economically disadvantaged groups, such as members of ethnic minorities wanting to start up a business. The consultancy operates as an autonomous unit within South Bank Polytechnic Centre for Employment Initiative.

Contact: Jonathan Emanuwa

PACE (PA Creating Employment),

c/o PA Management Consultants Ltd, Hyde Park House, 60a Knightsbridge, London SW1X 7LE. (01 235 6060)

This organisation aims at two particular areas: the managed 'industrial village'; and the attraction of jobs into the UK through the initiative of PA's international network of offices.

The Small Business Bureau, 32 Smith Square, London SW1P 3HH. (01 222 9000)

Formed in 1976, the bureau aims to serve the needs of the small business community. Membership costs £15 per annum, and gives you access to its Advisory Service and a copy of its bi-monthly newspaper, *Small Business*. It also represents the small business point of view to Government, organises trade delegations, and provides European opportunities through its involvement with EMSU (the European Medium and Small Business Union).

Small Firms Information Service, of the British Institute of Management, Parker Street, London WC2B 5PT.

The BIM runs a small firms information service to help with the management problems the smaller firm might encounter, and a sign-posting service to other sources of assistance in the area of general business information.

Setting up in Business, this is a package of articles, pamphlets, check lists, reading lists and other material put together for loan to the member who is considering setting up in business for the first time. The material highlights both the problems and the advantages of being self-employed, the various considerations involved in registering a company, tax planning, employing staff, credit control, obtaining finance and gaining help from bank managers and accountants.

The service is for members, although non-members may have photocopies of information sent to them for a modest cost.

The Union of Independent Companies, Alan Randall, 71 Fleet Street, London EC4. (01 583 9302; telex 298681 ComSerG)

This is a non-political organisation formed in 1977 by a number of small independent industrialists in the south-west of England. Its aim is to create an environment which will stimulate the independent sector of the economy and generally to further the interests of the small independent company, in both the manufacturing and servicing sectors.

The UIC works through small groups who run independent companies in many parliamentary constituencies, to research the problems affecting small independent companies and their potential growth and to develop methods of mutual assistance and combination. The UIC has a small effective headquarters in Fleet Street, London, where it maintains active contact with Whitehall, Westminster and the press. It disseminates literature, information and a monthly newsletter to members.

BUSINESS OPPORTUNITIES

If you know what kind of business you want and you plan either to start from scratch, or, if you are already in business, to grow from your existing base, then these ideas and opportunities may not be for you. There are, however, a very large number of people who simply know that they would like to work for themselves – quite what at they are not so sure.

There is nothing unusual about this phenomenon, sometimes an event such as redundancy, early retirement or a financial windfall may prompt you into searching for a business opportunity, or perhaps into extending the scope of an existing business idea. Business ideas themselves very often come from the knowledge and experience gained in previous jobs, but they take time to germinate. More usually people only really start to think seriously (and usefully) about an idea when it becomes an opportunity.

This section offers three main areas to examine and so increase your range of opportunities.

NEW PRODUCTS OR BUSINESSES

Although you may not know exactly what you want to do, you will have certain resources and skills. Contacting people with complementary 'features' is one way of getting into business, or expanding an existing business.

There are a number of organisations and publications that put people in touch with business opportunities and new products.

The Business Co-operation Centre, rue Archimède 17, B-1040 Brussels.

This centre was set up in 1972 to assist small and medium-sized firms to contact and co-operate with companies with similar interests in the Community. The centre was established on an experimental basis for a period of three years, but proved sufficiently popular to become a permanent service providing information to companies on economic, legal, tax and financial aspects of cross-frontier co-operation and integration. In addition, the centre acts as a 'marriage bureau' for small and medium-sized firms, putting potential partners in touch with one another and assisting in preliminary discussions.

Any firm seeking the centre's help is asked to provide certain information about itself, and to define exactly what type of partner or what type of co-operation it wants. All the information supplied, and any queries received, are treated as strictly confidential, and no names are revealed without the agreement of all parties. The centre will search its files for a suitable partner and, if the application cannot be matched, will, if the firm agrees, circulate a summary of its requirements, with no names mentioned, to its 'correspondents' in all EEC countries.

Ideas and Resource Exchange Ltd (IREX), Snow House, 103 Southwark Street, London SE1 OJF. (01 633 0424); telex 25187 SM1 W1LG)

IREX, founded in 1981, and extensively enhanced in January 1982, 'deals' in saleable resources. These are the elements of a business broadly classified as ideas, skills, finance, capacity and markets. These resources (or any combination of them) are offered or sought by members, using a computer-based exchange.

A member's entry in the exchange data box is called a proposition. This entry is based on a short statement written by the proposer giving the basic details of what he wants, either to receive or to offer. This information is coded, entered into the computer, which then carries out a matching run. When the computer finds that a member is offering what another is looking for, it records a match, after which the respective members' propositions are printed out. Contact can then be made in a way that ensures whatever level of security and confidentiality the respective members want.

Membership costs £25.00 per annum with a joining fee of £15.00 in the first year. The charge for putting a proposition into the exchange is £5.00, and first-time users are entitled to one free entry.

This seems a sound, economical and quick way of putting your under-used resources to work in exploiting a business opportunity. The Directors of IREX have an impressive past track record. They include Sir Alexander Smith (Chairman), who until 1981 was the Director of Manchester Polytechnic, and Colin Lyle, a Director of Tate & Lyle.

Since the index began in February 1981, members have recorded nearly 10,000 matches, and there is now over £8.5 million on IREX's data base available to help finance new or existing business.

Two other interesting IREX services are described below.

The Enterprise Counselling Service gives positive and supportive service to companies and their employees in periods of redundancy. IREX takes the view that many people leaving large companies are unlikely to return to the corporate environment, so they include alternative activities in their counselling – including of course, working for oneself or in a small business. For further details of this service telephone 01 633 0424 or write to Michael Bretherton, Director, at Snow House.

The Irex Clearing House puts people in contact with specialist help. It covers management, data processing, financial, technical, electronic and engineering consultancy and contracting services. Of course, it works the other way round too. So if you have specialist skills you can put them on offer. For further details of this service telephone 01 261 1543, or write to the Membership Secretary at Snow House.

Marriage Bureau, The London Enterprise Agency (LENTA), 69 Cannon Street, London EC4N 5AB. (01 236 2676/7 or 01 248 4444).

Each month a bulletin is produced in which subscribers can advertise anonymously, either offering a resource, product, service or idea, or appealing for one themselves. Companies or individuals interested in a box number – in this way things are kept confidential – write to the bureau, who then set about arranging contact between the parties.

LENTA has no involvement in any negotiations resulting from the 'Marriage Bureau' introduction. Nor do they accept responsibilities for what happens later. Their service costs £12.00, and with over 100 advertisements in one issue you should find an interesting range of new opportunities.

There are also organisations that provide new products or business opportunities in the area of high technology. More details of these are given in Section 4.

Publications
Business Ideas Letter. This is published by the Institute of Small Business, 13 Golden Square, London W1R 4AG. (01 437 4923)

Each month this publication reviews, step by step, the process of starting up a selection of businesses. For example, in one month their articles included 'How to Start a Small Hotel' and 'Starting a Picture Framing Business'. All the critical steps were examined and useful advice was given. Contact addresses for finding more detailed information is provided at the conclusion of each article. Reading this you would certainly have a good idea about the nature of the business you might be getting into.

Buying a Company. This is a checklist guide to successful acquisitions for the smaller company; it gives you 260 questions to ask before you decide to take up a business opportunity. Published in 1982 by the British Institute of Management, Parker Street, London WC2B 5PT. Price £3.00 (40 pages).

Chartsearch Ltd, 11–12 Bloomfield Street, London EC2M 7AY. These are publishers of a series of books on starting or improving a small business. Prices range from £4.00 to £15.00.

Enterprise A monthly, published by Research Associates, PO Box 125, Oxford.

Entrepreneur Published by Chase Revel Inc, 2311 Pontins Avenue, Los Angeles, California 90064, USA. UK price is £1.50 per issue (monthly). The publication gives a very invigorating view of American business opportunities, by the hundred. Some are not really appropriate, but very many are. Each issue has a 'Millionaire of the Month' article, which should put you to shame! Apart from opportunities it has perhaps the world's most comprehensive list of books on every aspect of evaluating and starting a small new business venture.

Innovators' News Journal Larsavon Publications, York House, 27 Tenby Street, Birmingham B1 3EE. Ten issues each year, on subscription for £8.00.

International New Products Newsletter PO Box 37, Esher, Surrey KT10 0QN.

International New Product Newsletter, PO Box 191, 390 Stuart Street, Boston, Mass. 02117, USA.

New Products International 15 Selvage Lane, Mill Hill, London NW7 3SS. Claims the 'Fastest, Fullest, Widest coverage' of any source of new product information. It gives details of over 100 new products per issue, together with news of major new products 'in the pipeline'. The subscription is £69.00 per annum however; the first two issues are free and arrive before you have to pay your subscription, so you can judge for yourself.

New Product/New Business Digest, published by General Electric USA, Business Growth Services, 120 Erie Boulevard, Room 144, Schenectady, New York 12305, USA.

The digest began twelve years ago as an outlet for GE's developments only, but now it is an extensively researched book. It describes, and in many cases illustrates, over 500 products and processes that are available for acquisition or licensing. The products/businesses, large and very small, range from new inventions, and R & D spin-offs, to fully developed and tooled-up products. The opportunities come from Universities, R & D firms, USA Government agencies (such as the Small Business Bureau), entrepreneurs and major companies (including GE). A very useful source either to get you started or to extend your existing product range.

The digest consists of sixty-seven pages and costs $60.00 including postage to the UK.

Occupation Self Employed, by Rosemary Pettit, published in 1981 by Wildwood House Ltd, Gloucester Mansions, Cambridge Circus, London WC2 8HD.

I think this is a unique before-and-after look at new small business. The author takes a return visit to seventy people who started up in 1976 to see how they were getting on in 1980. Each business area is different, and although many of the problems and experiences were also different, some very important common lessons appear to have been learned. It is a very good way both of gaining an insight into a very wide range of business opportunities, and a look at what problems the first few years might hold. Price £4.50.

Opportunities, A Handbook of Business Opportunity Search, by Edward de Bono, published by Penguin Books (1980) 536 King's Road, London SW1, price £1.95. This will certainly get you started. The whole book is thought-provoking, and the final part, 'Thinking for Opportunities', has a hundred pages that set out to answer two vital questions: 'How do you set about looking for business opportunities?' and 'Where do you start to look for those opportunities?' It is mind-bending but it will open your eyes. An opportunity only exists when you can see it.

Venture Capital Report, 2 The Mall, Bristol BS8 4DR. (0272 737222)

This is a publication that gives details of entrepreneurs and their business ventures, inviting people with money to invest, often on a partnership basis.

Working for Yourself, by Godfrey Golzen, published by Kogan Page, 120 Pentonville Road, London N1.

This is the very successful *Daily Telegraph* book, in its fifth edition (August 1982). Apart from useful sections on the general mechanics of starting a business, tax, raising money, etc., there is a Directory of Opportunities. In this section you are given an insight into the pros and cons of some 60 different types of business, together with addresses and contact points to follow up those of interest to you. Price £4.25. (This is a good starting point in the opportunity search.)

Newspapers One of the best ways to keep abreast of current business opportunities is to read a selection of national and local papers. Start off with as wide a range as you can afford (or visit your library), to get the flavour of each. Then once you have made a selection, keep searching. Many articles give details of useful follow-up addresses.

Paper	Day and Writer	Section
Birmingham Mail (884 236 3366)	Monday–Friday Bob Jebcott	*Business page* Business Mail except Wednesday

Birmingham Post (021 236 3366)	Monday–Friday Graham Sidwell	*Business page* Finance page
Bradford Telegraph *and Argus*	Monday–Friday Chris Holland	*Industry page*
Coventry Evening *Telegraph* (0203 25588)	Monday–Friday	*Business News*
Daily Express (01 353 8000)	Wednesday Roy Assersohn	*Express Money*
Daily Mail (01 353 6000)	Wednesday Patrick Sergeant	*Moneymail* Moneywise; 2 & 3; Questions Answers; Current Accounts
Dalton's Weekly (01 540 8211)	Thursday	Extensive coverage of businesses for sale and business oppor- tunities, partnerships, etc.
Exchange & Mart	Thursday	Business opportunities sections
Financial Times (01 248 8000)	Tuesday Christopher Lorenz	*The Management* *Pages* 2 pages of business opportunities and companies for sale and wanted
The Guardian (01 278 2332)	Friday Clive Woodcock	*Small Business* *Section* Frequent stories of small business success and the new sources of help and advice
Hull Daily Mail (0432 27111)	Wednesday John Simpson	*Industrial Note Book*
Lancashire Evening Post (0524 66226)	Wednesday Mr Heal	*Business Post*
Liverpool Post (051 227 2000)	Monday–Friday Keith Ely	*Business News* Business supplement 1st Wednesday of every month
Manchester Evening *News* (061 832 7200)	Monday–Friday Mr Lomax	*Business World*

Newcastle Journal (0632 327500)	Monday–Saturday Ronnie Harrison	*Business News* Money on Monday, Business Journal, Tuesday, Thursday, Friday and Saturday; Northern Business, Wednesday
Nottingham Evening Post (0602 45521)	Monday–Saturday Peter Skinner/Duncan Elliott	*Business Post* Bi-monthly Business Magazine
The Observer (01 236 0202)	Sunday Melvyn Marckus	*Observer Business*
Sheffield Telegraph (0742 78585)	Monday–Saturday Fraser Wright	*Business* Business extra, Wednesday
Sunday Telegraph (01 353 4242)	Sunday Ivan Fallon	*City Page*
Sunday Times (01 837 1234)	Sunday	*Business News* Business to Business section, extremely comprehensive range of Business opportunities
Western Mail (Cardiff & S. Wales) (0222 33022)	Monday–Friday Ken Rice/John Foscolo	*Business News*
Wolverhampton Express (0902 22351)	Monday–Friday Gordon Key/Brian Blakley	*Business Page*
Yorkshire Post (0532 432701)	Monday–Saturday Bernard Dineer/Charles Pritchard/Robin Morgan	*Business Post*

CO-OPERATIVES

Although the most commonly known co-operatives are the high street shops and supermarkets, there is another, lesser-known variety, the workers' co-operatives – where workers share control and decision-making equally, and not in relation to their financial stake. They split off from the more successful retail movement, reached a peak of a hundred or so outlets at the turn of the century, then declined (almost to the point of extinction).

The Industrial Common Ownership Act, 1976, and the formation of the Co-operative Development Agency (and subsequently the local CDAs) in 1978 gave workers' co-operatives a much-needed shot in the arm. Various estimates put the current population of workers' co-operatives at around four hundred, with seven thousand people working in them. Certainly, if the growth of supporting organisations and agencies is anything to go by, this seems a conservative estimate.

In order to meet the legal requirements a co-operative must conform to the following rules.

Conduct of business The members must benefit primarily from their participation in the business, i.e. as workers, not merely as investors.

Control Each member has equal control through the principle of 'one person, one vote'. Control is not related to the size of financial stake in the business.

Interest repayments A co-operative cannot pay an unlimited return on loan or share capital. Even in good years, interest payments will be limited in some specified way.

Surplus This may be wholly retained in the business or distributed in part to the members in proportion to their involvement – e.g., according to hours worked.

Membership This must be open to anybody satisfying the qualifications for membership.

The main attraction to co-operatives lies in the belief that shared control and decision-making leads to a greater level of work satisfaction. It is an unlikely path to wealth. There may be many partnerships and limited companies that operate close to the lines of a co-operative. They usually recognise that, in order to grow and survive, the door to larger funds than co-operatives can attract must be kept open.

The Co-operative Development Agency and local CDAs are a good starting point in the search for more information on workers' co-operatives.

Co-operative Development Agency, 20 Albert Embankment, London SE1 7IJ. (01 211 3000). The agency was established by Parliament in 1978 with all-party support, to promote the concept of co-operatives. It gives advice on the mechanics and philosophy of co-operatives to people starting a new business or wanting to convert an existing business that might otherwise be sold or closed down.

Either from the central office or through its growing network of local Co-operative Development Agencies, the CDA can advise on local opportunities for co-operatives, and with evaluating specific projects from a commercial as well as a co-operative point of view. It can also give advice on sources of finance, legal and taxation problems, education, training and publicity. The CDA has no money of its own to finance co-operatives, and it charges those able to pay, the cost of the advice and assistance given.

Details can be sent on request of a series of publications which cover various aspects of the co-operative movement.

Local Co-operative Development Agencies A variety of bodies have been set up in local areas to promote co-operatives. Some have full-time staff funded by a local authority; some are based on existing co-operatives; others are run solely by volunteers. None of them is an agent of the national Co-operative Development Agency, but many have close working relationships with it.

Bradford: 4 Grove Terrace, Bradford. (0274 394083) Contact: Richard Jowett, ATEC.

Brent CDA, c/o 192 High Road, Willesden, London NW10 2PB. (01 451 3777) Contacts: Greg Cohn and Bill Ball

Bristol CDA, c/o CRS Ltd, Fairfax House, Newgate, Bristol BS99 7PP. (0272 291041 ext. 297) Contact: Mr John Blizzard

Camden: 12 Fleet Road, London NW3. (01 267 6608) Contact: Will Pollard

Cleveland CDA, 10a Albert Road Middlesbrough TS1 1QA. (0642 210224) Contact: P Corne.

Devon & Cornwall CDA, 21 Fore Street, Bradiner, Exeter, Devon. (039 288679) Contact: Mr J Robertson c/o Cosira, Malford Lane, Exeter, EX2 4PS (0392 52616)

East Midlands Association of Common Ownerships and Co-operatives, c/o Northampton Industrial Commonwealth Ltd., Church Street, Moulton, Northampton. (0604 499664) Contact: Brian Battye.

Greenwich Employment Resource Unit, 105 Plumstead High Street, London SE18. (01 855 9817)

Gwent Common Ownership Association, 78 Bridge Street, Newport, Gwent NPT 4AQ. (0633 51868) Contact: Barrie Cooper

Hackney Co-operative Developments, 16 Dalston Lane, London E8 3AZ. (01 254 3743) Contact: Mr Nick Mahoney

Kirklees C.D.A., Taylor Hill Road, Huddersfield. (0484 48811) Contact: Mr Haywood

Humberside CDA, Not operational until 1983 c/o The Member Relations Committee, Hull & East Riding Co-operative Society, 2 Jameson Street, Hull, Humberside HU1 3LX.

Islington CDA, 326–328 St Pauls Road, London N1 2LS. (01 226 2783) Contact: Mr Roberts

Lambeth/South London CDA, c/o Lady Margaret Hall Settlement, 460 Wandsworth Road, London SW8 3LX. (01 720 1466) Contacts: John Berry

Lewisham Co-operative Development Group, c/o Voluntary Action Lewisham, 120 Rushey Green, Catford, London SE6. (01 690 4343 Ext 630) Contact: Ms Judy Bartlett, Sarah Glen

Employment Resource Group, 64 Mount Pleasant, Liverpool L3 5SH. (051 709 6858) Contact: Stuart Steeden

Milton Keynes CDA, Open University, Walton Hall, Milton Keynes, (0908 653303) P. Milford.

North Wales Employment Resource Centre, Bangor, Gwynedd, N. Wales (0248 54128)

North West Co-operative Development Council, c/o Co-operative Union, Holyoake House, Hanover Street, Manchester M60 0AS. (061 832 4300) Contact: Mr A. Pemberton

North Region Co-operative Development Association, 37 Woodbine Road, Gosforth, Newcastle upon Tyne LE3 1DD. (0632 859517) Contact: Mr N. Watson

Scottish Co-operatives Development Committee (SCDC), Senior Development Officer, 100 Morrison Street, Glasgow 65. (041 554 3797) Contact: Mr Cairns Campbell

Sheffield Co-operative Development Group, Sheffield Industrial Development Office, Palatine Chambers, 22 Pinstone Street, Sheffield S1 2HN. (0742 734563) Contact: Mr Bill Jordan

South-east Wales Co-operative Development Association, C.R.S. Regional H/Q, Moorland Road, Cardiff (0222 20361) Contact: K. Bignal

Southwark CDA, Southwark Council for Voluntary Service, 135 Rye Lane, London SE15. (01 732 9776/7) Contact: Mark Neuman

South-west Co-operatives Group, 149 Lower Cheltenham Place, Bristol BS6 5LB. (0272 555172) Contact: George Micklewright

Telford Working Alternatives, 30 Smith Crescent, Wrockwardine Wood, Telford, Shropshire TF2 7AK. (0952 612740) Contact: Mr Stuart Davis

Wandsworth Enterprise Development Agency (WEDA), Unity House, 56-60 Wandsworth High Street, London SW18 2PU (01 870 2164) Contact: Ms Manuela Sykes

West Glamorgan Common Ownership Development Agency, 2 Christina Street, Swansea SA1 4EW. (0792 53498) Contact: Ms J. Lynn

West Yorkshire Co-operative Development Group, Leeds Building Centre, 4 Knowle Road, Leeds 4 (0532 785253) Leeds. Contact: Raymond McArdle, Anna Whyatt

Department of Development Planning, Town Hall, King Street, London W6. (01 749 3020 ext. 5319) Contact: Andy Flockhart

Kensington & Chelsea: Group Plans Marketing, 37–39 Great Marlborough Street, London W1. (01 434 1461) Contact: Peter King

The Cottage, 6 Tunnel End, Preston-on-the-Hill, via Warrington Cheshire WA4 4JX. (0928 715087) Contact: Stephen Price

---

Beechwood College, Elmete Lane, Roundhay, Leeds LS8 2LQ (0532 72025)

The College, itself an independent co-operative, was founded in 1979 to meet the growing demand for education and training. Their courses are modestly priced, at around £12.00 per day, and cover most topics from how to start a co-operative to how to cope with expansion.

They also have a consultancy service, available to co-operatives, networks, voluntary groups and unemployment centres.

A leaflet is available which sets out the course programmes for each quarter, and also a booklist.

The Commonwork Centre, Bore Place, Tiddingstone, Edenbridge, Kent TN8 7AR. (073 277 255)

Commonwork is based on a farm in the Kent countryside, and was formed in 1976. It has gathered together learning material, and is using this in courses and workshops for co-operators. The centre can be used for groups of up to seventeen to stay for 'tailor-made' courses at very modest prices.

The Co-operative Bank PLC, Head Office, 1 Balloon Street, Manchester, M60 4EP. (01 832 3456 ext. 2803/2)

In 1978 this bank launched a special start-up scheme, aimed at encouraging viable new co-operatives. This consisted of an offer by the bank to match, pound for pound, the capital raised by members. Interest and other charges are at the prevailing commercial rate. Although this offer in itself is not particularly generous (given a sound business proposition any bank would lend in this ratio), their appreciation of the mechanics of a co-operative may make them a more understanding audience.

The Co-op Bank has been looking after the banking requirements of the co-operative movement for over 100 years. The full range of 'clearing bank' services are also available, including the Government Loan Guarantee Scheme. There are also more bank outlets than you may have thought: 75 regional branches (rising to over 100 over the decade), and 1,000 Handybanks.

Co-operative Enterprise Centre (Hartlepool) Ltd, Oaksway, Hartlepool Trading Estate, Hartlepool, Cleveland TS24 0JX. (0429 34617)
Manager: Dr Peter Slowe.

The centre opened in May 1982 as a European Commission pilot project with £320,000 from the EEC, The Manpower Services Commission and Cleveland Council. A further £5,000 has been raised by local churches.

The centre is intended to house new co-operative ventures for a year. During that time they will get training in business methods, and other help to establish their business on a sound basis before moving out. This will make room for the next intake.

Six co-operatives are in the centre at the moment, making and marketing both consumer and industrial products.

The Co-operative Union Ltd, Publication Sales Section, Holysake House, Hanover Street, Manchester M60 0AS. Their booklist is probably the most comprehensive on the subject in the UK, covering both the theory and the practice.

The Co-operative Union Ltd, Education Department, Stanford Hall, East Leake, Loughborough, Leicestershire LE12 5QR. (050982 2333) This is the supreme body in the traditional co-operative movement. The Co-operative College is based here, and it offers a variety of courses for managers. In 1982 it launched a new one-year course for mature students from inside or outside the co-operative movement (grants available).

This is also a contact point for the union's 50 full-time and 70 part-time education secretaries. They cover the country, and are a useful starting point for anyone wanting to find out more about co-operatives, courses, books or organisations.

Industrial Common Ownership Finance Ltd, 4 St Giles Street, Northampton NN1 1AA. (0604 37563)

Formed by ICOM (Industrial Commmon Ownership Movement) in 1973, ICOF Ltd now operates independently. It provides short- to medium-term loans from six months to six years and repayments can be made at regular periods – for example, monthly or in a lump sum at the end. The minimum sum it will consider is £500, and the maximum is £50,000, though usually loans range between £2,500 and £10,000.

The loan application form itself is a refreshingly simple but effective document. ICOF Ltd is quite a modest operation, having made a total of around 40 loans, with a little over half of these still outstanding, totalling some £130,000. Deposits in ICOF come in the main from larger co-operatives, such as Scott-Bader, and the Department of Industry.

Sources of Finance for Small Co-operatives by John Pearce, is ICOM pamphlet No. 7, price 25p.

Job Ownership Ltd, 9 Poland Street, London W1V 3DL. (01 437 5511) Chairman: The Rt. Hon. Jo Grimmond, M.P.; Director of Operations: Robert Oaksholt. Job Ownership was formed in 1978 to encourage the formation of all types of worker-owned business.

Apart from promoting the ideas of worker ownership, JOL is a consultancy. It advises people who are considering what sort of 'co-operative' to set up (for there are several quite different forms of worker ownership, of which the JOL model is only one). JOL's advice may include the preparation of a feasibility study/business plan, to help with a presentation to a source of loan funds, or help in forming a network of contacts. Normally they do not charge for initial consultation, and if they do their charges are modest compared with those of more conventional management consultancies.

Registry of Friendly Societies, 17 North Audley Street, London W1Y 2AP. (01 629 7001). The register can give information about the legal requirements of forming a co-operative.

Assistant Registrar of Friendly Societies, 19 Heriot Row, Edinburgh. (031 556 4371)

Publications

A Handbook for Workers' Co-operatives This is a simple and understandable guide to starting up and running a co-operative venture. It is published by Aberdeen People's Press, 1980, and written by Peter Cockerton, John Pearce, Ian Gilmour White and Anna Whyatt.

Work Aid — Business Management for Co-operatives and Community Enterprises was written by Tony Naughton. This book covers the legal, accounting, taxation, financial and marketing aspects of running a co-operative, and is published by Commonwork.

FRANCHISING

Franchising accounts for about a third of retail sales in the USA including household names such as Coca-Cola, Avis Rent-a-Car and the ubiquitous McDonalds (over 5,000 franchisees in the US alone). It is also viewed as one of the safest types of business (in the USA) with only fifty firms failing in 1981. To quote the US Department of Commerce: 'compared to total business format franchising sales of $85 billion, the $206 million turn-over of the fifty failures should be regarded as minimal'.

Between 1978 and 1980, retail franchise outlets in the UK doubled, from approximately 2,000 to 4,000. By 1983, the 120 or so UK franchise organisations are expected to be operating 6,000 outlets, with sales approaching £500 million. These include such names as Pronta Print, Home Tune and Kentucky Fried Chicken.

The franchise method involves three elements: a business (franchisor), which grants to others (franchisees) a right or licence (franchise).

Franchising is a marketing technique used to improve and expand the distribution of a product or service. The franchisor supplies the product or teaches the service to the franchisee, who in his turn sells it to the public. In return for this, the franchisee pays a fee and a continuing royalty, based usually on turn-over. The advantage to the franchisee is a relatively safe and quick way of getting into business for himself, but with the support and advice of an experienced organisation close at hand. The franchisor can expand his distribution with the minimum strain on his own capital and have the services of a highly motivated team of owner-managers. Franchising is not a path to great riches, nor is it for the truly independent spirit, as policy and profits will still come from 'on high'.

Before taking out a franchise it is *essential* that you consult your legal and financial advisers. You must also ask the franchisor some very searching questions to prove his competence. You will need to know if he has operated a pilot unit in the UK – an essential first step before selling franchises to third parties. Otherwise, how can he really know all the problems, and so put you on the right track?

You will need to know what training and support is included in the franchise package, the name given to the start-up kit provided by franchisors to see you successfully launched. This package should extend to support staff over the launch period and give you access to back-up advice.

You will need to know how substantial the franchise company is. Ask to see their balance sheet (take it to your accountant if you cannot understand it). Ask for the track record of the directors (including their other directorships).

In the USA there are specific disclosure rules that oblige a franchise organisation to give very extensive details of its operations to prospective franchisees; details are available from the Federal Trade Commission, 6th and Pennsylvannia Avenue NW, Washington DC 20580.

In the UK there are no such rules; however, the British Franchise Association (more details below), does lay down some guidelines. They can let you know something of the reputation of the organisation you are negotiating with.

It might also be useful to ask one of the banking organisations (also listed below) if the franchisor has been vetted by them and given a clean bill of health.

Associations

The British Franchising Association, 15 The Poynings, Iver, Bucks SLO 9DS. (0753 653546) The association was formed in 1977 to establish a clear definition of ethical franchising standards, and to help members of the public, press, potential investors and government bodies to differentiate between sound business opportunities and suspect business offers. It currently has some fifty members. Although being a member of the BFA does not guarantee the likely success of a franchise, it does show acceptance of a code of practice.

The association will provide a check-list of questions to ask a franchisor, and will answer questions on non-BFA companies if they have the information.

The International Franchise Association, 1025 Connecticut Avenue NW, Suite 1005, Washington DC 20036, USA. Founded in 1960, this is a non-profit organisation representing 350 franchising companies in the USA and around the world. It is recognised as the spokesman for responsible franchising.

It could be particularly useful in providing information on the growing number of 'new' franchises arriving in the UK with claims of USA parentage.

National Franchise Association Coalition, PO Box 366, Fox Lake, Illinois 60020, USA. The coalition was formed in 1975 by *Franchisees* in order to provide a centre for the expression of the franchisees' viewpoint, as distinct from that of the franchisors. No such organisation exists in the UK, but the American experiences provide some interesting lessons. There are areas of problems and dispute even between ethical and established franchise organisations and their franchisees. If you do run into such problems, this association may be able to give you some ideas and advice.

Banks and Financial Institutions

Barclays Bank PLC, Corporate Business Department, 5th Floor, Bucklersbury House, 3 Queen Victoria Street, London EC4P 4AT. (01 626 1567). Contact: F. P. Salaun, Franchise Marketing Manager. Either through a term loan, or a business expansion loan, Barclays can provide anything from £5,000 to £500,000 to new or established franchisees. Of course, the business proposal must meet certain standards of performance and finance.

Barclays has built up a considerable amount of experience in assisting franchisees, and they know the opportunities and advantages that exist in the 'right' franchise operations.

Lloyds Bank PLC, 71 Lombard Street, London EC3P 3BG. Lloyds expect to appoint someone to manage their franchise operations late in 1982. The manager will be located in the bank's well-established Small and Medium Finance Department, headed by John Kirkwood.

National Westminster Bank PLC, 4 Eastcheap, London EC3. (01 606 6060 ext. 2248) Contact: Tim Knowles: Franchise Marketing Manager

These organisations, as well as the banks listed above, can put together finance for suitable franchises.

Company Services (Canterbury) Ltd, Anzeec House, 6 Stour Street, Canterbury, Kent CT1 2NR. (0227 612188) Contact: D. M. Branton

First National Securities Ltd, First National House, College Road, Harrow, Middx HA1 1FB. (01 861 1313) Contact: Mr Owen, General Manager

First National have agreed a finance package with over two dozen franchise companies. This package can form part of the franchisor's offer to prospective franchisees.

Education

The following organisations regularly run courses on franchising, which are intended to explain the process to potential franchisees.

Crown Eagle Communications Ltd, 2 Bloomsbury Place, London WC1A 2QA. (01 636 0617) Contact: J. K. Van Wycks (Seminars Division)

Franchise World, James House, 37 Nottingham Road, London SW17 7EA. (01 767 1371)

Thames Polytechnic, School of Business Administration, Riverside House, Beresford Street, London SE18 6BH. (01 854 2030). Contact: Colin Barrow See also the education section.

Publications

This field is still dominated by American publications. The American books listed here have direct relevance to the UK.

UK

Franchise Opportunities Directory, available from Unit 10, Wreford Yard, Ransome Road, Northampton. (0604 68691). Up-dated and published each quarter, price £20.00 p.a. Gives the names and addresses of around 100 UK franchisors, a couple of lines description of the business and the minimum investment required.

Franchise Reporter, published by Franchise Publications, James House, 37 Nottingham Road, London, SW17 7EA has eight issues a year; cost £15.00 per annum. It is intended to keep you up to date with UK franchise news between the quarterly issues of *Franchise World.*

Franchising and the Total Distribution System, by D. Izraeli, published by Longman, 5 Bentick Street, London W1 (01 935 0121) 1972. It sets franchising in its position in the economic environment. A good back-drop to see where franchising really fits in.

Franchise World, published by Franchise Publications, James House, 37 Nottingham Road, London SW17 7EA has all the latest news on new franchise opportunities, new consultancies and sources of finance. Each issue has a franchise directory, which describes the franchise organisations and gives some idea of the cost of entry.

A Guide to Franchising, by Martin Mendelsohn, 3rd edition 1982, published by Pergamon Press, Heddington Hill Hall, Oxford, (0865 64881). A very sound introduction to advantages and disadvantages of franchising, it covers the basic principles, including the 'franchise contract' which formalises the relationship between the franchisor and the franchisee. Price £12.50.

Handbook of UK Franchise Opportunities, to be published by Kogan Page Ltd, 120 Pentonville Road, London N1 9JN in 1983, by Godfrey Golzen, Jackie Severn and Colin Barrow. Shows how to evaluate a franchise proposal as well as describing the structure of franchising in the UK. It contains a
major section on current opportunities and an analysis of franchise companies.

The Law and Practice of Franchising, by Martin Mendelsohn and Arthur Nicholson, available autumn 1982 from Franchise Publications. The book has three parts: an overview of franchising; precedents of franchising agreements and clauses with commentary; and the law applicable to franchising. The precedents include a specimen contract for a fast food franchise, and an international area franchise agreement. The areas dealt with range from trade marks, trade names and goodwill to the UK and EEC competition laws.

Planned Savings, Vol. 17, No 3, March 1982. The article 'Franchising – avoiding the pitfalls' presents a useful view of the UK franchising scene.

Sunday Times, Business to Business section has a small but growing Franchises sub-section which started in June/July 1982.

USA

The Complete Handbook of Franchising, by David D. Selz, published by Addison–Wesley. Price $35.00. This book is not for franchisees, but if you want to turn your existing business into an equally successful franchise organisation, the handbook may help.

The Dow Jones–Irwin Guide to Franchises, by Peter G. Norback and Crain Norback, May 1982. This is a thorough investigation of franchising, organised by franchise categories. Once again it covers only the American scene, but it does provide some useful pointers.

Franchising in the Economy 1980–1982, published in January 1982 by the US Department of Commerce, Bureau of Industrial Economies, Washington, DC, USA. Although completely based on the USA, it provides an extremely authoritative view of the role of franchising in an advanced industrial economy. It describes the business environment and the successes and failures in each sector of franchising.

Franchising and the ominous buy back clause, by Burr, Burr and Bartlett, in the *Journal of Small Business Management*, Vol. 13 (4), October 1975. The article helps with the crucial question: What happens if I want to sell out?

The Franchise Opportunity Handbook, published by US Government Printing Office, Administrative Division (SAA), Washington DC 20402, USA. Price $9.50. The handbook provides an interesting insight into the official American views on franchising, and also gives an idea of the scope of the franchising phenomenon.

Franchise Rights, a Self Defense Manual for the Franchisee, Alex Hammond, Hammond and Marton, 1185 Avenue of the Americas, New York, New York 10036, USA. Published in 1980, price $29.95. The manual contains perceptive insight into franchisee/franchisor relationships – forewarned is forearmed.

The INFO Franchise Newsletter, from INFO Press, 736 Center Street, Lewiston, New York 14092, USA. Does for the world (mainly North America) what *Franchise Reporter* sets out to do for the UK. INFO gives advance information on what new franchises are intending to start up in the UK, so it is a way of keeping ahead of the game.

Consultancies Some management consultancies have specialised in the franchising field. They are usually experienced both in launching new franchise businesses and in finding suitable opportunities for those wanting to take out a franchise. They are not necessarily legal and financial experts, so it is still important to get independent professional advice before acting.

The AFL Deeson Partnership Ltd, 151 Dulwich Road, London SE24. (01 733 6201/4, telex 916317) Contact: Dr A. F. L. Deeson
Andrew James, Franchise Consultant, Hilltop house, 24 Cairnmuir Road, Edinburgh EH12 6LP. (031 334 8040) Contact: Andrew James
The Centre for Franchise Marketing, 34 Jarvis Street, London W1M 5HS. (01 486 9957) Contact: John Gooderham
Caltain Associates Ltd, Rothamstead, Broken Gate Lane, Denham, Uxbridge, Middlesex, UB9 4LB (0895 834 200). Contact: Dick Crook
Franchise Concepts Ltd, 118 High Street, Sevenoaks, Kent TN3 1GL. (01 228 4743) Contact: Bryan Wilkes
Franchise Development Services Ltd, 3 Tombland, Norwich, Norfolk NR3 1HE. (0603 20301) Contact: Roy Seaman
The New World Consultants Ltd, 25 Queen Street, Glasgow G1 3EF. (041 221 6790) Contact: Charles Wadham
Raye Elliott Associates Ltd, 185 Great Tattenham, Tattenham Corner, Epsom Downs, Surrey. (07 373 59419) Contact: Raye Elliott

Franchise Organisations There are over a hundred franchise organisations in the UK. Only half of them are members of the BFA, and, collectively, little is known of them. *The Handbook of UK Franchise Opportunities,* to be published in 1983 by Kogan Page, will go some way towards remedying this situation. This directory, based on research work carried out at the Thames Polytechnic, provides a basic insight into the scope of UK franchising. Using this guide at the side of each entry you will see how long the franchise has been established, whether or not it is a BFA member, how many UK outlets it has, and whether or not it has a pilot operation, how much you will need in order to purchase and start up each franchise.

Franchise Directory Franchising is an extremely dynamic market, so things change very rapidly. Use the information as a rough guide only. For example, the investment required in a franchise outlet in Oxford Street, London w1, will be very different from that for a similar operation in a small town. If you think the business area is interesting, get more information on *all* the franchises in that field and compare them. Do use professional advice before entering into any agreements.

	Average investment required £	Date of 1st UK franchise	Company-operated/pilot	Franchisee-operated	BFA member or associate Yes/No
	1	2	3	4	5
The Acupuncture Centre, 185 Great Tattenhams, Tattenham Corner, Epsom Downs, Surrey. (07373 59419) Contact: Raye Elliott Aims to relieve and cure a wide range of pains, such as fibrositis, migraine and blood pressure. A shop premises is required and full technical training is given. A medical background is useful but not essential.	12,000	1981	Yes	N/A	No
Anicare Group Services (Veterinary) Ltd, 203 Old Shoreham Road, Southwick, Brighton, Sussex BN4 4LS. (Brighton 591042) Contact: Mr John P. Sheridan, via BFA Provides premises and a range of management services to graduate veterinary surgeons to enable them to provide small animal veterinary services in a group situation.	18,500	1975	Yes	4	Yes

	1	2	3	4	5
Apollo Window Blinds Ltd, Johnstone Avenue, North Cardonald Estate, Glasgow G52 4YH. (041 810 3021) Contact: James Watson, Franchise Manager Manufacturers of venetian, roller blinds and louvre curtains marketed through shops. A total service is offered from measuring the window to installing the blinds. Market includes homes, offices, factories and schools.	7,000	1975	Yes 3	60	Yes
Area Tent Hire, 185 Great Tattenhams, Tattenham Corner, Epsom Downs, Surrey. (07373 59419) Contact: Raye Elliott A marquee hire service for social and commercial events. A unique design of modular, hexagonal shaped marquees which can be linked together.	11,000	1981	Yes	11	No
Autopro, Badminton Road Trading Estate, Yate, Bristol BS17 5JS. (0454 314971) Contact: Nick Brayshaw, Managing Director A van-operated tools sales franchise, making weekly calls on garages to sell to mechanics. The company is a member of the RTZ group of mining and industrial companies.	4,000	1979	N/A	50	Yes
Badgeman Ltd, 544 Chiswick High Road, London W4. (01 994 0826) Contact: David Mackie A fast service for high-quality, personalised name badges on laminated plastic in any quantity. Can be operated from home. Customers range from large companies to local companies and retailers.	6,000	1980	N/A	7	Yes
Baskin-Robbins Ice Cream Europe Ltd, Glacier House, Brook Green, London W6 7BT. (01 603 2040) Contact: Susan Brocklehurst, Operations Manager Choice of type of outlet from complete shops, shops within shops or kiosks. A constantly changing range of 31 flavours of ice cream. Full training and support given.	15,000	1976	N/A	25	No
Bathcare Ltd, 22 Bell Hill Road, St George, Bristol BS5 7LJ. (0272 793443 or 541377) Contact: Mike Scanes Bathcare resurfaces and, if required, recolours baths on site using the Tufglaze process. Operates from a fully equipped van.	7,500 (min)	N/A	N/A	N/A	No

	1	2	3	4	5
Breath of Spring 185 Great Tattenhams, Tattenham Corner, Epsom Downs, Surrey. Contact: Raye Elliot, Peter Guntrip Provides a range of cut flowers and plants for sale in grocers, supermarkets etc.	9,000	1982	Yes	1	No
The British Centre, Cyriakspring 55, 3300 Braunschweig, W. Germany. (010 49531 82500). Contact: barry Schiller A total business unit incorporating an Olde Worlde English pub, a travel agency, a language school and and a business services office.	23,000	1982	N/A	None	No
British School of Motoring Ltd, 81/87 Hartfield Road, Wimbledon, London sw19 3tj. (01 540 8262) Contact: David Acheson Nationwide group of driving tuition schools. Detailed information available to people seriously considering taking out a franchise.	*(Contact direct for details)*				Yes
Bruce & Co., 43 Bridge Street, Leatherhead, Surrey, kt22 8bn (0372 375161). Contact: C. B. Jermyn, I. W. Lynch Business transfer agents for the sale of businesses, shops, hotels etc.	15,000	1981	N/A	7	No
Budget Rent-a-Car International Inc., International House, 85 Great North Road, Hatfield, Herts al9 5ef. (0702 68266) Contact: Charles Clark, Franchise Sales Manager A car- and van-hire company. The franchisee requires a reception facility, space for ready-to-rent vehicles and space for servicing and cleaning vehicles.	50,000	1966	Yes	90	Yes
Burger King Ltd, 10 Stratton Street, London w1x 5fd. (01 629 7571) Contact: Max Booth, UK Franchising Manager One of the world's largest fast food chains, founded in 1954. Burger King provides advice in marketing site, staff training and accounting. *In Europe	300,000	N/A	Yes	Yes 404*	
Burgerland, 24 Cornmarket Street, Oxford ox1 3ey. (0865 42876) Contact: Jeff O'Sullivan An American-style fast food hamburger restaurant. Has eight company-owned restaurants in UK and Eire.	350,000	1976	Yes 8	2	No

	1	2	3	4	5
Buyers World Ltd & Local Traders & Services Ltd, 221 & 194 Lower Addiscombe Road, Croydon, CRO 9RB (01 656 8411) Contact: D. R. Bunker Promote businesses particularly local trades and services by action 2 colour display	3,875	1981	Yes	12	No
Captain Courageous Restaurants, 53 Fife Road, Kingston Upon Thames, Surrey, (01 546 1724). Contact: Mr. John Connell A chain of low cost restaurants providing a low cost menu and prompt service for busy lunchtime service while also incorporating serving techniques for evening trade.	30,000	1982	Yes	2	No
Carmart, Car Market (Holdings) Ltd, Hilton House, The Downs, Altringham, Cheshire WA14 2QD. (061 928 9766) Contact: Roger Fairbrother, Director A Sunday car market bringing together sellers and buyers on one site. For a fixed rental fee the seller is provided with space in which to display his car.	16,000 (min)	1978	Yes 1	4	No
Centaur Electronic Sustems (Fuelsafe), 16 Shaw Road, Oldham, OL1 3LQ. Contact: George Hobday A monitoring system that analyses the use and allocation of fuel to vehicles that form part of a fleet.	9,500	1982	No	None	No
City Link Transport Holdings Ltd, 13/14 Ascot Road, Clockhouse Lane, Fettam, Middx. TW14 8QF. (Ashford 43721) Contact: Robert Thomas Parcel delivery service same day & overnight to and from Red Star Railway Stations.	20,000	1976	Yes 3	100	Yes
Colour Counsellors Ltd, 187 New Kings Road, Parsons Green, London SW6. (01 736 8326) Contact: Mrs Virginia Stourton Interior decorators who offer a colour-match service to match wallpapers, carpets and curtains.	1,500	1974	Yes	50	Yes
The Compleat Cookshop. 60–61 Rabans Close, Rabans Industrial Estate, Aylesbury, Bucks. (0296 31296). Contact: Ron Faulkner Retail opportunity featuring pottery, glass and gifts.	28,000	1980	Yes	5	No
Comprehensive Security Limited, Simpson Street, Hepton, Burnley, Lancs. (0282 78431). Contact: G. D. Thompson	5,000	1981	Yes	10	No

	1	2	3	4	5
Installation of security equipment for commercial, industrial and domestic use. **The Cookie Coach (UK) Limited**, J. Liquorish Associates, Firlands, Kingwood Common, Henley-on-Thames, Oxon (04917 262). Contact: Jack Liquorish	13,000	1982	N/A	None	No
Idea based on the 1906 bakers delivery van and services corner shops, petrol stations, work canteens etc. with a wide variety of exclusive food products. **Cookmate Reject Kitchen Shop,** Cookshop Supplies Ltd, Unit 5, Southern Road, Aylesbury, Bucks, HP19 3AW. (Aylesbury 20695) Contact: Jeff Franklin	25,000	1975	Yes	40	Yes
Retail chain of kitchenware shops, selling giftware, bankrupt stocks of china and glass, and practical cookware. **Copygirl Ltd,** Box 20, Gestetner House, 210 Eustonn Road, NW1 2GA. (01 388 9787) Contact: John Gregory, Divisional Manager.	15,000	1980	Yes	15	No
Franchised by the well-known reprographics company, Gestetner. Provides instant print services and sells Gestetner equipment and office supplies **Cover Right Ltd.**, Unit 10, Bancombe Industrial Estate, Martock, Somerset. (0935 824866). Contact: Mr. P. O'Leary.	7,000	1981	Yes	2	No
Suppliers and installers of high quality wall and floor systems. **Despatch Post,** TNT Despatch Post, TNT House, 102 Long Street, Atherstone, War. CV9 1BS. (08277 5322) Contact: John L. Ovens	4,400	1981	N/A	150	Yes
Posts where people can leave parcels for guaranteed delivery anywhere in UK the next day. A despatch post requires only about 30 sq. ft. but must be in a convenient and visible site. (£4,400 – or around £40.00 per week for 3 years) **Dip'n Strip,** Unit C, 9/23 Third Cross Road, Twickenham TW2 5DY. (01 898 9898) Contacts: Ivor Chivers, Franchise Director; Alan Mackenzie, Managing Director	11,000 (min)	1980	Yes	10	Yes
The largest furniture-stripping company; the process will completely strip paint, varnish, enamel and laquer from wood or metal.					

	1	2	3	4	5
The process takes place in cold baths as opposed to conventional hot caustic soda baths.					
Drainmasters (London) Ltd, 443 Brighton Road, South Croydon CR2 6EV. (01 668 6189) Contact: Mike Barry Primarily a business of inspecting and repairing drains without excavation. The company also offers drain-cleaning and unblocking services. The inspection is carried out by closed-circuit TV equipment which pinpoints the position of any defects.	8,850 (min)	1979	Yes	12	No
Drips Plumbing, 143 Maple Road, Surbiton, Surrey KT6 4BJ. (01 549 9711), Contact: Peter Slinn, Chief Executive and Managing Director A 24-hour, seven-day-a-week, instant plumbing service. Carries out emergency plumbing services and also installs dishwashers, washing machines, radiators and showers. (Out of Dyno-Rod stable.)	4,000	1981	Yes	20	No
Dyno-Rod, 143 Maple Road, Surbiton, Surrey KT6 4BJ. (01 549 9711) Contact: T. Morgan, M. Cowler The largest and best-known drain- and pipe-cleaning company, established in 1963. Provides a 24-hour service seven days a week to industry, commerce and homes.	20,000 (min)	1965	Yes	58	Yes
Fuelsafe, Franchise Concepts Ltd, 118 High Street, Sevenoaks, Kent TN3 1QL. (01 228 4743) Contact: Brian Wilkes Centaur Electronic Systems Ltd are franchising their Fuelsafe System. This monitors fleet vehicle users' fuel 'drawing' 24 hours a day. Centaur's Fuelsafe customers include the police, Reed International and W. H. Smith.	9,500	1981	Yes	N/A	No
Global Cleaning Contracts, Global Franchise Services Ltd, Global House, 4–6 Lind Road, Sutton, Surrey SM1 4PJ. (01 642 0055) Contact: Kevin Wearn, Managing Director The Global franchisee sells cleaning contracts to contractors. The contractor then has to supply the labour, equipment and materials.	12,000	1980	Yes	8	No

	1	2	3	4	5
GKN Autoparts (UK) Ltd, Cavalry Hill Industrial Estate, Weedon, Northants NN7 4JP. (0327 42020) Contact: Colin Oliver Retailing of motor parts and accessories.	N/A	1982	Yes	0	Yes
Highway Windscreens (UK) Ltd, Southend Road, Woodford, Essex IG8 8HD. (01 551 0131) Bob Fitzjohn A London-based windscreen replacement service with a fleet of radio-controlled, mobile workshops.	20,000	1980	Yes	10	No
Holiday Inns (UK) Inc., Windmill House, Windmill Road, Brentford, Middx. TW8 0QH. (01 568 8800) Contact: John Duncan A modern hotel facility offering quality accommodation and service throughout the world. A unique concept in hotel marketing and management. *$300 per room with minimum franchise fee of $30,000. The hotel itself will cost rather more.	*	1969	5	9	Yes
Holland & Barrett (Franchising) Ltd, Heathways House, 45 Station Approach, West Byfleet, Surrey KT14 6NE. (093 23 41133) J. H. Fellingham Britain's largest health food retailer. Health food division manufacturers, markets and distributes wide range of health foods including wholefoods, vitamin and mineral supplements, natural herbal remedies and natural cosmetics.	30,000	N/A	Yes 160	N/A	No
Home Tune Ltd, Home Tune House, Guildford Road, Effingham, Leatherhead, Surrey KT24 5QS. (Bookham 56656) Contact: Duncan Whitefield, Managing Director The world's first and largest mobile car engine tuning service. The company offers a vehicle, equipment, spares and training.	5,000	1968	Yes	250	Yes
Identicar Ltd, Identicar House, 963 Wolverhampton Road, Warley, West Midlands B69 4RL. (021 541 1141) Contact: D. A. Morcom, Managing Director Comprehensive vehicle securing systems, based on permanent vehicle identification. *44 mobile/104 fixed.	12,500	1979	N/A	* 44 104	No
Intacab Ltd, Clock House, High Road, Laindon, Basildon, Essex SS15 6NU. (0268 415891) Contact: Peter Dance, Franchise Director	50,000	1981	Yes	N/A	No

Operates in the style of the Chicago Yellow Cab Co. It is based on a taxi and private hire service run in Basildon since 1975.

Isodan (UK) Ltd, 12 Mount Ephraim Road, Tunbridge Wells, Kent TN1 1EE. (0892 22491) Contact: John Holt, Managing Director

A system of cavity-wall insulation using dry granules. It involves no on-site hazards or expensive equipment.

Isolarm, 12 Mount Ephraim Road, Tunbridge Wells, Kent TN1 1EE. (0892 44822/3) Contact: Michael Kerstein

Based on radio waves, the Isolarm provides effective security for homes, offices and shops and factories without the need for wiring, which means installation can be carried out simply and cleanly without damage to decor.

Jet Cleen Ltd, 11 Ludgate Circus, London EC4 7LQ. (01 248 7088) Contact: Richard Collett, General Manager

A mobile steam-jet cleaning service for commercial vehicles. Working mainly on a contract basis. Jet Cleen cleans the body and chassis. Operates from home with a purpose-designed trailer behind car or van. (Jet Cleen is a division of Alfred Marks.)

Jetmaster Fires Ltd, Winnall Manor Road, Winnall, Winchester, Hampshire SO23 8LJ. (Winchester 2918/3008) Contact: Nicholas Muers Raby, Managing Director

A range of open fires, stoves and cookers including hot-water systems. All can be equipped to burn coal, smokeless fuels, wood, gas or even peat.

Juliet Carpet Groom (UK) Ltd, Franchise Concepts, 118 High Street, Sevenoaks, Kent. (01 228 4743)

A stylish carpet and furniture-cleaning system which is easily run from home. A flexible time-table means that this franchise is ideal for women with family commitments.

Kall Kwik Printing, K K Printing (UK) Ltd, Kall Kwik House, Tennyson Road, Hanwell, London W7 1LH. (01 840 3222) Contact: John Atkinson, Franchise Manager

Company	1	2	3	4	5
Isodan (UK) Ltd	4,750	1979	No	44	No
Isolarm	4,000	N/A	N/A	N/A	No
Jet Cleen Ltd	2,500	1981	Yes	12	No
Jetmaster Fires Ltd	14,000	1977	N/A	N/A	No
Juliet Carpet Groom (UK) Ltd	5,500	N/A	N/A	N/A	No
Kall Kwik Printing	42,500	1979	Yes	43	Yes

	1	2	3	4	5
A chain of individually owned instant print shops. Kall Kwik provides full training, site selection, conversion and equipping.					
Kenprest, R. E. Tyre & Rubber Co Ltd, Mill Lane, Alton, Hants. GU34 2QG. (0420 82122) Contact: Mr R. J. Rara	20,000	1961	Yes	36	N/A
Operates a tyre retreading franchise with full package of materials, equipment and training.					
Kentucky Fried Chicken (GB) Ltd, Hawley Lane, Farnborough, Hants, TU14 8EG. (0252 516251) Contact: Julien Fletcher, Franchise Sales Manager	60,000	1963	Yes	339	Yes
The largest fast food franchise in the world, majoring in chicken. Expanding product range includes corn on the cob and barbecue spare ribs. One of the largest advertisers in the fast food market.					
Lyons Maid Franchise Division, Glacier House, Brook Green, London W6. (01 603 2040) Contact: Vincent Smith	5,000	N/A	Yes	2,000	No
A van-operated ice-cream business. A high-quality range of ice-cream products produced in modern, hygienic factories.					
Marlborough Hampers Ltd, Caddick Road, Knowsley Industrial Estate, Merseyside. (051 548 9322). Contact: Mr E. Duckworth, Mr. F. Roberts	4,500	1982	N/A	None	No
Packs and distributes Christmas hampers					
Masterserve, CMC House, Bumpers Farm Industrial Estate, Bristol Road, Chippenham, Wiltshire SN14 6LH. (0249 56521) Contact: G. R. Bray, Managing Director	11,000	1979	Yes 6	90	No
On-the-spot no-delay complete vehicle service and maintenance plus emergency call-out					
Med-Ped Moped Hire, Med-Ped S.A., San Cayetano 5, Palma de Mallorca, Spain. (34) (71) 21 20 46 Contact: Daniel C. Denby, President	30,000	N/A	N/A	N/A	No
Offers franchises in Mediterranean resorts hiring mopeds to tourists. Mopeds can be ridden in Spain without licence and offer a cheap and fun holiday transport. It has 12 offices in Spain and over 4,000 mopeds in its world-wide fleet.					
Midas Exhaust Centres, 107 Mortlake High Street, London SW14 8HH. (01 878 7803)	30,000	1979	Yes 60	28	Yes

	1	2	3	4	5
Contact: Mike Finn, Development Executive A joint venture between the Midas International Corp. of Chicago and TI Silencers, Britain's largest manufacturer of exhaust systems. Full training and continuing support given.					
Mister Softee Ltd, Glacier House, Brook Green, London W6 7BT. (01 603 2040) Mister Softee claims to be the best-known soft ice-cream company. Mister Softee is sold from catering establishments, kiosks, fast-food sites and vans.	N/A	1962	N/A	N/A	No
Mixamate Ltd, Station Yard, Hayes, Bromley, Kent, BR2 7EY. (01 462 8011) Contact: Peter Bates, Managing Director A new method of supplying ready-mix concrete to the small builder and do-it-yourself market. It is based on a unique lorry which carries all the materials to enable the driver to mix the concrete on site.	40,000	1979	Yes	9	No
Mobile Tuning, 7a Nelson Road, Greenwich, London SE10 9JB. (01 853 1520) Contact: Mr A. R. Roundtree A reconditioned van and new Crypton equipment is supplied to enable the franchisee to tune car engines at the customer's home.	6,000	N/A	N/A	N/A	Yes
Motor Buy, 15/16 Hampshire Terrace, Portsmouth, Hants (0705 739211) Gordon Powell. Local advertiser specifically for car sales. Franchisees canvas local used car dealers etc for sale of advertising space.	11,500	1982	N/A	None	No
Mr Slade Franchising Ltd, Maritime Chambers, 1 Howard Street, Northshields, NE2 1AR. (0632 596421) Dry cleaning units inside House of Fraser and other departmental stores. *Agents	30,000	1982	Yes 19	* 90	No
Nature's Way Ltd, 1 Clifford Road, Bex Hill, East Sussex TN40 1QA. (0424 431124) Contact: Barry Howell An independent health-food shop chain operating in the South of England only.	15,000	1975	N/A	12	No
Olivers Hot Bread & Coffee Shops, Olympic House, 142 Queen Street, Glasgow	30,000	1982	Yes	Yes 1	No

G1 3BU. (041 226 3333) Contact: Ian Mackechnie

Named after the Oliver Twist of Charles Dickens. Available as either bakery shops or bakery and coffee shops combined. The products are freshly baked from natural ingredients and have the appearance of home baking. Established in 1977 and franchised in 1982.

	1	2	3	4	5
Panarama Sunroofs Ltd, Ashville Trading Estate, Nuffield Way, Abbingdon, Oxon OX14 1IU (0235 33355)	1,500 (min)	N/A	N/A	250	No

A division of Tuff-kote Dinoll

Panarama glass sunroofs are designed and manufactured in Britain. They make the vehicle feel lighter and more airy, and greatly increase ventilation. Panarama makes an ideal additional service for body shops, rust-proofing centres, tyre and exhaust centres and car dealers. (Investment figure covers stock only.)

	1	2	3	4	5
PDC Copyprint, 68 Wigmore Street, London W14 9DL. (01 935 3478) Contacts: D. Campbell Nisbet, Managing Director; Harry Stokes, Franchise Manager	15,000	1981	Yes 8	3	No

A copyprinting service offering quick printing with design and artwork. Also a 'while you wait' photocopying and duplicating service.

	1	2	3	4	5
Phildar (UK) Ltd, 4 Gambrel Road, Westgate Industrial Estate, Northampton NN5 5NF. (0604 583111) Contact: John Shannon	10,000	1979	Yes	5	Yes

A knitting-wool and DIY products and accessories franchise, retailing and the company's own products.

	1	2	3	4	5
Photoco Snapshop & Photocare, 427–431 London Road, Sheffield S2 4HJ. (0742 53351) Contact: John Mottershaw, Managing Director	7,500	N/A	N/A	N/A	No

A fast and convenient colour-film processing service which also sells films, photo albums, picture frames and inexpensive cameras

	1	2	3	4	5
Pip Instant Printers, Pip UK, 166–168 West End Lane, London NW6 1FD. (01 794 7850) Contact: Ivor Freedman, Franchise Sales Director	35,000	1981	Yes	6	Yes

Shops provide a full instant-print service from copiers and offset presses; with over

700 locations worldwide it is the largest instant printers.

Pizza Express Ltd, 29 Wardour Street, London w1v 3HB. (01 437 7215) Contact: Ian S. Neill, Franchise Controller
These restaurants offer a choice of 14 pizzas, a selection of desserts and Italian wines and beer. Comprehensive training is given and advice on all aspects of running a Pizza Express.

Pizza Hut (UK) Ltd, 10 Old Court Place, London w8 4PL. (01 937 9649/9638) Contact: Peter Bassi
A division of Pepsi Co., family orientated restaurants offering a wide range of pizzas, soft-drinks, sandwiches, beer, wine & dessert.

Playtime Foods Ltd, Sizers Court, Hernshaw Lane, Yeadon, Leeds LS19 7DP. (0532 504339) Contact: Michael Land, Joint Managing Director
Franchises in the distribution of popcorn. There are three types of merchandiser: a counter-top unit, mobile trolley or large-volume self-standing unit.

Power Rod Ltd, Lidgra House, 250 Kingsbury Road, London NW9 0BT. (01 206 0766) Contact: B. Imrie, Franchising Director
Established in 1971, Power Rod has 35 service centres in operation throughout the UK, providing a 24-hour service to industrial and commercial and domestic users in drainage and pipework.

Prontaprint Ltd, Coniscliffe House, Conniscliffe Road, Darlington DL3 7EX. (0325 55391–4) Contact: Peter Drennan, Trevor Smith, Director of Franchising
High-speed printing and instant copying shops. Printing experience is not required, as full training is offered and all equipment is tested for suitability.

Pronuptia & Youngs (Franchise) Ltd, 70–78 York Way, Kings Cross, London N1 9AG. (01 278 7722) Contact: Edward Young, Managing Director
Leading bridal specialists with more than 275 outlets throughout the world.

	1	2	3	4	5
Pizza Express Ltd	50,000	1972	Yes 6	20	Yes
Pizza Hut (UK) Ltd	50,000 (min)	N/A	N/A	N/A	No
Playtime Foods Ltd	1,350	1976	N/A	N/A	No
Power Rod Ltd	8,500	1976	Yes	35	Yes
Prontaprint Ltd	10,500	1973	Yes 14	180	Yes
Pronuptia & Youngs (Franchise) Ltd	21,500	1977	Yes	35	Yes

	1	2	3	4	5
Retail Shop & Business Sales (Franchise) Ltd, 319 Barking Rod, Plaistow, E13 (01 474 7000). Contact: Rhonda Brooke – Taylor Professional business transfer agents buying and selling a wide range of businesses.	15,000	1977	Yes	32	No
Safeclean International, D. G. Cook Ltd, Pound House, Upton, Didcot, Oxon OX11 9JG. (0235 850387) Contact: Desmond Cook, Managing Director Offers an on-site hand cleaning service for carpets, curtains and upholstery and a range of treatments which provide stain and soil retardancy, fire retardancy and re-move spots and stains.	3,600	1972	Yes	35	Yes
Scottish & Newcastle Inns PLC, Abbey Brewery, Holyrood Road, Edinburgh EH8 8YS. (031 556 2591) Contact: Andrew H. James, Commercial Development Manager A subsidiary of Scottish & Newcastle Brewer-ies, have a number of retail public houses, some of which are operated as a franchise	10,000	1979	Yes 900	5	yes
Seekers Property Shops, Seekers, Owls Lodge, Chatsworth Road, London NW2 5QT. (01 444 5971) A fast-growing chain of shops introducing home buyers to home sellers offering a low-cost alternative to the established estate agents.	8,000	N/A	N/A	N/A	No
Selectacar Autorentals, 10 Plaistow Lane, Sunridge Park, Bromley, Kent BR1 3PA. (01 460 8972/3) Contact: Jim Brown Car and van hire.	12,000	N/A	N/A	22	No
Servicemaster Ltd, 50 Commercial Square, Freemans Common, Leicester LE2 7SR. (0533 548620) Contact: Derek W. Kirk, Market Expansion Manager A carpet and upholstery cleaning organisa-tion specialising in on-site cleaning of car-pets and upholstery in domestic, commercial and disaster situations.	6,750	1958	Yes	170	Yes
Servotomic Ltd, 199 The Vale, Acton, London W3 7RB. (01 743 1244) Contact: Pe-ter Welsh, Franchise Manager Installers of gas central heating. Design, manufacture, sale and installation of dom-estic heating systems.	14,500	1972	N/A	47	No
Servowarm, 99 The Vale, London W3 7RB. (01 743 1244) Ted Brammer & P. S. Welsh A gas central heating installation franchise.	6,000	N/A	N/A	N/A	No

	1	2	3	4	5
Shape Health Studies Ltd, 11 Broadwater Road, Worthing, Sussex BN14 8AD. (0903 200177) Contact: John Bubb or Ric Pitkethly, Directors Purpose-built health studios containing fully equipped gymnasium, sauna, steam room, whirlpool, showers and sun-tanning and beauty facilities	100,000 (min)	1979	N/A	7	No
Silver Shield Windscreens Ltd, 38–42 Holbrook Lane, Coventry, CV6 4AB. (0203 661311) Contact: John Oliver A 24-hour emergency windscreen replacement service for cars and commercial vehicles throughout the UK. Equipment, stationery, marketing materials etc, are supplied by Silver Shield	15,000	1978	Yes 1	42	Yes
The Singer Co (UK) Ltd, 255 High Street, Guildford, Surrey GU1 3DH. (0483 571144) Contact: Brian Peet, National Marketing Manager The world's largest sewing machine manufacturer, and thought to be the first company in the franchising field.	4,000	N/A	Yes 100	150	No
Snap-on-Tools, Derbyshire House, Lower Street, Kettering, Northants. Contact: Michael Ward, Financial Director A mobile, professional tools sales franchise requiring ownership of a van. A subsidiary of a US company established 60 years ago	1,500	1968	No	6	Yes
Spud-u-Like Ltd, 81/87 Hartfield Road, Wimbledon SW19 3TJ. (01 540 8262) Contact: David Acheson, Chairman A fast-food chain, offering baked potatoes with a variety of fillings	30,000 (min)	1980	Yes	16	Yes
Steiner Products Ltd, Broadway Cottages, 57–65 The Broadway, Stanmore, Midx. HA7 4DU. (01 954 6121) Contact: Ian Macaulay, Franchise Director An international group of companies offering a range of the best-known hair-care names in the world. Hairdressing experience is not necessary, as Steiner provide staff training.	25,000 (min)	1978	Yes 5	8	Yes
Strikes Restaurants, 8 Cranley Gardens, London SW7 3DB. (01 370 6964) Contact: Stuart Thompson, General Manager A licensed table service family restaurant which offers a range of popular meals, steaks, hamburgers, chicken and fish.	25,000 (min)	1982	Yes 30	No	No

	1	2	3	4	5
Tan-at-Home Rentals, Queen Anne House, Queen Anne Street, Southport PR8 1DT. (0704 35156 and 43514) Contact: Jim Gudgeon, Franchise Controller A sun-bed hire service which is delivered by the franchisee to the customer's home on weekly rental. There is also opportunity to sell sun-beds in a variety of finishes to match customer's furnishings.	5,000	N/A	Yes	80	No
Tandy, Tandy Corporation (Branch UK), Tameway Tower, Dealership Division, Bridge Street, Walsall, Staff. (Walsall 648181) Contact: Bob Cleaver, National Manager A retailer of consumer electronics, whose range includes hi-fi, radios, microcomputers, electronic components and general electronic durables.	17,000	1973	Yes 212	82	No
Tao Skin Care Clinics, 153 Brompton Road, London SW3. (01 581 3127) Contact: Andrew Ingram, Director A wide range of facial and body treatments, including removal of unwanted hair by electrolysis, and a range of own-brand skincare products. The clinics are mainly for women and are run by women. Company began operation in 1935 and plan to start franchising in 1983.	20,000	1983	Yes 32	0	No
Thermobead, G. C. Insulation Ltd, 12 Mount Ephraim Road, Tunbridge Wells, Kent TN1 1EE. (0892 22491 or 44822) Contact: John Holt, Managing Director Claimed to be the only cavity-wall insulation which can be installed on a do-it-yourself basis. The franchisee inspects the site, provides the customer with a work schedule and hires out the equipment and supplies the materials.	4,875	N/A	N/A	N/A	No
Thorntons, J. W. Thorntons Ltd, Derwent Street, Belper, Derbyshire, DE5 1WP. (077 382 4181) Contact: Mr R. E. Smith A confectionery manufacturer requiring prime-position high-street shops and supplying a vast range of attractively presented sweets.	10,000	1980	Yes 135	40	Yes
Thrifty Rent-a-Car Rentals (UK) Ltd, 144 High Street, Sandhurst, Camberley, Surrey, GU17 8HA. (0252 877333) Contact: John Morgan Car and van hire.	*(All details sent on request)*				

	1	2	3	4	5
Thuroclean International Ltd, 55 Bondway, London SW8 1SJ (582 6033). Contact: Ralph James Service includes cleaning of fine furnishings, carpet dyeing on site and salvaging water/smoke/fire-damaged carpets.	13,500	1975	N/A	N/A	Yes
Torlink, A retail consultancy within Clarks of Street, Somerset BA16 0YA. (0458 43131) Provides a management consultancy service to 300 independent shoe shops selling the Clarks brand. They plan to open 25 new outlets each year through their 'Acorn' programme.	20,000	1966	Yes	300	No
Tuff-Cote Dinol, Dinol (Car Care) UK Ltd, 185 Milton Trading Estate, Abingdon, Oxon OX14 4SR. Contact: south: Mike Chambers, north: Barry Hynes A vehicle rust-proofing treatment for use on new or used cars. Developed in Sweden, Tuff-Cote Dinol is the only process applied in two layers. The company can also offer a paint glazing and fabric protection service. Now incorporates Bodyshield Ltd and Dinitrol (Car Care) Ltd.	8,000	1963	Yes	140	Yes
Unipart, BL Cars Ltd, Unipart House, Garsington Road, Cowley, Oxford OX4 2PG. (0865 778966) Contact: Michael Mathews Retails motor accessories and replacement parts.	30,000	N/A	N/A	N/A	Yes
Uticolour (Great Britain) Ltd, Sheraton House, 31/35 North Street, York YO1 1JD. (0904 37798) Contact: Eric Bottomley, Managing Director An invisible repairing service for vinyl- or leather-covered furniture. The bonding technique is taught. Customers include schools, pubs, hotels and offices.	6,000	1978	Yes 2	25	Yes
Videotherapy, PO Box 29, 48 High Street, Saffron Walden, Essex CB10 1ED. (0799 24599) Contact: Barrington Lloyd, Marketing Manager A revolutionary concept which offers slimmers, smokers and sufferers of psychosomatic ailments a chance to combat their problems by undergoing professional treatment through the medium of video.	5,000	N/A	N/A	N/A	No
Vinyl Master (UK) Ltd, 8 Somerset Place, Tewkesbury, Glos. (0684 295511) Contact: Nick Scanlan, Managing Director	3,000	1979	N/A	10	No

	1	2	3	4	5
Vinyl Master offers an on-site repair and re-covering service for vinyl-covered upholstery. The market includes homes and businesses such as theatres, schools, pubs, restaurants and public transport.					
Willie Wurst Inns, Cloverbest Restaurant Associates Ltd, 9 Topping Street, Blackpool, Lancs FY1 3AX. (0704 44455) Contact: Ernest Horsfall A retail organisation specialising in the sale of a large selection of traditional German sausages.	1,500 (min)	N/A	N/A	N/A	Yes
Wimpy International Ltd, 214 Chiswick High Road, London W4 1PN. (01 994 6454) Contact: John Cutler, National Franchise Manager A world-wide network of hamburger restaurants. Wimpy offers franchise in its new counter-service style.	250,000	1958	Yes	300	Yes
Wordplex Wordprocessing Bureaux, Wordplex Ltd, Excel House, 49 Demonford Road, Reading, RG1 8LP (0734 584141). Contact: Miss M. Wright, Administrative Co-ordinator The bureau offers a word-processing service to local companies. They also sell word-processors and allied equipment. Full training is given.	25,000 (min)	N/A	N/A	30+	No
Young's Formal Wear, 70–77 York Way, London N1. (01 278 7722) Contact: Edward Young, Managing Director These shops sell and hire a range of men's wear including morning wear, formal lounge suits, dinner suits and accessories. *See Pronuptia	25,000	1979 11	Yes	34	*
Yves Rocher (London) Ltd, Chapel Court, 169B Borough High Street, London SE1 1HZ. (01 403 4944) Contact: Steve Partridge, Managing Director Attractively designed and equipped small shops which offer a complete range of cosmetic products and treatments. Over 580 outlets world-wide.	13,000	1980 1	Yes	14	Yes
Ziebart, Envirogarde Group Ltd, Ziebart House, Unit 1, Dominion Way, Worthing, Sussex BN14 8PE. (0903 204171) Contact: Peter Dunscombe, Managing Director Vehicle rust-proofing service and other vehicle services.	7,000	1970	Yes	115	Yes

EXPLOITING HIGH, AND NOT SO HIGH, TECHNOLOGY

Technology presents considerable opportunities to inventors and users alike. It also presents a number of problems. Inventors have difficulty in communicating their ideas to commercial organisations. These ideas are often a long way from being a recognisable product at the time when most help (financial or otherwise) is needed. A growing number of institutions, organisations and services now aim to provide just this understanding and assistance.

On the other hand, there are many small businesses which could make considerable use of new technology, if only they knew how. Microcomputers are the most obvious development, where dull, re-petitive tasks can be done quickly, leaving the entrepreneur free to perform more important tasks.

The following material should give you an appreciation of what is happening to solve these technological communication problems.

SCIENCE PARKS, INNOVATION AND TECHNOLOGY CENTRES

In 1973 an experiment began to encourage the growth of technical innovation in the USA. The basic idea was to bring inventors, entre-preneurs and academics together physically on or near the college campus. By adding some government funds to provide buildings, materials and equipment, it was hoped that the right environment to identify and stimulate new products and services would then be created. Although at the start these 'Innovation Centres' would be heavily subsidised, they were expected to become substantially self-supporting. This, no doubt, was the motivation in ensuring that a good business school was on the campus too (a lesson that UK emu-lators have not universally followed). The American experiment seems to show that the college-industry centres can and do flourish. By 1978 these centres had played a major part in forming some thirty new and largely technology-based businesses. They employed on average forty people each, and some had sales returns of well over $1 million per annum. By the end of 1983, some forty centres will be operating around the USA based on such colleges as Carnegie–Mellon and the Massachusetts Institute of Technology.

In the UK (and elsewhere) similar deliberations were taking place. For example, in 1969 a decision was taken to encourage the expansion of science-based industry close to Cambridge. This would take advantage of the considerable concentration there of scientific expertise, equipment and libraries. The resultant Science Park was officially opened in 1975.

A growing number of organisations are now concerned with improving the lot of the inventor-entrepreneur. Some of these seem to offer little more than premises and a sympathetic ear. Others are more obviously aimed at established businesses. Yet others are rather less than high-technology based. However, most of them are extremely young, and at least half have expressed a desire to provide practical as well as technological help to small, new, innovation-based businesses. This situation represents a considerable improvement when compared to the UK inventors' lot in the seventies.

Aston Industrial Science Park This was established by Aston University and Birmingham City Council late in 1982. It will make use of refurbished and adapted factory premises on a half-hectare site close to the campus. This will provide nursery accommodation for small firms in units from 538 to 5,380 square feet (50 to 500 sq.m.).

Aston is the largest technological university in the UK, with expertise available in the following fields: microprocessors, computing, biotechnology, biodeterioration, pharmaceuticals, tribology and robotics.

Other help to the users of the Science Park will include access to venture and loan capital, administrative services, business advice, technical support on product development, and advice on licensing and patenting.

Contact: Will Rogers, Business Employment Bureau, PO Box 50, Birmingham BA3 3AB. (021 235 4901/4824)

Birchwood Science Park This science park is not on a university campus, although Liverpool and Manchester Universities Joint Research Unit is nearby. The universities themselves, together with UMIST and Salford, are within a radius of 20 miles. The Northern Area Headquarters of the UK Atomic Energy Authority is based at Birchwood, as are British Nuclear Fuels, the Nuclear Power Company, the National Centre for Tribology, the European Space Tribology and the Risley Materials Laboratory.

Sites are available from 1 acre up to 13 (0.4 to 5.2 hectares). However, possibly of more interest to smaller firms is the Genesis Centre opened in the spring of 1982 on the science park. Phase 1 provides 43,670 square feet (4,058 sq.m.) in units from 500 to 5,000 square feet (46 to 460 sq.m.). The units can be tailor-made to meet the needs of a wide variety of science- and technology-based companies, and can be used as a laboratory, a workshop, sales office or demonstration area.

Contact: Tina White, Warrington and Runcorn Development Corporation, PO Box 49, New Town House, Buttermarket Street, Warrington WA1 2LF. (0925 51144, telex 627225)

Brunel Science Park, Brunel University, Uxbridge. In collaboration with the GLC, structural work on this science park starts in 1983. The first phase will consist of 20 small units of between 1,000 and 5,000 square feet (92 and 460 sq.m.). They are sited directly on the university campus.

Contact: Mr Burkitt of the University Industrial Services Bureau. (0895 39234)

Cambridge Science Park, Trinity College, Cambridge. (0223 358201)

Opened in 1975 with 14 acres (5.6 ha.) of land, it has gradually been extended to 52 acres (20.8 ha.) in 1982. The use of buildings on the park is limited to applied research and light industrial production that needs regular scientific consultation with the college or other local institutions and appropriate ancillary services.

The businesses are in the following fields, among others: genetic engineering, contract research and development, computer systems and software, specialist biochemicals, lasers and a firm that consults on the causes of fire, accidents and explosions.

The twenty-four companies on the park occupy units from 1,300 square feet (117 sq. m.) up to 122,600 square feet (11,034 sq. m.), employing from 4 to 200 people. The average is something like forty per company, with around 10 per cent being directors of the businesses.

Hull Innovation Centre, Guildhall Road, Queens Gardens, Hull HU1 1HJ. (0482 226348, telex 52531) Contact: Dr W. K. Donaldson

The centre was set up by the Kingston upon Hull City Council at the end of 1980, to operate as an advice office. Its objectives are to encourage and assist small firms, especially new ventures. From April 1981 the centre extended its services by taking on staff and converting a 603 square feet (56 sq.m.) warehouse in the city centre.

A total of 26 work spaces from roughly 160 to 500 square feet (15 to 45 sq.m.), is available in the building, and the assumed occupancy time is one year.

Although the Innovation Centre works closely with local firms, the University of Hull, the city's other colleges and the Department of Industry, it has some very useful 'self-contained' resources. The centre makes available floor space, engineering staff and well-equipped machine shop, electronics equipment, plastics machinery, operational support, technological consultancy and contact with other sources of advice, education and help. When they are established, clients move out to commercial premises, some of which are also being provided by the City Council. The licence includes an undertaking to pay, over the first seven years of successful operation, a levy calculated to make Hull Innovation Centre independent of public-sector help.

Merseyside Innovation Centre Ltd, 131 Mount Pleasant, Liverpool, L3 5TF. (051 708 0123) Contact: Dr A. O. Jakobovic, Executive Director. This independent company is sponsored by the University of Liverpool, Liverpool Polytechnic and Merseyside County Council. Its general purpose is to foster closer liaison between research activities of the polytechnic, the university and the economic development objectives of the county council. It provides a confidential facility to inventors, entrepreneurs and innovators, ranging from advice on protecting a new product through to its commercial exploitation. The centre can organise appropriate consultancy research, design and testing facilities, and take responsibility for project management. Its main fields of interest include micro-electronics, information and communication technology, biotechnology, energy sources and management, environmental protection and mineral and natural resources.

The Innovation Centre is in premises on the edge of the university precinct and close to the polytechnic's headquarters.

Salford Science Park, Wynne Street, Salford 6. Contact: Mr Henry, Commercial and Industrial Development Officer, Civic Centre, Chorley Road, Swinton M27 2AD. (061 794 4711) Together with Salford University, Salford City Council launched this science park in 1980. The first phase of 8 small industrial units of 1,250 square feet (116 sq.m.) was completed and occupied by business in 1982. In mid-1982 the next phase started with an additional 6 acres (2.4 ha.) of land being purchased for development.

Somerset Innovation Centre, 1 The Crescent, Taunton, Somerset TA1 4EA. (0823 76905) The Centre, launched in April 1982, is jointly sponsored by CoSIRA and Somerset County Council. It is intended to act as a focal point for those who have an invention but lack the expertise to make or market the product.

Confidential, impartial advice is available on technical evaluation, patent and licensing design, design and drawing facilities, models and prototype production, production planning, marketing finance, supply sourcing, and setting up a new business.

In particular, the following facilities are available to those inventors who can show that they have a potentially commercial product:

■ Engineering facilities: As well as having close links with local engineering colleges, CoSIRA has its own experimental workshops in Salisbury where staff specialise in engineering problem-solving. By making use of the skilled and professional staff at these centres, CoSIRA can help inventors realise their original ideas.

- Marketing: Advice can be given on test marketing, advertising, packaging and joint ventures with existing manufacturers.
- Finance: Apart from CoSIRA's own loan facilities, their accountants are familiar with all the many schemes available from the high street banks, the City and various government aids for investment. Budgeting and cash-flow forecasts can be prepared for presentation to other lenders. In addition, they are aware of individuals and firms looking for new products.
- Patents and other protection: Advice on patents, copyrights and trade marks is available through links with several local firms of patent agents. The initial discussion is free or at a low charge.
- What will it cost? An initial discussion costs nothing, and much of the necessary explanatory talks will be at no charge. Should engineering or prototype production be involved, then costs will be incurred but at a subsidised level. Patent fees and the full costs of employing a patent agent are your responsibility.
- The award scheme: In addition to the package of advice, a limited number of cash awards are made to help with the costs of patenting, market research or prototype production. Awards are made to a maximum of £500.00 per applicant. The awards are open to individuals, small firms and new businesses and companies of all sizes. The new product or process must incorporate an innovation but need not be patented or patentable. It must either not yet have come into production or have been produced within the last year. The awards given will be on the merits of commercial viability, market potential, originality and technical merit. Financial need may also be taken into account.

South Bank Techno-Park Contact Mr Jeffers, Project Director, Polytechnic of the South Bank, London SE1. (01 223 8977/8). The first phase consists of 75,000 square feet divided into units of less than 2,000 square feet. The services are aimed at new start high technology businesses that would benefit from interfacing with Polytechnics facilities, e.g. use of computer, laboratories, recreational facilities, etc.

South Bank Techno-Park company manage the development and provide professional back-up services such as book-keeping. Building started in September 1982 and the Park is due to open by Christmas 1983. The funding of £5.8m was provided by the Prudential.

Stowell Technical Park This technical park was developed by Fearney Industrial Development Ltd, in co-operation with the City of Salford. It is close to Salford University but is not on the campus.

However, there are links with the University's Research and Development Faculty. The site has the benefits of an enterprise zone, and is intended to provide 96,250 square feet (8,942 sq.m.) of offices, laboratory, workshop, research and development and servicing accommodation.

Initial contact can be made with Fearney, 445 Bolton Road, Pendlebury, Manchester M27 2TD. (061 736 4576)

Tyne and Wear Innovation and Development Co Ltd, Unit 3, Green Lane Buildings, Heworthway, Pelaw, Gateshead, Tyne and Wear NE10 0UW. (0632 380500) Contact: Dr J. A. Hedley, Manager (0632 382468)

This is the umbrella for the Innovation Centre, sponsored by Tyne and Wear County Council, the North Regional TUC, Tyne and Wear Chamber of Commerce and Industry, and Newcastle and Sunderland Polytechnics.

The centre includes among its objectives the introduction of new products and processes by inventors and small businesses, particularly those that will improve employment prospects in the county. It has space, advice, facilities and, most importantly, encouragement to offer, together with practical help in moving inventions or innovations to the prototype stage. Help is on hand with patent application procedures, and the centre has strong links with local companies on the look-out for new products to license.

Alternatively, the centre will introduce the innovator to other organisations who will help them to set up their business.

The first practical piece of advice comes with their introductory leaflet. Bold red type advises you to patent your idea as soon as possible, and warns you not to talk to anyone until they have signed a 'non-disclosure agreement'.

Unilink, Heriot-Watt University, Riccarton, Edinburgh EH14 4AS. (031 445 5111 ext. 2299 and 2330) Contact: Mr I. G. Dalton, Director

Unilink is the division of the university that works to establish links with both the private and state business communities. The Board of Management, headed by the university's Principal, has ten directors drawn in equal proportions from the university and the business community. Apart from an extensive range of consultancy activities, the Director of Unilink is responsible for the following:

The Research Park Here companies are encouraged to build their own research departments on the campus. The university's particular areas of expertise are electronics and micro-electronics, computer-aided engineering, offshore and petroleum engineering, and biotechnology.

At present the park covers an area of approximately 22 acres (9 ha.), which is 10 per cent of the total campus area. Unlike some science parks, this facility is not intended for production or mass manufacturing units. The site is available only to companies who want to establish their own research and development groups.

Upton Science Park, Metropolitan Borough of Wirral, Municipal Offices, Brighton Street, Wallasey, Wirral, L44 ATD. (051 638 7070 ext. 377) Contact: R. E. Shaw, Director of Development. Wirral Council has designated 50 acres (20 ha.) of pasture-land at Upton for a science park. Their literature forecasts 'prestige developments' and clean, low-level modern buildings. The map of the site shows the GPO site and Champion Spark Plugs, but there is no sign of the university. The sites on offer are between 5 and 50 acres (2 and 20 ha.), so it may not appeal to a small firm.

University of Warwick Science Park, Coventry CV4 7AL.

For more information, contact Mr M. L. Shattock, Academic Registrar on 0203 24011 ext. 2620. Warwick Science Park was launched in February 1982 with some £2 million put up by the university, Coventry City Council, West Midlands County Council and Warwickshire County Council. The 24-acre (9.6 ha.) site will be used to attract high technology firms wanting to take advantage of a close relationship with the university and other institutions, such as Lanchester Polytechnic, the Motor Industry Research Association; the National Agriculture Centre, the National Vegetable Research Station, Lucas Group Services, British Leyland, Rolls-Royce, Talbot, and Courtaulds.

Specific expertise includes biotechnology and bio-engineering; computer science; micro-electronics; robotics; high-technology manufacturing; instrumentation technology; NMR spectrometry; and the physics of materials and solid state physics.

Companies can either build their own premises, rent a unit or take a space in the 'incubator' building. This is a 25,000 square feet (2,322 sq.m.) building designed to house a number of small companies, sharing common central services such as administrative and computing services. Barclays Bank has invested £1 million in this project.

Residents of the science park may be able to get loan and equity capital from either the West Midlands County Council or Coventry City Council. The latter can provide loans of up to £100,000 at low-level interest rates, for the first two years. Otherwise, close relationships are maintained with ICFC, Technical Development Capital (TDC) and the British Technology Group (see next section for more details of these organisations).

Whitechapel Technology Centre, opened in 1982, is located at 75 Whitechapel Road, London E1 (close to Aldgate tube station). Contact: Steve Baker, Dept. TD/LIC/P, Richard Purssell (01 633 7635). The County Hall, London SE1 7PB. (01 633 2344) This is the first of a series of new technology centres that the GLC plan to open in

London. It is intended for small companies supplying technologically innovative products or services. There are nine units, ranging in size from 1,360 square feet (126 sq.m.) to 3,636 square feet (338 sq.m.) available on ten-year leases. A rent-free period of three months will be considered as a contribution towards the cost of fitting the units.

This unit is not on a university or college campus (though Queen Mary College Industrial Research Unit is close), but their innovation centre will help.

An innovation centre will occupy one of the units at the technology centre. This will provide information and advice on new technology, link firms to existing networks of advice, information and support, and generally help new ventures to get off the ground.

Genesis units, fourteen from 240 to 1,100 square feet (22 to 102 sq.m.) are provided. They are intended to appeal particularly to firms at an early stage of their development. This product or service should be based on a patented invention or a technological innovation.

FINANCIAL AND ADVISORY SERVICES FOR TECHNOLOGY

Apart from the science parks, there are a number of other organisations and services useful to the innovator. In this section you can find how to meet other inventors – how to get someone else to do all the work of developing, patenting and marketing your product, and then pay you a fee; how to find financial institutions that understand technology and can give more than just financial help.

British Technology Group, 12–18 Grosvenor Gardens, London sw1 0DW. (01 730 7600) (Funded by national government.) In 1981 the British Technology Group was formed out of the late National Enterprise Board and the National Research Development Corporation. The two organisations have a combined portfolio of 400 investments in industrial companies. In addition, about 200 research and development projects are being funded at British universities.

BTG can provide finance for technical innovation in any field of technology. This finance is available to any company or individual entrepreneur, either as equity or loan capital. BTG is the main channel for exploiting technology from universities, polytechnics, research councils, and government research establishments. It has a portfolio of 1,800 UK patents, 600 licences and over 400 revenue-earning innovations.

For small companies they have two schemes:

■ *The Small Company Innovation Fund* (SCIF) This was established in September 1980 to provide finance where the business as a whole is innovative. Despite having advanced only £1 million spread over two dozen projects since its inception, BTG are keen to hear from innovative entrepreneurs needing the services of SCIF.

- *Oakwood Finance Ltd,* established in March 1981, provides loans of up to £50,000 for technological or more traditionally based companies.

The Chartered Institute of Patent Agents, Staple Inn Buildings, High Holborn, London WC1V 7PZ. (01 405 9450) The institute does not itself run an advisory service, although it will give advice on patents, trade marks and designs where possible. It publishes *The Register of Patent Agents* (price, £1.00), which lists the names and business addresses of all the patent agents qualified to practise before the Patent Office.

The patent agent will be able to give advice on all aspects relating to making application for patents, trade marks and designs, as well as on infringement of these forms of protection and on passing off matters. He may also be able to give advice on the exploitation of an invention protected by patent, although this is not specifically within his field of operation. The patent agents will work to a fixed scale of charges relating to the work done, in the same way as a solicitor charges, rather than taking a share in the commercial success of an invention.

The Institute of Inventors, 19 Fosse Way, Ealing, London W13 0BZ. (01 998 3540) This is a self-supporting institute run by inventors for inventors. It can help with patent application, prototypes and commercialisation of suitable inventions.

The Institute of Patentees and Inventors, Staple Inn Buildings South, 335 High Holborn, London WC1V 7PX. (01 242 7812) The institute was founded in 1919 to further the interests of patentees and inventors. It gives advice and guidance to members on all aspects of inventing, from idea conception to innovation and development. Its journal, *The Inventor,* comes out quarterly and helps to keep members up to date. Its *New Patents Bulletin* acts as a liaison with industry, bringing members' inventions to the notice of specialised manufacturing firms.

Membership costs £15.00 per annum.

PA Patcentre International, Cambridge Division, Melbourn, Royston, Herts. SG8 6DP. (0763 61222, telex 81561). Patcentre has a comprehensive technology service, which can, for example, take a client's 'ideas' right through to commercialisation, or until they are licensed off to a third party, such as Prutec.

The service begins with a clear definition of the commercial and market constraints and extends through initial concept development, technical and commercial feasibility studies, ergonomic design and styling, prototype design and construction, production and manufacturing engineering, market research and market launch, packaging and supporting graphics.

Each project is managed by an experienced team of senior consultants who are recognised authorities in their field and have in-depth experience in international product and business development.

Patentec Ltd, 1 Rue de Pres, St Saviour, Jersey, Channel Islands. (0534 71040, telex 4192065) Patentec's specialised and successful business is based largely on its success at inventing, developing, patenting and then licensing the 'Workmate' to Black & Decker. They try to identify potentially good ideas, usually from outside inventors, which they believe can be turned into attractive and economic designs. Then they set about protecting them by applying for patents and/or design registrations in all the countries in which substantial sales might be expected.

If they are successful at both developing and protecting the idea, they look for a firm with the appropriate strengths to make a commercial success of the product. They then try to persuade the firm to take out a Patent Licence Agreement with them. The inventor can expect to get between 25 and 40 per cent of any net royalties from the product sales – that is, after development, patent and administrative expenses have been deducted.

This may be the only way in which an inventor with little money or commercial expertise can make any money out of his invention without taking on extra risks, such as borrowing the money and setting up in business himself.

If Patentec do not like your idea, they will tell you why. This explanation in itself may be worth getting.

Prutec, 33 Davies Street, London W1Y 2EA. (01 491 7000, telex 266431) Prutec is a wholly-owned subsidiary of Prudential Assurance. Since opening its doors for business in 1981 with some £20 million of venture capital, it has sought out investment opportunities in technological innovation in the UK. The company has close links with PA International, and has several PA executives on its board. The rest of the management consists of a small, highly qualified team with wide experience in science and technology, and in business methods. Prutec's investment strategies include basic research developing technological applications and commercialising such developments.

This is an unusual source of finance, with Prutec Executive setting out to speak the same language as technologists. They expect not just to invest money but to give technological and commercial expertise as well. They have a number of technology areas of particular strategic interest, and they will actively promote the development of products to meet market needs that they have identified.

QMC Industrial Research Ltd, 229 Mile End Road, London E1 4AA. (01 709 0066) QMC Ltd is a wholly-owned company of Queen Mary College, University of London, which makes available the invention expertise and equipment of the college to industry. They have available some 250 highly qualified staff and their supporting technicians.

QMC have very active links with the local small business community and have carried out work in the following fields:

- Testing Services. Chemical, physical and biological tests ranging from strength and fatigue of metals and plastics to safe development of crops in polluted waste ground;
- Materials Expertise. Safety of materials and products, particularly organic materials like upholstery foams exposed to fire; and substitution of cheaper new materials with adequate performance in traditional products;
- Engineering Expertise. Wide range of services, including strength of structures, more efficient energy utilisation, geotechnical surveys and soil mechanics, process improvements;
- Product Liability investigation. Advice and laboratory service from a reputable, independent, expert organisation (the university), which carries weight in court proceedings;
- Specialised ('one-off') services. Prototype development, project management, economic appraisals of technical markets, adaptation of computer software to specific needs, etc.

Technical Development Capital (TDC), This is an arm of Industrial and Commercial Finance Corporation (ICFC), the venture capital business owned by the leading clearing banks and the Bank of England. Since its formation in 1962, TDC has become the largest provider of venture capital to new technology firms in Europe. Funds are available, usually in the form of equity capital, in amounts from £5,000 to £2 million. TDC's services go beyond the purely financial; they have developed more specialised operation support systems covering the fields of industry, commerce and technology. In 1980–1981 they invested around £7 million in some 70 ventures. Since then they have been looking for propositions in four industry sectors: computers, micro-electronics, biotechnology and industrial automation.

Once the funds are invested, performance is monitored by TDC experts who look beyond the operating results to the performance of the venture as a whole.

Its close relationship with ICFC gives ready access to a total range of financing, advisory and other business services.

TDC is at 91 Waterloo Road, London SE1 8XP. (01 928 7822), and local contact can be made through branch offices of ICFC.

Technology Advisory Point, Department of Industry, Station Square House, St Mary Cray, Orpington, Kent BR5 3RF. (0689 72918; telex 896866) Contact: Ian Melville. TAP's primary purpose is to help UK industry to increase its productivity and profitability by taking advantage of the UK's vast R & D expertise. This service is not confined to the department's own research establishments, as TAP has detailed knowledge of the expertise, experience and facilities in associations and academic institutions.

The aim is simply to provide one point of contact for businesses looking for help when faced with a technological problem. In this way, they hope to remove the frustration felt when enquiries are passed from one person to another.

Information which TAP can provide includes the best contact to deal with a particular problem, establishments which can carry out work in a particular area; establishments which have a certain testing or calibration facilities; and laboratories which have available certain specialised equipment or facilities.

Three telephone lines are open for enquirers to contact TAP staff to discuss the details of their problems and the sort of expertise they are looking for. There is no charge for using TAP, and the same will normally apply to preliminary enquiries to the chosen organisation. Their charges will vary with the nature of the services provided and the charging policy of the establishment concerned. Information on this will normally be provided at an early stage.

The Technology and Innovations Exchange Ltd, 12 Ormonde Gate, PO Box 242, London SW3 4EY. (01 351 4753, telex 923421) Formed in 1982, the exchange is intended to bridge the gap between inventors and developers of new products and those with the technical expertise or the money to develop them. It has a heavyweight board, and Sir Denis Haviland, industrialist and senior civil servant, is Chairman.

TIE operates as follows. Inventors (referred to as 'sellers') contact the company, giving as much detailed information on their product or idea as they can. This information is assessed by technical and legal experts in the appropriate fields. They concentrate on such areas as patent protection, product development potential, financing requirements and market possibilities.

If the idea is accepted, outline details are placed on the TIE listing, which are sent to subscribing organisations (or 'buyers'). Each brief has a summary of the main advantages of the products, together with relevant facts.

If the buyer is interested, then after signing a non-disclosure agreement negotiation can start. By April 1982, 40 propositions were in hand. The starting price for the service is £65 for sellers and £86 for buyers (VAT excluded).

RESEARCH ASSOCIATIONS

There are some thirty-six research organisations in the UK, which are the centres of knowledge in their respective fields. If the product or idea that you are developing (or want to use) comes within their sphere of interest, they may well be of use. They have extensive information systems, and can usually guide enquirers to appropriate sources of data or other help.

ASLIB, (Association of Social Libraries Information Bureau), 3 Belgrave Square, London SW1X 8PL. (01 235 5050) Contact: Dr Dennis A. Lewis, Director

BHRA Fluid Engineering, Cranfield, Bedfordshire MK43 0AJ. (0234 750422) Contact: Mr G. F. W. Alder, Director

Brick Development Association, Woodside House, Winkfield, Windsor, Berkshire SL4 2DX. (0344 885651) Contact: Rear Admiral A. J. Monk, CBE, Director-General

British Brush Manufacturers' Research Association, c/o Department of Textile Industries, The University, Leeds LS2 9JT. (0532 31751) Contact: Mr D. I. Fothergill, Director

British Carbonization Research Association, Wingerworth, Chesterfield, Derbyshire S42 6JS. (0246 76821) Contact: Mr J. P. Graham, OBE, Director

British Ceramic Research Association, Queens Road, Penkhull, Stoke-on-Trent ST4 7LQ. (0782 45431) Contact: Dr D. W. F. James, Director

British Glass Industry Research Association, Northumberland Road, Sheffield S10 2UA. (0742 686201) Contact: Dr E. A. Kellett, Director

The British Internal Combustion Engine Research Institute Ltd, 111–112 Buckingham Avenue, Slough SL1 4PH. (75 27371) Contact: Mr I. A. G. Brown, Director and Secretary

British Leather Manufacturers' Research Association, King's Park Road, Moulton Park, Northamptonshire NN3 1JD. (0604 494131, or 0604 493990 after 5.15 p.m.) Contact: Dr R. L. Sykes, Director

Building Services Research & Information Association, Old Bracknell Lane West, Bracknell, Berkshire RG12 4AH. (0344 26511) Contacts: Dr D. P. Gregory, Director

Construction Industry Research & Information Association, 6 Storey's Gate, London SW1P 3AU. (01 222 8891) Contact: Dr L. S. Blake, Director

Cranfield Unit for Precision Engineering, Cranfield Institute of Technology, Cranfield, Bedfordshire MK43 0AL. (0234 750111) Contact: Professor P. A. McKeown, Director

Cutlery & Allied Trades' Research Association, Henry Street, Sheffield S3 7EQ. (0742 79736) Contact: Mr E. A. Oldfield, Director

Drop Forging Research Association, Shepherd Street, Sheffield S3 7BA. (0742 27463) Contact: Dr S. E. Rogers, Director

Fabric Care Research Association, Forest House Laboratories, Knaresborough Road, Harrogate HG2 7LZ. (0423 883201) Contact: Mr E. J. Davies, Director

Fire Insurers' Research & Testing Organisation, Melrose Avenue, Borehamwood, Hertfordshire WD6 2BJ. (01 207 2345) Contact: Mr R. W. Pickard, Executive Director

Furniture Industry Research Association, Maxwell Road, Stevenage, Hertfordshire SG1 2EW. (0438 3433) Contact: Mr D. M. Heughan, Director

HATRA, (Hosiery and Allied Trades Research Association), Thorneywood, 7 Gregory Boulevard, Nottingham NG7 6LD. (0602 623311/2) Contact: W. N. Bignall, Director

Lambeg Industrial Research Association, The Research Institute, Lambeg, Lisburn, Co. Antrim BT27 4RJ, Northern Ireland. (084 62 2255/6) Contacts: Dr W. W. Foster, PA to Director of Research/Director)

Machine Tool Industry Research Association, Hulley Road, Macclesfield, Cheshire SK10 2NE. (0625 25421/3 and 26189) Contact: Mr M. E. Hadlow, Director

National Computing Centre, Oxford Road, Manchester M1 7ED. (061 228 6333) Contact: Mr David R. Fairbairn, Director
London Office: 11 New Fetter Lane, EC4A 1PU. (01 353 4875) Contact: Mrs Fleming, Regional Officer

The Paint Research Association, Waldegrave Road, Teddington, Middlesex TW11 8LD. (01 977 4427/9) Contact: Dr G. de W. Anderson, Director

Paper & Board, Printing & Packaging Industries Research Association, Randalls Road, Leatherhead, Surrey KT22 7RU. (0372 376161) Contact: Dr N. K. Bridge, Director

Processors' & Growers' Research Organisation, The Research Station, Great North Road, Thornhaugh, Peterborough PE8 6HJ. (0780 782585) Contact Mr A. J. Gane, Director and Secretary

Production Engineering Research Association of Great Britain, Melton Mowbray, Leicestershire LE13 0PB. (0664 64133) Contact: Professor W. B. Heginbotham, OBE, Director-General

Rubber & Plastic Research Association of Geat Britain, Shawbury, Shrewsbury, Shropshire SY4 4NR. (0939 250 383) Contact: Dr J. P. Berry, Director

Shirley Institute, Wilmslow Road, Didsbury, Manchester M20 8RX. (061 445 8141) Contacts: Dr Alasdair Maclean, Managing Director; Dr J. Honeyman, Director of Research

Shoe & Allied Trades' Research Association, Satra House, Rockingham Road, Kettering, Northamptonshire NN16 9JH. (0536 516318) Contact: Mr J. Graham Butlin, Director

Spring Research and Manufacturers' Association, Henry Street, Sheffield S3 7EQ. (0742 760771) Contact: Mr J. A. Bennett, Director

Steel Castings Research and Trade Association, 5 East Bank Road, Sheffield S2 3PT. (0742 28647) Contact: Dr J. A. Reynolds, Director

Timber Research and Development Association, Stocking Lane, Hughenden Valley, High Wycombe, Buckinghamshire HP14 4ND. (0240 24 3091) Contact: Mr J. G. Sunley, Director

Water Research Centre, P.O. Box 16, Henley Road, Medmenham, Marlow, Bucks, SL7 2HD (049 166531) Contact: Mr J. L. van der Post, Chief Executive.

WIRA, (Woollen Industry Research Association), Wira House, West Park Ring Road, Leeds LS16 6QL. (0532 781381) Contact: Dr B. E. King, Director

COMPUTERS

If you have not already bought a computer then there are a number of organisations, periodicals and books that may help you to make the best decisions. You will need to know something of what a computer can and cannot do, and exactly what work you want done. If your business is or is likely to involve repetitious, routinised, time-consuming and usually boring tasks, the chances are that a computer could do them better. Typically, small businesses put their book-keeping, management accounts, payroll, mailing and price lists and, more recently, word-processing functions on to a computer. Systems are available to analyse customers: how long they take to pay up; how much on average they order; and when their next order is due.

Finding your solution Once you have decided what you want done, then you have to find the software and hardware to meet your needs. The software is the programme or instructions that have to be given to the computer in order to process your data and produce the information that you want.

Finding out about software means reading the computer magazines, talking to manufacturers and users, going to exhibitions and getting demonstrations from software houses.

An increasing number of 'standard' software packages are available for specific trades and professions. Packages include those for small shops, such as pharmacies, and for medical practices and estate agents. Your trade association will be watching these developments, and they should be able to help you find out more. Keeping a watch in your trade magazine will also show you what enterprising people are getting up to in this area. It is highly likely that your needs and the available software will not quite match. In this case you will need to, customise the software to your own requirements by writing, or having written, additional programmes.

Finally, you will have to decide on the hardware – the computer itself. Your choice of software will pre-select the computer best-suited to your needs, but you can still choose whether to buy (or lease) your own, or to use a computer bureau on a time-sharing basis.

It is very likely that the complexities and unfamiliarity of the field, combined with overwhelming apparent choice of systems, will leave you confused. Help is at hand, either from the following organisations, or by referring to the publication listed afterwards.

Organisations
Association of Independent Computer Specialists, c/o BEAMA, Leicester House, 8 Leicester Street, London WC2H 7BN. (01 437 0678, telex 263536) Contacts: AICS Public Relations Officer: Dr S. G.

Beech (0732 460420); AICS Marketing Services: John Braithwaite (0628 30748); AICS Microsystems Group: Alan Mayne (01 883 7703). The association was formed in 1972 with the twin objectives of improving the professional standards of computer consultants, and of making sure that clients receive independent advice. There are now some eighty members. Contact can be made either by sending for the *AICS Handbook* or by asking for a specific service. The handbook, as well as telling you about AICS, has the names, addresses and details of the fields of experience and specialisation of members. It also tells you when the members' consultancy was established, who the principals are, and the geographical area of operations.

AICS maintains links with similar organisations – for example the Association of Independent Computer Professionals. AICP was formed in Birmingham in 1981 and now has about 20 members.

Barclays Microprocessor Applications Unit, Department of Computer Science, University of Manchester, Oxford Road, Manchester M13 9PL. (061 273 7121)

Brixton Information Technology Centre, c/o ICFC Ltd, 91 Waterloo Road, London SE1 8XP. (01 928 7822, ext. 387) ICL, Freemans and ICFC are to sponsor this centre, which should be operational in 1983. Its primary purpose is to train young people in the micro-electronics and computing fields. However, it will offer products and services under contract to the immediate community. (Other London boroughs, including Southwark, Camden, Harringey and Hackney, are a few of the thirty places in the UK likely to have an Information & Technology Centre in 1983/94 (contact the Manpower Services Commission for local details).

City Technology Centre, 165 Shoreditch High Street, London E1 6HU. (01 739 8856) Contact: Mr R. Dowry. The centre was set up in 1982 to encourage and help firms in Hackney to make use of microcomputers in their business. The centre runs training courses and other education and awareness programmes.

Microcomputer Advisory Service, University of Manchester, Oxford Road, Manchester M13 9PL. (061 273 3333, ext. 3206)

Micro Systems Centres (MSC) A Federation of Microsystem Centres is being established, supported by the Government and the National Computing Centre. These centres are an independent, authoritative, practical and individual source of assistance, advice and information for anyone who is considering using a microcomputer in business. Small and new businesses will find the range of services particularly helpful.

The services of each centre will include:

- Training. The centres' flexible training programmes are aimed at specific needs, from clerical staff through to financial advisers. They run self-instruction and taught courses at most times including weekends, evenings and lunch-times.
- Consultancy and advice. This is available to help you choose the right computer; to analyse and select from available software; or to commission specific or modified software. This consultancy extends from the feasibility study designed to find out if a computer will help to solve your business problem, through to acceptance tests on installing any system you may decide to buy. The centres do not sell hardware or software, so the advice given *is* independent. The cost per hour for this consultancy advice is around £50.00.
- Demonstrations by their trained staff can be given of a range of microcomputer systems on permanent display at centres.
- Information is available from the centres' comprehensively stocked book shop, which carries a range of books, magazines and articles on most aspects of the subject.

At present one unit is fully operational:
Microsystems Centre, 11 New Fetter Lane, London EC4A 1PU. (01 353 0013/4/5) Contact: Colin Harris
However, the Department of Industry is making funds available to set up another twelve centres to cover the country. These will become operational in 1983/84, though up to three of them may be operational by the end of 1982.
At present the co-ordinating headquarters of the organisation is:

Federation of Micro Centres, The National Computing Centre Ltd, Oxford Road, Manchester M1 7ED. (061 228 6333, telex 668962) Contact: John Turnbull, Federation Manager
The other centres are most likely to be located as follows:
Avon (Bristol), Belfast, East Midlands, Glasgow, Home counties, Liverpool, Manchester, Newcastle, South Wales (Regional Management Centre, Polytechnic of Wales), South Yorkshire, West Midlands (Aston University), West Yorkshire.

Neath Information Technology Centre, contact Mr Emlyn Williams, ITEC Centre, Neath. (0639 4141 ext. 176) Jointly sponsored by Metal Box PLC and Neath Borough Council, with educational, administrative and technical support from the West Glamorgan Institute of Higher Technology. (See Brixton for details on ITEC's.)
As well as these centres, a network of associated centres will be set up, offering either a more limited or more specialised service. These centres will complement the activities of major centres and they will work closely with them. In this way both wider and deeper coverage will be attained quickly.

Publications

Computing Marketplace, Gower Press, 1981, 501 pp., Price £26.45, Gower House, Croft Road, Aldershot, Hants GU11 3HR. This is a directory of computing services, software suppliers, micros, minis, mainframes, computer training establishments, DP staff recruitment, computer equipment financing and leasing, system maintenance.

Guide to Small Business Computer Systems, Gower Press, Croft Road, Aldershot, Hants, GU11 3HR (0252 331551), 1981, 238 pp., price £24.00. The guide sets out how to choose and specify and systemise, how to find suppliers of hardware and software and how to choose between systems.

Making a Success of Micro-computing in your Business, by Pannell, Jackson and Lucas, published by Enterprise Books, 79 Osword Road, Manchester, N21 1QD 1981, price £4.95. Barclays Bank helped in the production of this extremely useful little book.

Following the main chapters there is a series of check-lists to guide prospective users through all the decisions involved in finding hardware, software, suppliers and advisers.

The Official Software Buyers' Guide, published twice yearly from Data Sources Enterprises, 84 Glen Carren Circle, Soarks NV 89431, USA, price $9.

Small Computers in Small Companies, December 1981, by Easton & Lawrence, Dept of Marketing, University of Lancaster, Gillow House, Lancaster LA1 4YX. (0524 65201)

It surveys the experiences of 100 small organisations that have installed small computer systems. It tells you how they chose, what they chose and how happy (or unhappy) they are with their decisions. Price £25.

INDUSTRIAL ORGANISATIONS

Further sources of information on the application of technology are listed below.

British Safety Council, 62–64 Chancellors' Road, London W6 9RS. (01 741 1231)

British Standards Institution, 2 Park Street, London W1A 2BS. (01 629 9000)

Cambridge Information and Research Services Ltd, the School House, Heydon, Royston, Herts. SG8 8PW. (076 383615) 'Publishers of the directory of Energy Saving Equipment'

Ergonomics Information Analysis Centre, Department of Engineering Production, University of Birmingham, PO Box 363, Birmingham B15 2TT. (021 472 1301 ext. 2731)

Institution of Industrial Managers, 45 Cardiff Road, Luton, Beds. LU1 1RO. (0582 37071)

Institute for Operational Research, Tavistock Centre, 120 Belsize Lane, Hampstead London NW3 5BA. (01 435 7111)

Institute of Production Control, National Westminster House, Wood Street, Stratford-upon-Avon, Warwicks. CV37 6JS. (0789 5266)

Institution of Production Engineers, 66 Little Ealing Lane, London W5 4XX. (01 579 9411)

Institute of Quality Assurance, 54 Princess Gate, Exhibition Road, London SW7 2PG. (01 584 9026)

Institute of Management Services, 1 Cecil Court, London Road, Enfield, Middx. EN2 6DD. (01 363 7452) Contacts: Jim Francis or Barbara Goreham. Leaders in the work-study field; their technical information service can give advice to small businesses.

Institute for Scientific Information, 132 High Street, Uxbridge, Middx, UB8 1DP. (0895 30085)

Institute of Value Management, c/o Delta Executive Development Centre, 22 Cavendish Avenue, Buxton, Derbyshire SK17 9AE. (0298 2284)

Intermediate Technology Development Group, 9 King Street, London WC2E 8HN. (01 836 9434)

Local Government Operational Research Unit, 229 Kings Road, Reading, Berks, RG1 4LS. (0734 661234)

Low Cost Automation Centres Established by the Department of Industry to encourage the use of low cost aids to automation, the centres now run independently, and have developed considerable micro-electronics expertise. Department of Industry, Electric Application Division, Room 406, 29 Bessenden Place, SW1E 5DT. Contact: Dr Flaherty on 01 213 5290. There are centres for Scotland (Paisley College of Technology – 041 887 1241); the North West (Stockport College of Technology – 061 480 3897), Yorkshire and Humberside (Leeds Polytechnic, 0532 462960, ext. 13, and Sheffield Polytechnic, 0742 20911, ext. 335); West Midlands (University of Birmingham, Department of Engineering Production – 021 472 1301, ext. 3404); London and the South-east (Kingston Polytechnic – 01 549 0115, ext. 241); the South-west (Bristol Polytechnic, 0272 41241, ext. 73, and Gloucester City College of Technology, 0452 21727); Northern Ireland (Queen's University of Belfast, Ashby Institute, 0232 661111, ext. 4281).

Manufacturing Advisory Service (MAS), PERA (Production Engineering Research Association) Melton Mowbray, Leicestershire LE13 OPB. (0664 64133) Open to small firms (80–100 employees) in certain sectors of manufacturing industry, the service includes free advice on methods of improving manufacturing efficiency; answers to three enquiries on technical problems in the manufacturing field; limited assistance with training.

Micro-Electronics Industry Support Programme (MISP), Department of Industry (same address as MAP, below). (01 213 5818) The scheme, announced in July 1978, is mainly intended to help UK firms create the capability to meet the demands for micro-electronic components and ancillary equipment, materials and services. MISP provides grants towards the cost of product/process development and manufacturing. The scheme will run until March 1984.

Micro Processor Application Project (MAP), Electronics Application Division, Room 514, 29 Bressenden Place, London SW1E 5DT. (01 213 3932) MAP's aim is to encourage UK industry to apply micro-processor techniques to a wide range of products and production processes. Grants are available for training, feasibility studies and product development.

National Industrial Fuel Efficiency Service Ltd (NIFES), Head Office, Nifes House, Sunderland Road, Broad Heath, Altringham, Cheshire. Altringham (061 928 5791) and at Birmingham WA14 5HQ. (021 454 4471); Buntingford, Herts. (0763 71154); Leeds (0532 505943); Newcastle upon Tyne (0632 813776); Nottingham (0602 625841); and Aberdeen (041 332 2453).

National Terotechnology Centre, c/o Assel Management Centre, British Institute of Management, Management House, Parker Street, London WC2B 5PT. (01 405 3456)

Operational Research Society, Neville House, Waterloo Street, Birmingham B2 5TX. (021 643 0236)

Small Engineering Firms Scheme, The Department of Industry. Under this scheme, eligible small firms will be able to call on a total of £20 million being made available by the Government to encourage them to invest in high-technology machine tools. Companies employing fewer than 200 people will be able to recover a third of the cost of some new capital equipment. Only machines costing more than £15,000 will qualify for the grant. An upper limit of two machines costing £200,000 in total has been set. Applications for grants can be made up to 31 March 1983, but the £20 million will be handed out on a 'first come, first served' basis. Tooling and accessory costs and installation and commissioning costs will be included up to 10 per cent of the cost of each machine.

The Small Firms Technical Information Service This was launched in June 1982 and is operated for the Department of Industry by the Production Engineering Research Association. A funding of £2.2 million has been made available for three years. Aid is obtainable to any small manufacturing firm employing no more than 200 people.
The service could be used, for example, in helping to find the source of a particular component, in improving the quality of a product, or in helping to increase the efficiency of a process, and for many other problems. Firms can make use of the service by ringing PERA at Melton Mowbray (0644 64133 ext. 444).

Technical Indexes Ltd, Willoughby Road, Bracknell, Berkshire RG12 4DW. (0344 26311) Specialists in producing or disseminating technical information. Founded in 1965, they provide essential technical data to design engineers, draughtsmen and buyers in the following fields: electronic engineering, chemical engineering, laboratory equipment, materials handling, engineering components and materials, British Standards, defence standards, American industry standards, Mil Specs, American catalogues and Japanese catalogues.

FINDING OUT ABOUT YOUR MARKET

In contrast to the raising of money, where problems and their solutions can be treated in a relatively general way, everyone's products and markets are specialised, if only geographically so. Unless you are prepared to spend a lot of cash early on, perhaps even before you are sure whether you have a product or service to sell, you will have to find out about your market yourself. Your market-place is made up of customers, actual and potential; competitors; suppliers; distribution channels; and communication media. In order to succeed, you will have to find out all you can about these elements of your market-place and use that knowledge to your advantage. There is a vast amount of information freely available, or at a comparatively low cost – much cheaper than the cost of a relatively small mistake, which could be fatal early in the life of a business.

There are also many organisations, which, though not expressly set up to help you, have services, facilities or resources that you can tap, and so improve your knowledge and skills.

To make this complex subject digestible it is divided into six topics. 'The Information Available' will give you a flavour of the great mass of data on companies, at home and overseas, and on products and markets. There are almost 4,000 current British directories, and this section pulls together the ones of most use to you.

'Finding the Information' tells you how to make use of the country's substantial information and library services. The main business libraries in London, for example, are the most extensive in their fields in Europe.

'Marketing Organisations and their Services' provides details of the prominent professional bodies in the field, and, where appropriate, how they might help you. One organisation, for example, can put you in front of a marketing expert in your field of interest for half a day at a cost to you of only £15.00.

There are also sections on exporting and importing, giving details of important organisations and services.

The final topic covers general marketing books and periodicals that can give you a broad background knowledge on the subject. These books have been chosen as much for their readability as for their direct usefulness.

THE INFORMATION AVAILABLE

You will need a regular flow of information on your market to help you make decisions about such matters as what to sell, at what price, your likely competitors, or to find what is going on in markets overseas. You will also need to know something on the size, shape, rate of growth and profitability of your chosen market.

In this section the hundred or so key directories, indexes, reference works and services that hold much of this valuable raw marketing data are identified and described. The ready availability of these publications has been as much a consideration in including them as their usefulness.

Interpreting that information is a harder problem, but some of these reference works contain analyses of the data provided. Otherwise, organisations in the other sections of this book may be able to help, particularly those offering a counselling or advice service, such as Enterprise Agencies, the Marketing Advisory service, or the Warwick Statistical Service.

This section is divided into four areas: Company and Product Data, UK; Company and Product Data, Overseas; Market and Industry data, UK; and Market and Industry Data, Overseas.

Company and Product Data provides information on home and overseas companies, their products or services, profiles and profitability. Market and Industry Data provides information on the markets serviced by those companies, their size, growth and other characteristics. There are a number of reference sources that do not rest easily in one section, and they will have been placed in the most suitable location and cross-referenced in order to help you find your way around.

Company and Product Data The range of readily held data on UK companies is bewildering, and on overseas companies only a little less so. At first glance many of the directories and information sources seem to duplicate one another's efforts, or at any rate to overlap. However, once you are faced with a particular problem their differences become apparent. *Kelly's Manufacturers & Merchants Directory* is a most useful tool for finding suppliers or competitors on a national basis. Their *Regional Directories*, however, go into much finer detail for each region, but they omit the global picture.

The Retail Directory will tell you, street by street, the names and business of every shop, and another section will tell you each buyer's name. None of these will tell you much about who owns the business or about their financial performance. This information is given in *Who Owns Whom* and the Extel Card Services, respectively. If you want to compare one company with another in the same line of business, *Jordans* or *ICC Business Ratios* are two useful sources. To find out what has been said in the press about a company, you could use *McCarthy's Information Services* or *Research Index*. If you want to confine your search to comment in the *Financial Times*, then their monthly index provides a cross-reference by company, general business area and by personality.

If you want to know who has gone bankrupt lately, then *The London Gazette* gives out an official notice.

For overseas companies, much the same information is available, but some of the sources' names are different. There is very little you cannot find out about a company or business if you set your mind to it. The publications listed below are not exhaustive, but they are among the most important and authoritative.

Company & Product Data, UK

The Centre for Interfirm Comparison Ltd, 8 West Stockwell Street, Colchester, Essex co1 1hn (0206 62274), and 25 Bloomsbury Square, London wc1a 2pj (01 637 8406) This is a non-profit-making organisation, established in 1959 by the British Institute of Management and the British Productivity Council to meet the need for a neutral, expert body to conduct interfirm comparisons on a confidential basis, and to help managers to improve business performance. Participating firms feed a range of information into the centre, who in turn feed out yardsticks for them to compare systematically the performance of every important aspect of their business with other, similar firms. Together with the yardstick ratios come written reports on the findings and ideas for action – but only, of course, to the participating firms, and even then only on a 'comparative' basis so that no one company's data can ever be identified.

The uniqueness of this method rests in part on the data itself. It goes far beyond anything supplied in companies' annual returns to Companies House or production monitor figures.

Thousands of companies, large and small, have participated, and comparisons are made in over 100 industries, trade, services and professions both in the UK and abroad.

The centre publishes a number of free booklets that explain their activities, the ratios they use, why they use those particular ratios and, more importantly, how you can use them to improve performance.

Credit Ratings Ltd, 51 City Road, London ec1y 1ay. (01 251 6675/6) This company provides an *ad hoc*, subscription service Credit Report. The cost varies from £15.00 to £12.00 for each report, which can normally be provided within 24 hours.

Each Credit Report provides a company profile, financial performance figures for the past two years, and 8 credit ratios (including an estimate of how long they normally take to pay their bills). These ratios are then compared with the average for that industry, and are followed by a short commentary bringing important factors to the reader's attention.

Companies Registration Office keeps records of all limited companies. For England and Wales these records are kept at Companies House, 55 City Road, London EC1 (01 253 9393), and for Scotland at the Registrar of Companies for Scotland, 102 George Street, Edinburgh EH2 3JD. For Northern Ireland the same service is available from The Department of Commerce, Chichester House, 43/47 Chichester Court, Belfast BT1 4PJ. (0232 34121)

The records kept include financial statements, accounts, directors' names and addresses, shareholders, and changes of name and structure. The information is available on microfiche at £1.00 per company, and can be photocopied at 10p per sheet. This service is available to visitors only. There are a number of commercial organisations who will obtain this information for you. Two such organisations are:

The Company Search Centre, 1/3 Leonard Street, London EC2A 4AQ (01 251 2566); and

Extel, 37/45 Paul Street, London EC2A 4PB. (01 253 3400)

The charges for this service are about £3.00 to £3.50 for a microfiche of each company, or for a photocopy of the report and accounts, around £8.00.

Extel Quoted Service, cards published each year by the Exchange Telegraph Co Ltd. Cards for each of the 3,000 UK companies quoted on the Stock Exchange contain the following information: name and business of the company together with details of subsidiaries and associates; the date on which the company was registered (formed), along with any change of name or status (e.g., private to public); directors – their positions (chairman, managing director, etc.) and their shareholdings, as well as the names of the company secretary, bankers, auditors and solicitors. Ten years' profit and loss accounts and at least three years' balance sheets are given, together with a sources and applications of funds statements. The highest and lowest share price over the ten-year period is also given, as well as the chairman's latest statement on the company position.

A news card is published three or four times a year, giving details of dividends declared, board changes, acquisitions, liquidations, loans raised and other elements of operating information. A selection of these cards is held in many reference libraries. Individual cards can be bought for £1.95 from Extel Statistical Services Ltd, 37/45 Paul Street, London EC2A 4PB. (01 253 3400, telex 262687, or Manchester Office, 061 236 5802)

Extel's *Handbook of Market Leaders,* brings together details on 750 major quoted companies. Though not a substitute for the cards it does provide a quick reference guide to the financial performance of major companies. Published twice a year, in January and July, at £30.00 an issue.

Extel Unquoted Service provides a similar service for some 2,000 ordinary companies. These cards cost £5.85 each, as considerably more work has to be done to get at this information, and the call for it is less.

Financial Times Index, introduced in 1981, provides a monthly and yearly index to the references to some 35,000 companies. Instead of thumbing through back issues, you can locate the abstract of each story by using the corporate index, the general index covering products and industries, or the personality section covering key people. This series costs £240.00 per annum, and is available from Financial Times Information Ltd, Minster House, Arthur Street, London EC4R 9AX. The index is also available on microfiche, floppy disc and magnetic tape.

ICC Business Ratios produce 150 business sector reports analysing the performance of some 12,000 leading UK companies over a three-year period. For each sector (for example, window manufacturers, retail chemists, the toy industry or computer equipment) key performance ratios are shown for each company in the sector and an average for the sector as a whole. You can therefore use this information to compare your performance, actual or projected, against an industry standard. There are nineteen key ratios, and they cover profitability, liquidity, asset utilisation, gearing, productivity and exports. Growth rates are monitored, including sales, total assets, capital employed, average wages and exports. It is thus possible to see quickly which company is growing the fastest in your sector, and to compare your growth against the best, the worst or the average. Reports are priced at about £100.00 each, and further details are available from The Business Ratio Manager, ICC Business Ratios, 23 City Road, London EC1Y 1AA. (01 638 2946)

Jordan's Business Information Service, Jordan House, 47 Brunswick Place, London N1 6EE. (01 253 3030) They also have offices in Bristol, Cardiff, Edinburgh and the Isle of Man. Their Company Search Department can get you information on any UK company in 'Companies House', and their Rapid Reply Service can guarantee despatch within a few hours. Alternatively, if you really are in a hurry, they have a telex and telephone service. They also produce a range of annual business surveys covering some eighty industries. These are priced between £8.00 and £85.00.

Jordan's new Companies Service could be particularly useful for a small company looking for sales leads. Over 5,000 new companies are incorporated each month, and Jordans reports on about half. They eliminate the companies with convenience directors and registered offices (each of which offers no contact point), which leaves several thousand 'genuine' new potential customers each month. Naturally, these companies could be anywhere in the UK, so in order to make the service more useful to small business, they have produced a county by county service, with London split into eight. These selected services cost from £60.00 to £600.00 per annum. The whole UK service could cost around £4,000.00, and London alone around £2,000.00. At just over 13p a 'lead', this could prove a cost-effective way to expand sales.

Kelly's Manufacturers & Merchants Directory, published by IPC Business Press, 40 Bowling Green Lane, London EC1R ONE has an alphabetical list of manufacturers, merchants, wholesalers and firms, together with their trade descriptions, addresses, telephone and telex numbers. In addition, entries are listed by trade classification. A section lists British Importers under the goods they import. Exporters are listed by the products they export and the continent and countries in which they sell.

The directory covers 90,000 UK firms classified under 10,000 trade, product or service headings.

Kelly's Regional Directory of British Industry is published in eight volumes each October. It provides an exhaustive, town-by-town guide to industry and the products and services offered. This really is most useful if you want to confine your interests to one particular area, perhaps as an aid to a concentrated sales blitz.

Kelly's Post Office London Directory provides business listings by street, so a company's immediate neighbours can be identified. It is useful for finding concentrations of a particular type of business, or for finding gaps in provisions of a particular type of business.

Key British Enterprises, published by Dunn and Bradstreet Ltd., 26/32, Clifton Street, London, EC2P 2LY (01 247 4377). Information on 20,000 UK companies that between them are responsible for 90 per cent of industrial expenditure. *KBE* is very useful for identifying sales prospects or confirming addresses, monitoring competitors and customers or finding new suppliers. As well as giving the names, addresses, telephone and telex numbers of the main office of each company, it gives branch addresses, products indexed by SIC code, sales turn-overs (UK & overseas), directors' names and responsibilities, shareholders, capital structure, trade names, and number of employees.

KBE is in two volumes, alphabetical and geographical. By using the directory you can quickly establish the size of business you are dealing with and what other products or services they offer. It is very often important to know the size of a firm, if, for example, your products are confined to certain types of business. A book-keeping service is unlikely to interest a large company with several hundred employees; they would have their own accounts department. Conversely, a very small company may not need a public relations consultant.

Kompass is published in association with the CBI in two volumes: Volume I is indexed by product or service to help find suppliers, indicating whether they are manufacturers, wholesalers or distributors. It can be very useful indeed on certain occasions to be able to bypass a wholesaler and get to the manufacturer direct.

Volume II gives basic company information on the 30,000 suppliers identified from Volume I. These include the addresses, telephone and telex numbers, bankers, directors, office hours and the number of employees.

The London Gazette, published by HMSO four times a week, provides the official notices on companies, including bankruptcies and receiverships. It may be too late for you to do much by the time it reaches the *Gazette.*

McCarthy Information Services provide a comprehensive press comment service monitoring the daily and financial press. From some fifty papers and journals they extract information on quoted companies each day and unquoted companies each week.

The service is provided on subscription, and a modestly priced Back Copy Service seems the most likely one to appeal to small business. The subscription is £35.00 per annum, and 55p per page copied. McCarthy Information Ltd, Manor House, Ash Walk, Warminster, Wilts. BA12 8PY. (0985 215151)

Research Index is an index to news, views and comments from the UK national daily papers plus around 150 periodicals in every field. The material is chosen carefully to include most items that would interest the business user, both on individual companies and on industries. Over the period of a year it includes around 130,000 items, and since the first edition over a million references have been made.

Research Index has always given good value at a modest price, currently £83.00 per annum, including binder and postage. By using it, even the smallest business can have at its fingertips the knowledge for information retrieval equivalent to the most sophisticated libraries. Published by Business Surveys Ltd, PO Box 21, Dorking, Surrey RH5 4EE. (0306 87857)

The Retail Directory, published by Newman, 48 Portland Street, London W1 (01 439 0335), gives details of all UK department stores and private shops. It gives the names of executives, and merchandise buyers as well as addresses and telephone numbers, early closing days, etc. It also covers multiple shops, co-operative societies, supermarkets and many other retail outlets. If you plan to sell to shops, this is a useful starting point, with around 1,305 department stores and large shops and 4,821 multiple shop firms and variety stores listed in 1,346 pages. If you are already selling retail, this directory could help you expand your prospects list quickly. The directory also identifies high turn-over outlets for main product ranges. There is a useful survey, showing retail activities on each major shopping street in the country. It gives the name and nature of the retail businesses in each street.

A separate volume contains shop surveys for the Greater London area, with 27,830 shops listed by name, street number and trade. The head offices of 1,130 multiples are given, as are 233 surveys showing what sort of shops are in any area. This can be used for giving sales people useful contacts within their territory.

Sell's Directory Sells Publications Ltd, Sell's House, 39 East Street, Epsom, Surrey KT17 1BQ, and the Institute of Purchasing Management. It lists 65,000 firms alphabetically, with name, trade, address, telephone number and telex numbers. Using a classified cross-reference system, it covers 25,000 products and services. There is a guide to several thousand trade names cross-referenced back to each company. The two remaining sections include a contractors' section, advertising firms seeking contract work, and a business information section.

If you only know the trade name and want to find out who makes the product, then this directory will help you. You can then use it to find competitive sources of supply of similar products or services.

Stubbs Directory, published by Dunn and Bradstreet Ltd, lists 130,000 UK firms, their addresses, phone numbers and the product or service provided. Some 4,000 categories of suppliers of goods and services are given, making this the most useful tool for identifying competitors and suppliers throughout the whole country – a sort of one-edition Yellow Pages. Although it does not have the depth of information of some other directories, it certainly has one of the widest spreads. You can use this as a starting point to find what companies you would like to look at in much more detail, or it may well be enough in itself.

Who Owns Whom, (U.K.) pub. David Bradstreet. Vol I lists parent companies, showing the structure of a group as a whole and the relationship with member companies. Vol II lists subsidiaries and associates showing their parent companies.

Company and Product Data, Overseas

DTI Export Data Branch holds 50,000 status reports on overseas businesses. As well as telling you what the company does, each report gives a guide to the company's local standing and suitability for acting on behalf of a UK business. It is very useful if you want an overseas agent or wish to establish their reliability generally, for example as a customer (p. 139).

European Companies is a comprehensive guide to sources of information on business enterprises throughout Europe. Published by CBD Research Ltd, 154 High Street, Beckenham, Kent, BR3 1EA. (01 650 7745)

European Report (A 4/6) (published in Europe and available in main UK business) comes out twice a week and provides a brief review of business and economic events.

Extel European Companies Service See listing in UK section for more details.

Funk and Scott International & European Indexes provide a worldwide index to company news appearing in several hundred English language papers and journals. They have an index for the USA too. You can use this service to find out what has been happening to a company that has not shown up in its figures, for example, new products cancelled, strikes, acquisitions, divestments and board changes.

ICC American Company Information Service, 81 City Road, London EC1Y 1BD. (01 251 4941) They can provide reports on 12,000 US public companies. The report includes the Annual Report and Accounts and the IOK Corporate Structure report on subsidiaries, directors, prominent shareholders and company properties. These cost £25.00 and £17.50 respectively for each company.

ICC European Company Information Services, 81 City Road, London EC1 1BD. (01 251 4942) Through company registries and information services throughout Europe, ICC can provide various reports, including financial accounts, status reports and annual returns on companies registered in Belgium, Denmark, France, Germany, Holland, Norway, Sweden, Channel Islands, Italy, Portugal and Spain. A thousand European company accounts are kept on file in the UK ready for immediate despatch.

The cost of the information ranges from £10.50 to £35.00 per company.

Jordan's Overseas Company Information, (See page 123, for address) covers the whole world with an international network of agents and information sources. Information on companies varies from country to country, as does the speed with which that information can be retrieved. Still, this is certainly one of the best ways of finding out about a company that is not included in a general directory either because it is too small or too new. Of course, you may need much more detailed information on a particular company than is normally provided in a directory, and this information service may be able to provide it.

KOMPASS Directories, similar to the UK directories, are available for Belgium and Luxemburg, Denmark, West Germany, France, Holland, Italy, Australia, Brazil, Indonesia, Morocco, Norway, Singapore, Spain, Sweden and Switzerland. (see page 124).

McCarthy's European Information Service
McCarthy's Australian Service
McCarthy's North American Service
See listing in UK section for more detail of above three services, (see page 125).

Principal International Business, published by Dun and Bradstreet, gives the basic facts about 50,000 businesses in 135 countries. As well as the business name, address and telex and its main activities, it tells you if the company is a subsidiary of a larger corporation; whether they import or export; how many employees they have; their latest sales volume; and the name of the chief executive. Its cover of companies in each country is not great: nearly 8,000 in the USA; 6,000 in Germany; 5,500 in France; 4,000 in Japan; and 2,000 businesses in the UK. This represents only a small percentage of the businesses in any one country, but they are the principal ones.

Standard and Poor's Register of Corporations, Directors & Executives. The *Corporation Record,* Volume I, has a wealth of information on the financial structure and performance of 38,000 of the most significant American corporations. There is also a list of the subsidiary companies cross-referenced to parents. Volume II contains the individual listings of 70,000 people serving as officers of these corporations, together with some personal details on their education and fraternal membership. Volume III contains a series of indexes that complement the first two volumes.

Stores of The World Directory, 1982/83 edition, covers 7,550 department stores, chains, co-ops and variety stores in 121 countries. (See *Retail Directory UK* for sources and more details, page 125.)

Thomas's Register of American Manufacturers, consists of sixteen volumes, making it probably the most comprehensive directory on the market. Volumes 1–8 list products alphabetically, giving the manufacturer's name. Volumes 9 and 10 give company names, addresses with zip codes and telephone numbers listed alphabetically, together with branch offices, capital ratings and company officials. An American trade-mark index is given in Volume 10.

Volumes 11–16, called *Thomcat,* contain catalogues of companies, bound alphabetically and cross-referenced in the first ten volumes. In all a formidable work, this is useful either to find an American source of supply or a potential customer for your product. The catalogues provide an insight into the way in which American companies market their wares.

Wall Street Journal Index provides a monthly and annual review of published material on the USA. It is in two sections. The first gives company news, and second gives general business news. Both are alphabetical and provide brief abstracts of the activities in question. It is somewhat similar to what the *FT* has to say about a company, product or personality.

Who Owns Whom (Australasia and Far East). Details are as below.

Who Owns Whom (Continental Europe). This is published in two volumes. The first is similar to the UK volume, and the second volume has a section on foreign investment. (See listing in UK section for more details.)

Who Owns Whom (North American edition) is perhaps the definitive directory of US multinational subsidiaries. Canadian companies are also covered.

Market and Industry Data

Businesses have to take part in censuses in much the same way as do individuals. This information, showing purchasers, stocks, capital expenditure and so on, is available for all the main UK industries, in the Annual Report on the Census of Production. The *Business Monitor Series* covers this and other areas in considerable detail each month and quarter. *Mintel Retail Business* is a monthly publication that examines consumer goods markets. By taking an area at a time it can produce quite comprehensive studies on spending patterns and the underlying reasons for them. The market share held by various businesses is given in *The A–Z of UK Marketing Data* and *UK Market Size* lists the output of the UK manufacturing industry under thousands of headings.

If you want a piggy back on someone else's research, then *Reports Index* is a quick reference guide to several thousand market studies, carried out on UK products and markets, available for purchase at quite modest prices. If you do not find a reference book in this section covering the field you are interested in, then the *Guide to Official Statistics* from HMSO, or *Sources of UK Marketing Information* by Tupper and Wills, will probably show you where to find it.

Overseas markets are particularly well covered with the *Euromonitor* publications, which provide comprehensive comparative information on European and international markets. *Market Data Reports on European Industries* shows growth and size trends of twenty-four industries in eight countries over the past seven years. *The International Directory of Published Market Research* provides a useful insight into who has done what in the market research field, and a number of useful indexes on other international data sources are also identified.

Market and Industry Data, UK

The A–Z of UK Marketing Data, published by Euromonitor Publications Ltd, 18 Doughty Street, London WC1N 2PN.

It provides basic market data for several hundred UK markets, from adhesives to zip fasteners, by product area, market size, production, imports, exports, the main brands, their market share and a market forecast. A good glimpse at a wide range of markets.

Annual Abstract of Statistics, published by the Central Statistical Office, is the basic source of all UK statistics. Figures are given for each of the preceding ten years, so trends can be recognised.

ASLIB Directory, Volume I. Information sources in science, technology and commerce, edited by Ellen M. Coldlin, 5th edition, 1982. A valuable reference tool if you need to track down information over a wide range of subjects. This edition has over three thousand entries from a large number of sources, professional, amateur, big and small. A major factor in including sources was their willingness to make the information available.

BBC Data Enquiry Service, Room 3, The Langham, The British Broadcasting Corporation, Portland Place, London W1A 1AA. This is a personal information service drawing on the world-wide resources of the BBC. It is an inexpensive and speedy way of checking facts and drawing on a statistical data bank which covers people, products, countries and events. The service could tell you the price of a pint of milk in 1951 or the current state of the Dutch economy. *Ad hoc* enquiries can cost as little as £5.00, or an annual subscription, £100.00.

Benn's Press Directory, published by Benn Publications Ltd, Sovereign Way, Tonbridge, Kent TN9 1RW. (0732 364422)

Published in two volumes. Volume I is the standard reference work on the UK media, giving detailed descriptions. Volume II covers the media in other countries.

British Business, published weekly by the Department of Industry and Trade (£1.10) provides basic statistics on UK markets. These include retail sales, cinemas, hire purchase, engineering sales and orders, industrial production, catering, motor trade, textiles and man-made fibre turn-overs.

British Rate & Data Advertisers & Agency List is produced four times a year, and lists all advertising agencies, their executives and their customers' brand names. It also covers market research and direct mail companies.

British Rate & Data, updated monthly. Whatever market you are interested in, it is almost certain to have a specialised paper or journal. These will be an important source of market data. BRAD lists all newspapers and periodicals in the UK and Eire, and gives their frequency and circulation volume, price, their executives, advertising rates and readership classification. There is also information on company acquisitions, liquidity and insolvencies.

Business Monitors are the medium through which the Government publishes the business statistics it collects from over 20,000 UK firms. They are the primary, and very often the only source of detailed information on the sectors they cover. The *Monitors* can help businessmen to monitor trends and trace the progress of 4,000 individual products, manufactured by firms in 160 industries. *Monitors* can also be used to rate your business performance against that of your industry and measure the efficiency of different parts of your business.

The *Monitors* are published in three main series. The *Production Monitors* are published monthly, quarterly and annually. The quarterly is probably the most useful, with comprehensive yet timely information. The *Service and Distributor Monitors* cover the retail market, the instalment credit business, the motor trade, catering and allied trades and the computer service industry, amongst others. Finally, there are *Miscellaneous Monitors* covering such topics as shipping, insurance, import/export ratios for industry, acquisitions and mergers of industrial and commercial companies, cinemas and tourism.

The *Annual Census of Production Monitors* cover virtually every sector of industry, and include data on total purchases, total sales, stocks, work in progress, capital expenditure, employment, wages and salaries. They include analyses of costs and output, of establishments by size, of full- and part-time employees by sex, and of employment, net capital expenditure and net output by region.

You can use the information – particularly that from the size analysis table – to establish such ratios as gross output per head, net output per head, net to gross output, and wages and salaries to net output. With these as a base, you can compare the performance of your own business with the average for firms of similar size and for that with your particular industry as a whole. For example, you can discover your share of the market, and compare employment figures, increases in sales and so on.

Most of the libraries listed later in this section will have a selection of the *Business Monitor Series.* Individual monitors can be bought from HMSO Books, PO Box 569, London SE1 9NH. They are all individually priced.

Financial Times Business Information Service, published by the *FT* at Bracken House, 10 Cannon Street, London EC4P 4BY. (01 236

4000) (More details are given under Information Services in the next section.)

Guide to Official Statistics is the main guide to all government-produced statistics, including *ad hoc* reports. It is published by HMSO at £18.50. However, a brief, free guide is available from the Press and Information Service, Central Statistical Office, Great George Street, London SW1 3AQ.

Key Note Publications. Publishers of the same name at 28–42 Banner Street, London EC1Y 8QE. (01 253 3006), produce concise briefs on various sectors of the UK economy.

Each *Key Note* contains a detailed examination of the structure of an industry, its distribution network and its major companies; an in-depth analysis of the market, covering products by volume and value, market shares, foreign trade and an appraisal of trends within the market; a review of recent developments in the industry, highlighting new product development, corporate development and legislation; a financial analysis of named major companies, providing data and ratios over a three-year period together with a corporate appraisal and economic overview; forecasts on the future prospects for the industry, including estimates from *Key Note's* own database and authoritative trade sources. There is a very useful appendix detailing further sources of information – recent press articles, other reports and journals.

Over 100 market sectors are covered, including such areas as adhesives, after-dinner drinks, bicycles, butchers, commercial leasing, health foods, road haulage, public houses, travel agents and woman's magazines.

Each *Key Note* costs £35.00, falling to £17.00 for users of their voucher system.

Marketing & Distribution Abstracts, published eight times a year by Anbar Publications Ltd, PO Box 23, Wembley HA9 8DJ. (01 902 4489). This surveys 200 journals world-wide and provides an index to abstracts of appropriate articles and reports in the field.

McCarthy's Industrial Services provides a similar service on products and markets as their service on quoted and unquoted companies. The industry service is classified into thirteen industry groups: agricultural and animal and vegetable raw materials; building and civil engineering; finance; general engineering; electrical and electronic engineering; chemicals and chemical engineering; miscellaneous industrial manufacturers; consumer goods manufacture; transport and transport equipment; marketing; distribution and consumer services; communications and communications equipment; mining and minerals and energy. Within the main industry group lie about 350 subsections. Marketing for example, ranges from auto vending, franchising to street markets, as well as the more predictable department stores and supermarket groups.

Press cuttings are provided at 55p per copy. A phone call to McCarthy will tell you how many pages are involved, as naturally the size varies with the volume of news in a given area. The Back Numbers Service seems good value for small businesses.

MGN Marketing Manual, published by the Mirror Group of Newspapers (01 353 0246), provides a survey of UK social and economic conditions, including market data on ninety products.

Mintel is a monthly publication providing reports on the performance of new products and a wide range of specific areas of consumer expenditure. It covers five specific consumer goods markets each month, combining published data and original research to make the studies as exhaustive as possible. Comparative data on overseas markets is also given when appropriate.

Further details from Mintel, 20 Buckingham Street, The Strand, London WC2N 6EE. (01 839 1542)

Office of Population, Census and Surveys produce demographic statistics for each county in England and Wales from the 1981 census. These provide data not only on total populations in each area, but also on occupations, economic groups, etc. Similar reports for Scottish and Northern Ireland regions are also available. There is a reference library at OPCS, St Catherine House, 10 Kingsway, London WC2B 6JP. (01 242 0262)

More information and answers to general enquiries on these reports are also available from this number on ext. 2009/2013.

Overseas Trade Statistics published by the Department of Industry and Trade, provide a monthly statement of UK imports and exports by volume and value for each product group and individual country.

The Bill Entry Services, operated by HM Customs and Excise, Portcullis House, 27 Victoria Avenue, Southend-on-Sea SS2 6AL (49421 ext. 310), will provide more detailed information at a fee.

Principal Sources of Marketing Information, by Christine Hull, The Times Information and Market Intelligence Unit, New Printing House Square, Gray's Inn Road, London WC1. (01 837 1234), price £2.50.

Reports Index. More recently Business Surveys Ltd introduced its bi-monthly *Reports Index.* This is an index to reports in every field published and available for sale. Its sources include Government publications, HMSO as well as non-HMSO, market research organisations, trade and professional associations, public bodies, stockbrokers, educational establishments, EEC, industrial and financial companies. Again, at £94.00 per annum, the cost is modest. (Address: see *Research Index* page 125.)

Retail Business, published monthly by the Economist Intelligence Unit, covers the economic aspects of the UK retail trade, with emphasis on consumer-goods market research, distribution patterns and sales trends.

Retail Intelligence is a quarterly publication also from Mintel, covering the consumer goods marketed in considerable depth.

Sources of UK Marketing Information, by Tupper & Wills, published by E. Benn, 24 New Street Square, London EC4, 01 353 3212. A comprehensive guide to the main source of data on over 1,000 products. Price £20.00.

UK Market Size, published by IMAC Research, Lancaster House, More Lane, Esher, Surrey (Esher 63121). This report lists the output of UK manufacturing industry under 5,000 separate headings. It costs £75.00 and is produced each year.

Market and Industry Data, Overseas

British Business, weekly news from the Department of Trade & Industry. *British Business* magazine's European Community Information Unit offers a free service to businesses in Britain by answering general enquiries about EEC matters and referring business enquiries to experts in official circles on detailed points.

Concise Guide to International Markets is now published in four volumes, covering Europe, the Americas, the Far East and Australia, and the Middle East and Africa. It is updated every two years, and contains 4,000 facts about 109 world markets. There are 550 pages of up-to-date information on population, literacy, languages, religion, climate, working hours, currency, main towns, income, retail and wholesale structures, advertising agencies, commissions, associations, advertising controls, advertising expenditure, media of all types, market research facilities, together with over 100 maps.

This guide provides a useful overview to markets, and could be helpful in choosing markets to look at more closely later.

It is published by Leslie Stinton & Partners, 39a London Road, Kingston-upon-Thames, Surry KT2 6ND, in conjunction with the International Advertising Association.

Economist Intelligence Unit produces each quarter some eighty-three separate reviews covering 160 countries, evaluating growth prospects, assessing opportunities and examining local and international problems. It provides a business-orientated analysis of the economic state of the countries examined.

European Marketing Data & Statistics, published by Euromonitor Publications Ltd, is an annual handbook containing comparative information about European Markets. *International Marketing Data &*

Statistics is a companion volume that covers North and South America, Asia, Africa and Australasia.

Findex, published by ICC Information Group Ltd, 23 City Road, London EC1Y 1AA. (01 638 2946)

This is a reference guide to 7,000 world-wide market research reports, polls, studies and surveys from 300 leading research publishers. It gives rather more details on each research study than some other publications. It is extremely well cross-indexed, by subject, geography and publisher.

It is produced in the spring of each year, and an update is produced between publications. The price is £110.00

International Directory of Published Market Research, 6th edition, 1982, by British Overseas Trade Board in association with Arlington Management Publications Ltd, 87 Jermyn Street, London SW1 6JD.

The directory is in three parts. Part I is the Master Index, assigning a code number to each product. Part II contains 6,000 study listings in numerical order according to the British Standards Industrial Classification Scheme. This has the advantage of keeping related subjects close together. The studies themselves cover industrial and consumer markets and are briefly described together with the date when they were completed, how much each study costs and who is selling it. Part III gives the names, addresses and phone numbers of the 375 research firms who carried out the studies. None of the studies is earlier than 1977, and some were produced in 1982.

Market Data Reports on European Industries are published by Market Studies International, 81 City Road, London EC1Y 1BD. (01 250 3922, telex 23678).

Twenty-four European industries are included in this series. Each study gives the growth, size and competitive potential over seven years, in eight European countries. The studies are priced between £75.00 and £175.00.

Published Data on European Industrial Markets, published by Industrial Aids Ltd, 14 Buckingham Palace Road, London SW1W 0QP. (01 828 5036)

Part I lists over 1,900 market research reports available for purchase at prices from as low as £10.00 up to several thousand pounds. Although the directory is entitled 'industrial', the interpretation is fairly wide. It covers consumer goods as markets for industrial products, and financial and economic planning studies, where they are considered of possible interest to industry. This could be a relatively inexpensive way of finding out about a distant market-place. The market studies are indexed, and the most frequent entries are food and drink, machinery and equipment, chemicals, plastics and polymers, transport, pharmaceutical, medical, veterinary and dental, metals, metal powders, paper board, paper chemicals, computers and data processing, fuels, oil, energy, feedstocks, furniture and fittings, electronic, electrical, building and construction packaging, printing and graphics (including inks and publishing), fibres and textiles, clothing and agriculture (excluding fertilisers).

Part II is a guide to other sources of information on European industrial markets. It covers East Europe and the USSR as well as the more obvious European countries. It gives sources of international statistics and a few pages on each country's key sources of information. These are grouped under six main headings: national statistics, government and non-governmental organisations, the press, banks, company information, libraries and similar organisations.

Statistics – Europe, Africa, Asia and Australasia are four guides to sources of statistics for social, economic and market research. They are published by CBD Research Ltd, 154 High Street, Beckenham, Kent. (01 650 7745)

Subjects Index to Sources of Comparative International Statistics (SISCIS). For any activity or commodity it shows in what form the statistics are presented, in what unit and for what countries. From this it is possible to identify which of 350 major statistical serials contain the required figures. Also published by CBD Research Ltd (see above for address).

FINDING THE INFORMATION

Now that you have an idea of the considerable mass of data that is available about companies, their products and markets, the next problem that remains is to track it down. Fortunately, many of the directories and publications are kept in reference sections of major libraries up and down the country.

If you know exactly what information you want, then your problem is confined to finding a library or information service that has that information.

Specialist Libraries
Apart from your local library there are hundreds of specialist libraries concentrated in government departments, major industrial companies, trade organisations, research centres and academic institutes.

Two useful publications that will help you find out about these are listed below.

ASLIB Economic and Business Information Group Membershire Directory, published by the group and available from the London

Business School Library, Sussex Place, Regent's Park, London NW1 4SA. (01 262 5050)
It provides a list of over 300 specialist business libraries throughout the country, and gives a very useful guide to their area of specialist interest.

Guide to Government Departments and Other Libraries. The 25th edition, published in 1982, is the latest, and it is available from the Science Reference Library, 25 Southampton Buildings, Chancery Lane, London WC2A 1AW, price £9.00. As the title indicates, this book concentrates on libraries in government departments and agencies, and particularly avoids duplicating the ground covered by the *ASLIB Directory*. The entries are arranged by subject covered, supplemented by an alphabetical index of the libraries, their locations, phone numbers and opening hours.

Not all the libraries covered in these directories are open to the public for casual visits. However, many will let you use their reference facilities, by appointment.

British Institute of Management Library, and Management Information Centre, Management House, Parker Street, London WC2B 5PT. (01 405 3456 ext. 126/7/8/9), open Monday–Friday, 09.15 to 17.15. The Library houses one of the largest specialised collections of management literature in Europe. This includes much valuable information not generally available. The services are for BIM members who can use the library in person or make enquiries by letter or telephone.

The Library also produces extremely valuable reading lists covering a wide range of topics. These provide a selective guide to books, directories and periodicals in any of 170 specific areas. They also publish *A Basic Library of Management*, which lists 300 or so of the more useful books in the management field.

Business Statistics Office Library, Cardiff Road, Newport, Gwent NPT 1XG. (0633 56111 ext. 2973, telex 497121/2), open Monday–Friday, 09.00 to 17.00. This Library keeps all the data produced in published form by the Business Statistics office, together with a substantial quantity of non-official material. The coverage extends beyond UK statistics to include foreign information and an extensive range of company data and trade directories. The library is freely open to the public, who can enquire personally or by telephone, telex or letter.

Science Reference Library, Department of the British Library, 25 Southampton Buildings, Chancery Lane, London WC2A 1AW. (01 405 8721 ext. 3344 or 3345; patent enquiries, ext. 3350, telex 266959) This is the national library for modern science and technology, for patents, trade marks and designs. It has the most comprehensive reference section of this type of literature in Western Europe. If you do not have an adequate library close at hand a visit here could save you visits to several libraries. It should also be able to provide you answers if most other places cannot do so.

The library's resources are formidable. It has 25,000 different journals, with issues back to 1960 on open shelves and the rest quickly available. It has 85,000 books and pamphlets and 20¼ million patents. It has a world-wide collection of journals on trade marks, together with books on law and design. Most of the major UK and European reports are held, as is trade literature and around 1,000 abstracting periodicals.

The services are equally extensive. It is open from Monday to Friday, 09.30 to 21.00, and on Saturday from 10.00 to 13.00. You can visit without prior arrangement or a reader's ticket. Telephone requests for information, including the checking of references, are accepted. Once at the library, staff are available to help you find items and to answer general queries. Scientific staff are also on hand for specialised enquiries. There is even a linguist service to help you inspect material written in a foreign language, though for this service you must make an appointment.

The Business Information Service of the Science Reference Library (01 404 0406) This was set up in January 1981, primarily to support the activities of other business and industrial libraries. However, it will help individual users as much as possible. Staff here can extract reference information quickly, advise on the use of business literature and suggest other organisations to contact. For extensive research you will have to call in person, but they can let you know if a visit would be worth while.

There are three locations, the first is at Southampton Buildings (address above), which holds company information, industry, country and market surveys. The other two are listed below.

Official Publication Library, The British Library, Great Russell Street, London WC1B 3DG. (01 636 1544 ext. 234/5), open Monday, Friday and Saturday from 09.30 to 16.45, and Tuesday to Thursday 09.30 to 20.45 (please phone first). Virtually all official British publications are held here, together with an extensive intake from all other countries of the world from international organisations. All the UK and major overseas series complementing the Statistics and Market Intelligence Library are here too. An extensive world-wide collection of legislative publications and a complete set of all current UK electoral registers are kept here.

The Newspaper Library, The British Library, Colindale Avenue, London NW9 5HE. (01 200 5515) A comprehensive set of British (national and local) newspapers and most major foreign and commonwealth newspapers are kept here. It is best to telephone and check they have what you want, or you can send for a catalogue and price list.

Statistics and Marketing Intelligence Library, of The Overseas Trade Board, 1 Victoria Street SW1. (01 215 5444/5, telex 8811074DTHQG). Reading room open 09.30 to 17.30, Monday to Friday.

This library is primarily concerned with statistics and directories from overseas countries and import/export data on the UK. As such, it is the most important source of international statistics and business information. It also has a very comprehensive collection of other UK statistics and directories.

In addition to these special libraries, major chambers of commerce, such as those in London, Birmingham, Manchester and Glasgow, have their own substantial business collections.

Local Reference Libraries For most purposes you will find that one of the major local libraries with a good business information section will do. Among the libraries with a strong commitment to business information and experienced staff are the following:

ABERDEEN
Central Library, Rosemount Viaduct, Aberdeen AB9 1GU. (0224 634622) Open: 9 a.m.–9 p.m. Monday–Friday, 9 a.m.–5 p.m. Saturday

BIRMINGHAM
Central Libraries, Chamberlain Square, Birmingham B3 3HQ. (021 235 4511) Open: 9 a.m.–6 p.m. Monday and Friday, 9 a.m.– 8 p.m. Tuesday, Wednesday and Thursday, 9 a.m.–5 p.m. Saturday

BRISTOL
Central Library, College Green, Bristol, BS1 5TL. (0272 276121) Open: 9.30 a.m.–8 p.m. Monday–Friday, 9.30 a.m.–5 p.m. Saturday

CAMBRIDGE
Central Library, 7 Lion Yard, Cambridge, CB2 3QD. (0223 65252) Open: 9 a.m.–7 p.m. Monday–Saturday

CHATHAM
Chatham Library, Riverside, Chatham, MA4 5SN. (0634 43589) Open: 9 a.m.–7 p.m. Monday, Tuesday and Friday, 9 a.m.–5 p.m. Wednesday, Thursday and Saturday

EXETER
Central Library, Castle Street, Exeter, EX4 3PQ. (0392 77977) Open: 9.30 a.m.–8 p.m. Monday–Friday, 9.30 a.m.–6 p.m. Wednesday, 9.30 a.m.–4 p.m. Saturday

GLASGOW
Commercial Library, Royal Exchange Square, Glasgow. (041 221 1872) Open: 9.30 a.m.–5 p.m. Monday–Saturday

IPSWICH
Central Library, Northgate Street, Ipswich, IPI 3DE. (0473 214370) Open:

10 a.m.–5 p.m. Monday–Thursday, 10 a.m.–7.30 p.m. Friday, 9.30 a.m.–5 p.m. Saturday

LEEDS
Central Library, Calverley Street, Leeds LS1 3AB. (0532 462067) Open: 9 a.m.–5 p.m. Thursday–Friday, 9 a.m.–9 p.m. Monday, Tuesday and Wednesday, 9 a.m.–4 p.m. Saturday

LIVERPOOL
Commercial Library, William Brown Street, Liverpool, Merseyside L3 8EW. (051 2072147 and 2070036) Open: 9 a.m.–9 p.m. Monday–Friday, 9 a.m.–5 p.m. Thursday and Saturday

LONDON
City Business Library, Gillett House, 55 Basinghall Street, London EC2B 5BX. (01 638 8215) Open: 9.30 a.m.–5 p.m. Monday–Friday

Deptford Reference Library, 140, Lewisham Way, Deptford, London SE14 6PF. (01 692 1162) Open: 9.30 a.m.–8 p.m. Tuesday–Friday

Holborn Library, 32/38 Theobalds Road, London WC1X 8PA. (01 405 2706) Open: 9.30 a.m.–8 p.m. Monday–Thursday, 9.30 a.m.–6 p.m. Friday, 9.30 a.m.–5 p.m. Saturday

Westminster Reference Library, St Martin's Street, London WC2H 7HP. (01 930 3274) Open: 10 a.m.–7 p.m. Monday–Friday, 10 a.m.–5 p.m. Saturday

LUTON
Reference Library, Bridge Street, Luton. (0582 30161) Open: 9 a.m.–8 p.m. Monday–Friday, 9 a.m.–5 p.m. Saturday

MANCHESTER
Central Library, St Peter's Square, Manchester M2 5PD. (061 236 9422) Open: 9 a.m.–9 p.m. Monday–Friday

NEWCASTLE UPON TYNE
Central Library, Princess Square, Newcastle upon Tyne, Northumberland NE99 1HC. (0632 610691) Open: 9 a.m.–9 p.m. Monday–Friday, 9 a.m.–5 p.m. Thursday and Saturday

NOTTINGHAM
Central Library, Angel Row, Nottingham, NG1 6HP. (0602 43591) Open: 9.30 a.m.–8 p.m. Monday–Friday, 9 a.m.–1 p.m. Saturday

OXFORD
Central Library, Westgate, Oxford, OX1 1DJ. (0865 815509) Open: 9.15 a.m.– 7 p.m. Monday–Friday, 9.15 a.m.–5 p.m. Thursday and Saturday

PETERSFIELD
Central Library, 27 The Square, Petersfield, GU32 3HH. (0732 3451) Open: 10 a.m.–5 p.m. Monday, Tuesday and Friday, 10 a.m.–7 p.m. Wednesday, Closed all day Thursday, 10 a.m.–1 p.m. Saturday

SOUTHAMPTON
Central Library, Civic Centre, Southampton, SO9 4XP. (0703 23855) Open: 9 a.m.–7 p.m. Monday–Friday, 10 a.m.–4 p.m. Saturday

Before making a special journey it would be as well to telephone and make sure the library has the reference work you want.

Do not neglect your local library. A recent visit to Kensington and Woolwich libraries was a very pleasant surprise. Gloucestershire is also among a growing band of progressive County Libraries aiming to serve local business needs in the information field. Their librarian has produced a very useful guide to their free commercial service for the county's business communities.

Information Services

In addition to the many excellent business libraries up and down the country, there are an increasing number of organisations that will do the searching for you. The benefits to you are twofold: professionals search out the data, and can alert you to sources that you may not have thought of; they save you time, not just the time you would spend searching. If you are not near a good business reference library you may have a considerable and expensive journey to make. Mostly, these organisations have substantial libraries of their own, but, for example Warwick, will search elsewhere if they cannot find it in their stocks. They claim the largest statistics collection in the UK, after the Statistics and Market Intelligence Library in London, and they have access to several on-line data bases.

ASLIB, 3 Belgrave Square, London SW1X 8PL. (01 235 5050, telex 23667) Their referral service is available to non-members of ASLIB for a fee of £25.00 plus VAT per enquiry. For this fee, ASLIB will assist enquirers by identifying sources of information on any subject; compiling short bibliographies; verifying details of publications; tracing details of translations from their unique index; and supplying lists of specialist translators or specific subject/language dictionaries.

The Financial Times Business Information Service, 102–108 Clerkenwell Road, London EC1M 5SA. (01 251 9321) The service offers impartial, authoritative facts – facts about companies, industries, statistics and people. They keep press cuttings on some 25,000 prominent people in industry, politics and business. They also have a Business Information Consultancy, which can offer an on-demand information service to meet individual information requirements.

The service costs £32.00 per hour, with a minimum charge of £3.00. Subscriptions can be taken out on a six-month or annual basis. The annual rate is £250.00, plus VAT. This is, in effect, a deposit, with charges for using the services debited against it.

Industrial Aids Ltd, Enquiry service at 14 Buckingham Palace Road, London SW1W 0QP. (01 828 5036, telex 918666 CRECON G.) This service is geared to supply commercial and technical information, such as Who makes what/where/how much? Who is company

A's agent in country X? Where are custom manufacturing sources? Details are given of company financial data, affiliations, product literature, consumption patterns, end users, prices, discounts and trading terms, as well as new legislation and standards, trade and industrial economic statistics, conference papers, proceedings and lists of delegates.

The cost is £29.00 per enquiry, excluding VAT. You can use the service by telephone, telex or by letter, and the response is fast.

Market Location Ltd, 17 Waterloo Place, Warwick Street, Royal Leamington Spa, Warwicks. CV32 5LA. (0926 34235) Contact: M. J. Griffiths. Market Location is a research organisation studying manufacturing industry in the UK. It gathers its information through field research. Its team of researchers travel the country, marking each manufacturing unit on maps and conducting a face-to-face interview with a representative of the company in order to obtain accurate, first-hand information.

The data gathered is published on a series of large-scale maps with accompanying indexes, giving the company name, address and telephone number; the name of the location manager and his position; the activity of the company and its SIC main-order heading; the size of the work-force and its group structure.

Clients of Market Location are usually companies with a sales force selling to manufacturing industry. They use the service to improve their sales performance by finding new prospects, by increasing salesmen's call rates, reducing travelling expenses, and eliminating potentially abortive cold-calling.

Market Location produces statistics tables for each county, showing the number of factories, broken down by SIC code and number of employees (including percentages).

Copies of the statistics tables for all the counties researched cost £50.00.

The Marketing Shop, 18 Kingly Court, Kingly Street, London W1R 5LE. (01 434 2671, telex 262284). This organisation provides a wide range of marketing services, but its Information Service is perhaps the most useful facility for small businesses. It can provide data on practically any topic, either using its own library or outside sources, and will also monitor the media for information on companies, products or markets. Charges are £35.00 an hour for *ad hoc* work. The more usual arrangement is for customers to take a block of hours to be used over the year. Block fees start at around £500.00, which works out at £30.00 per hour.

The Trade Openings Bureau (TOB), confederation of British Industry, Centre Point, 103 New Oxford Street, London W1A 1DU. Tel 01 379 7400. The aim of this free service is to help British Companies, particularly, but not exclusively CBI members by identifying purchasing and tendering opportunities for their goods and services in the UK and abroad.

The service covers a comprehensive range of trading and commercial matters including Raw materials- Trade names; New and existing products; Industrial and commercial services and consultancies; Research and commercial organisations; Trade associations; Journals and directories; Exhibitions and trade fairs.

To make contact with the TOB either phone or write to the address above. The bureau's staff are there to help you find the answer to your particular enquiry and the service is completely free of charge.

Warwick Statistics Service, University of Warwick Library, Coventry CV4 7AL. (0203 418938, telex 31406) Contact: Jennifer Carr or David Mart.

The service offers a range of commercial and economic information based on published sources including international statistics, both official and non-official, market research, periodicals, reports, directories, company reports and on-line services. The service can be particularly helpful to a small business with information on market size and share, locating particular types of company and finding out about them, tracing recent articles on a particular product or process, on consumer expenditure data, imports and exports, economic conditions, price trends, advertising expenditure and production and sales figures.

The service will also undertake analysis of the data in question, and provide a written report on their desk research. In general, enquiries are dealt with on the telephone, telex or by post; however, personal visits are welcomed. If you telephone beforehand, documents can be assembled for you to look at.

Annual subscribers to the service pay £300.00 for 25 hours' search time and publication. Occasional users of the service can get information or research assistance on an *ad hoc* basis at a cost of £20.00 per hour *pro rata*, with a minimum charge of £5.00.

All in all, it is very good value.

Their monthly journal, *Warwick Statistics News*, provides a regular source of information on statistical and marketing topics, and costs £25.00 per annum.

The service holds regular one-day seminars on Information Sources for Business Planning and Market Research, costing £30.00.

Three on-line, computer-based business information retrieval systems are Dialog, Data star and Textline. They require the user to have a terminal (keyboard) and a Modem or Accoustic coupler. That is the device that lets you use your telephone to connect up to the data base.

Dialog and Data star have extensive American information data bases, and are building up their UK information file. They could be worth a look for a small business if you already have the hardware, and are very interested in the USA business scene.

Data star, 199 High Street, Orpington, Kent BR6 0PF. (0689 38488, telex 898239)

Dialog, Information Retrieval Service, PO Box 8, Abingdon, Oxford OX13 6EG. (0865 730969, telex 837704 Inform G)

Textline is a computerised business information service provided by Finsbury Data Services, 68–74 Carter Lane, London EC4V 5EA. (01 236 9771) Users can retrieve summaries of daily press stories on financial, business and industrial matters. The service covers the business news published in the leading UK daily and weekly newspapers, and from other sources.

Abstracting Services If you do not know exactly what you are looking for but know the subject area, then you need to find out what is in print on that subject. Simply to scan the shelves, apart from being time-consuming, will not produce direct results. Only a fraction of the books, periodicals, directories and other reference works are likely to be in any one library. For these reasons you need to use one of the main abstracting systems. An abstract is a brief summary of the publication itself, usually just enough to let you know if it is worth reading. Only a few are mentioned here, but one or more such services are available at many major county libraries. Alternatively, you could search the one that best suits your needs by reading:

Inventory of Abstracting and Indexing Services Produced in the UK, by G. Burgen, A. Vickery and S. Keenan, published by the British Library Research and Development Department. This is the definitive guide to abstracting and indexing services. Otherwise, useful abstracting services are listed below.

Anbar Bibliography gives details of the main business management books published each year. Anbar Publications, 65 Wembley Hill Road, Wembley, Middx. (01 902 4489)

Anbar Abstracting Journals cover accounting and data processing; marketing and distribution; personnel and training; top management; work study and O & M.

These abstracts are a selective guide through the literature, provided by subject experts, and include brief summaries of the articles listed from the 200 or so journals searched.

British National Bibliography, published weekly by the British Library Bibliographic Services Division, provides a subject list of all books published in Britain.

Business Periodicals Index, published by G. H. W. Wilson (New

York), provides a guide to articles published in some 300 international business journals, and are indexed by the service.

London Business School Small Business Bibliography, arranged under appropriate subject headings, lists and indexes about 2,600 books and articles on small business management. First published in 1980, it is up-dated at nine-monthly intervals.

SCIMP (Selective Co-operative Index of Management Periodicals) is produced by the Manchester Business School Library, but covers mainly European periodicals.

It may be useful to know something of other types of written information that is not generally published. Two such abstracts are:

Research in British Universities, Polytechnics and Colleges, from the British Library Lending Division. There is a section on business and management with a comprehensive guide to current research indexed by topic and college.

Selected List of UK Theses and Dissertations in Management Studies, compiled by N. R. Hunter, University at Bradford Library.

Three useful books on researching for business information are:

Business Information Services, published in 1981 by Clive Bingley Ltd. The author is Malcolm J. Campbell of the City Business Library. It is an extremely useful book and illustrates clearly the range of business information that is available.

The Manager's Guide to Getting Answers (1980), The Library Association, 7 Ridgmount Place, London WC1E 7AE. (01 636 7543) Price, £2.50.

Use of Management and Business Literature, edited by K. D. C. Vermont, published by Butterworths.

MARKETING ORGANISATIONS AND THEIR SERVICES

The organisations that look after the interests of professional marketeers can also give considerable help to newcomers and small businesses. At least two of these organisations, the Institute of Marketing and the British Overseas Trade Board, have unrivalled libraries and information banks in their respective fields. The Institute of Marketing, with its unique low-cost advisory service, is one particularly useful organisation. Many others, including the Market Research Society, the Institute of Management Consultants and the Society of Business Economists, provide specialist members' directories. These can put you in touch with someone with recent experience in the area of your concern. Although you will have to pay for their services, you will improve the chances of solving your problem first time round.

Education is also a strong point of many organisations. The Institute of Sales and Marketing and the British Direct Marketing Association hold frequent short courses on most aspects of sales and marketing, as does the Institute of Marketing itself.

The Advertising Association, Abford House, 15 Wilton Road, London SW1V 1NJ. (01 828 2771). The association was formed in 1926, and is primarily a federation of organisations with a major interest in advertising. As such it sets out to promote greater awareness of the effectiveness and purpose of all types of 'paid-for-space' in the media. Two services of possible interest are its publications of advertising expenditure statistics and forecasts in all media; and its education programme, run through CAM, listed later.

British Consultants Bureau, Westminster Palace Gardens, 1–7 Artillery Row, London SW1P 1RJ. (01 222 3651) This is an independent, non-profit-making association of British consulting firms of all disciplines. BCB's main purpose is to promote the interest of British consultants overseas. However, the bureau publishes a comprehensive directory, giving detailed information about all their members, their experience and their expertise. This is available to commercial firms.

The British Direct Marketing Association, 1 New Oxford Street, London WC1A 1NQ. (01 242 2254) The association brings together the three main groups of people who influence the way in which products and services are marketed direct to customers. These groups are: direct mail houses, who prepare and market lists of prospective customers; financial, insurance, commercial and manufacturing firms; publishers and professional organisations that market direct (i.e., not via retailers), and advertising agencies and consultancies that specialise in direct marketing methods.

The BDMA is growing rapidly both in size and stature. It has played an important role in helping the customer to choose whether or not he wants to receive more advertising mail through the post. Its education programmes of short courses and work-shops, covering the use of direct mail, is extensive. In October 1982 the first Diploma in Direct Marketing programme was launched at Kingston Polytechnic.

The BDMA also produces a number of useful books that introduce the subject to the novice, or sharpen up older hands.

British Institute of Management, Management House, Parker Street, London WC2B 5PT. (01 405 3456)

Their services to members include information and advisory functions, and a research and education programme. They also have a Centre for Physical Distribution Management, which covers transport, warehousing, inventory control, materials handling and packaging matters.

This is more an institute for professional managers than just for marketeers, but its wider vision is particularly useful for small business.

Communication Advertising and Marketing Education (CAM) Foundation, Abford House, 15 Wilton Road, London SW1V 1NJ. (01 828 7506) This is the authoritative body on what and where to study in the marketing field.

Institute of Management Consultants, 23–24 Cromwell Place, London SW7 2LG. (01 584 72856) The institute has 3,000 individual members, and publishes the journal *Innovation and Management*. As a free service to industry it operates a professional register, putting enquirers in contact with members with appropriate skills.

Institute of Marketing, Moor Hall, Cookham, Maidenhead, Berks. SL6 9HQ. (06285 24922) The institute has nearly 23,000 members, and is the largest and most comprehensive body in the field. It has a substantial library and a wide range of publications, including its series *Checklists for Sales and Marketing* (details from Leviathan House Ltd, 80 East Street, Epsom, Surrey KT17 1HF. (Epsom 28300)

Its annual *Marketing Year Book* also provides a useful range of information sources.

There are few subjects in the field to which the institute cannot provide a useful pointer.

The Marketing Advisory Service, reachable at the Institute of Marketing, was established to enable British companies of any size to get marketing advice from highly experienced professional marketeers. The service itself is free, although an administration charge of £15.00 is made, and you will have to meet any travelling expenses incurred by the advisers.

It works like this; you get a list of fifty advisers, a brief description of their qualifications, experience and areas of particular knowledge and skill, and from that list you choose who you would like to speak to. Seeing that list, it is hard to think of an area of marketing or type of product that is not covered.

Your meeting with the adviser will not resolve all your marketing problems, but it will help you decide what to do next. If you think that some professional consultancy is needed, then your advisers should be able to put you in touch with the right people. It is important to note that these advisers are not consultants themselves. If you want to discuss the scheme before committing yourself, first send for their booklet, then talk to Peter Blood, the Director General of the Institute.

Industrial Market Research Association, 11 Bird Street, Lichfield, Staffs, WS13 6PW. (05432 23448) The association represents some 800 members of the profession of Industrial Market Research in the UK. Although it does produce a directory of members, this is not generally available.

The Institute of Public Relations, 1 Great James Street, London WC1N 3DA. (01 405 5505) The institute is mainly concerned with keeping professional standards high and promoting general awareness of the role of public relations. It produces a useful guidance paper, *Choosing a PR Consultancy.*

Institute of Purchasing and Supply, IPS House, High Street, Ascot, Berks, SL5 7HU. (0990 23711) Not strictly a marketing organisation, it is, however, an authority on finding information in its field. As such, its services can be of use to the smaller business.

The Institute of Sales Promotion, Panstar House, 13–15 Swakeleys Road, Ickenham, Middx, UB10 8DS. (London 71; STD 08956 74281/2)

This is the recognised professional body of their branch of marketing. Their *Consultants' Register* is available to non-member prospective clients, as is their information service, which holds a comprehensive reading list on the subject.

The Marketing Society, Derwent House, 35 South Park Road, London SW19 8RR. (01 543 5191) The society was formed twenty years ago. One of its main objectives is to raise the reputation and understanding of marketing among general management, government, the Civil Service, trade unions and educationalists.

The Market Research Society, 15 Belgrave Square, London SW1X 8PF. (01 235 4709) This is the professional body for those concerned with market, social and economic research. It has 3,500 members, and is the largest body of its kind in the world.

Apart from a programme of education, research and publications of primary interest to members, the society produces a directory of organisations providing market research services. The directory provides background information on the 210 research agencies, their executives, experience and the size in sales turn-over. Some of the organisations are quite small, with turn-overs below £50,000 per annum, whereas others have a turn-over of several million pounds.

Also published (autumn 1982) is the *International Research Directory.*

Public Relations Consultants Association, 37 Cadogan Street, Sloane Square, London SW3 2PR (01 581 3951) The association produces a wide range of guidance papers and other publications, which extend from the useful – *Selecting a PR Consultancy and Consul-*

tancy/Client Agreement – to the esoteric – *How to Set up for a Royal Visit.*

It publishes, together with the *Financial Times*, the most authoritative book in the field, *Public Relations Yearbook*. This gives profiles of 150 PR consultancies and their clients. There are also several useful articles on other aspects of public relations.

Price £15.00 from Financial Times Publishing, 2 Greystoke Place, Fetter Lane, London EC4. (01 405 6969)

The Society of Business Economists, 11 Bay Tree Walk, Watford, Herts. WD1 3RX. (Watford 37287) The society was formed in 1953 to allow businessmen and other economists to discuss ideas, problems and other matters of common interest.

It produces a register of Freelance Economists who are members of the society. The register costs £5.00, and contains details of some thirty economists, their experience, specialist skills and fees.

The fees range from around £100.00 to £250.00 per day, and several express a specific interest in the small business field.

SPECIALIST SERVICES FOR EXPORTING

The British Overseas Board, with its wide range of expertise and services, is of considerable use to first-time exporters. Apart from a wealth of information and statistics, its Market Entry Guarantee Scheme can provide an important part of the funding which a small firm needs to enter a new market.

The Institute of Export is the professional body in the field, and two other services are particularly interesting. Scanmark, run from Buckinghamshire College of Higher Education, undertakes research into overseas markets at a fraction of the cost of the commercial research organisations. The Export and Overseas Trade Advisory Panel Ltd performs a rather different role. Using their panel of expert advisers, they not only help you to evaluate an overseas market opportunity but will guide you through the red tape, too.

SITPRO (the Simplification of International Trade Procedures Board) will also be able to help with export documentation systems that will save exporters time and money, and the BBC Service to Exporters is always keen to hear interesting exporting stories.

Organisations

BBC Data Enquiry Service, Room 3, The Langham, British Broadcasting Corporation, Portland Place, London W1A 1AA.

This service draws on the world-wide resources of the BBC to provide up-to-the-minute, accurate information, fast. It can provide information on the social, economic and political aspects of every country in the world. It can also supply career details of leading foreign politicians and other public figures overseas. It is quite inexpensive too; a relatively simple enquiry could cost as little as £5.00.

BBC Service to Exporters, Export Liaison Unit, BBC External Services, Bush House, London WC2B 4PH. (01 240 3456 ext. 2039/ 2295) Which of your products could make a good story? Which programme would be the right one for you? Any overseas enquirers will be put in touch with you.

British Overseas Trade Board, 1–19 Victoria Street, London SW1H OET. (01 215 7877). The board provides a considerable amount of information, advice and help to the exporter. In particular it gathers, stores and disseminates information on overseas markets; gives advice and help to individual firms; organises collective trade promotions; and stimulates export publicity.

The board really does know all there is to know about the process of exporting, and it can help with some of the costs. For example, its Export Market Research Scheme can provide up to a third of the costs of carrying out market-research studies overseas. The Market Guarantee Scheme can fund a large part of the cost of your export drive. Half of such costs as overseas office accommodation, staff costs, training, travel expenses, sales promotions, overseas warehousing and commercial and legal costs can be met by the board, which could pay up to £150,000 towards such costs.

The board's Export Intelligence Service costs £52.50 for a subscription. This will keep you up to date on events in any market area you choose. The service publishes a very comprehensive booklet outlining its services, and can provide more information on any area of particular interest (details from the Publicity Office at the above address).

Regional Offices:

North-eastern Regional Office, Stanegate House, 2 Groat Market, Newcastle upon Tyne NE1 1YN. (0632 324722, telex 53178)
Yorkshire & Humberside Regional Office, Priestley House, Park Row, Leeds LS1 5LF. (0532 443171, telex 557925)
West Midlands Regional Office, Ladywood House, Stephenson Street, Birmingham B2 4DT. (021 632 4111, telex 337919)
North-west Regional Office, Sunley Buildings, Piccadilly Plaza, Manchester M1 4BA. (061 236 2171, telex 667104)
East Midlands Regional Office, Severns House, 20 Middle Pavement, Nottingham NG1 7DW. (0602 56181, telex 37143)
South-west Regional Office, The Pithay, Bristol BS1 2PB. (0272 291071, telex 44214)

Export Houses See under their heading in the finance section (page 173 in the Finance Section). These provide the most comprehensive range of services to exporters and potential exporters.

The Export Overseas Trade Advisory Panel Ltd, World Trade Centre, London E1 9AA. (01 481 1962) This company has a panel of advisers with substantial knowledge of overseas markets. They have experience of finding and developing profitable opportunities for exporting and trading overseas. They also have experience in handling all aspects of finance, insurance and shipping. The panel themselves have among their number recently retired members of the Diplomatic Service, the Department of Trade and the Export Credit Guarantee Department. Their service could be particularly attractive to a company exporting for the first time, or considering a move into a new market.

It will cost £75 per day for each panel member forming the advisory team, plus any out-of-pocket expenses. This could be a lot cheaper than going to the country in question.

The Institute of Export, World Trade Centre, London E1 9AA. (01 488 4766) The institute aims to contribute to profitable exporting by providing a forum for the exchange of experience and information between exporters. It also promotes education and training throughout the whole field of exporting. Its regular journal, *Export*, is a good way of getting into the export picture.

Institute of Freight Forwarders Ltd, Suffield House, 9 Paradise Road, Richmond, Surrey TW9 1SA. (01 948 3141)

International Business Unit, University of Manchester Institute of Science and Technology (UMIST), PO Box 88, Sackville Street, Manchester M60 1QD. (061 236 3311)

International Chamber of Commerce, Centre Point, New Oxford Street, London WC1. (01 240 5588)

The London Chamber of Commerce, runs residential beginners' courses in French, Arabic, German, Spanish and Portuguese (and Mandarin Chinese from 1982), which guarantee to teach you to speak and write 450 words of the new language in six days. It does not sound a lot, perhaps, but when used in multiple combinations 450 words provide an extremely useful basic preliminary vocabulary of expressions and phrases.

The courses have been designed by Professor Robert Boland specifically for the mature student, and make a complete departure from the school language-lab routine.

For more information contact Mrs K. Allerman, LCCI, 69 Cannon Street, London EC4A 5AB. (01 248 4444 ext. 337)

The North West Industrial Development Association (NORWIDA), Brazenose House, Brazenose Street, Manchester M2 5AZ. (061 834 6778)

The association maintains a file of companies in the North-west who are interested in entering business agreements with foreign firms. The file contains anonymous details of each company looking for an overseas partner for a joint venture. This information is circulated by NORWIDA among firms and commercial organisations in the USA and Western Europe. The aim is to promote joint ventures that will result in increased investment and employment in Northwest England.

Scanmark, Buckinghamshire College of Higher Education, High Wycombe, Bucks. HP11 2JZ. (0494 22141 ext. 35) Contact: S. E. M. Roberts, Chairman. Established in 1974, Scanmark is a team of postgraduate students in the final year of an export marketing course. Their first disciplines include accountancy, agriculture, business studies, chemistry, economics and psychology. They also have a combined fluency in French, Spanish, German, Russian, Italian and Portuguese.

Recognised by the British Overseas Trade Board and the London Chamber of Commerce, Scanmark has carried out over 100 research projects in twenty countries.

Its clients have included small businesses launching their first product, and larger companies moving into new markets. This really is a low-cost way of getting the fundamental facts on overseas markets.

Simplification of International Trade Procedures Board, SITPRO, Almark House, 26–28 King Street, London SW1Y 6QW. (01 214 3399, telex 919130 Sitrog) This is an independent body set up by the Department of Trade. Its objective is to simplify trade documents and procedures and so make international trade easier for British companies.

The board would like to know of any persistent problems in international trade documents and procedures, to help it decide on future priorities for action. *SITPRO News* is available on request. SITPRO also produces a range of publications, one of which, *Systematic Export Documentation*, is a useful guide through a complex process.

The board has an advisory consultancy service which will visit sites and help with specific problems.

Technical Help to Exporters, from the British Standards Institution, Marylands Avenue, Hemel Hempstead, Herts. HP2 4SQ. (0442 3111, telex 82424 BS1HH1G)

Marketing any product overseas means that you will have to comply with all the technical requirements of the country to which you want to sell. You will have to comply with the laws of the land (safety and environmental); national standards; certification practices; and customer needs. This service can supply detailed information on foreign regulations; identify, supply and assist in the interpretation of foreign standards and other technical requirements; provide translations; and help with obtaining foreign approval.

A technical enquiry service is operated specifically to deal with the day-to-day problems of exporters, many of which are answerable over the telephone. The charge depends on the amount of research and the time involved. Many queries are answered free of charge to members. Membership costs £120 plus VAT per annum, with an initial registration fee of £20.00 plus VAT. A publications list is issued twice a year, free of charge.

Publications

Barclays Bank International, Barclays House, 1 Wimborne Road, Poole, Dorset BH15 2BB.

Barclays Bank International has produced a new (1982) series of booklets entitled *Introduction to Exporting, Export Finance – Barclays and ECGD* and *Documentary Letters of Credit.* The publications deal in detail with such subjects as how to find markets abroad; where to obtain reliable, up-to-date information about those markets; the British Overseas Trade Board and export factoring; the Export Credits Guarantee Department; buyer/supplier credits; documentary letters of credit; and bills of exchange. Specimen documents and diagrammatic guides complement the text.

These booklets were produced not only for companies thinking of exporting for the first time but also for those already established in the overseas markets. They explain, in a clear, concise manner, the steps along the export road. Copies of the booklets are available to companies through any branch of Barclays or by writing to the Marketing Department (address above).

Croner's Reference Book for Exporters, from Croner House, 173 Kingston Road, New Malden, Surrey KT3 3SJ.

This is a loose-leaf and regularly up-dated service that keeps exporters up to date on all exporting procedures. It is available on a ten-day free approval offer. Price, £30.00.

Directory of Export Buyers, 1983, published by Trade Research Publications, 6 Beech Hill Court, Berkhamstead, Herts. HP4 2PR. (044 27 3951) Price £29.00.

The conventional wisdom of successful exporting recommends that you should travel abroad to contact buyers. However, increasingly firms abroad are establishing buying offices in this country – amongst other reasons, to look for new sources of supply. It is estimated that orders for about 20 per cent of British exports are negotiated and signed in the UK, and mainly by people listed in this directory. The entries are indexed by countries bought from, products bought and foreign firms bought for.

Handbook of International Trade, from Kluiver Publishing Ltd, 1 Harlequin Avenue, Great West Road, Brentford, Middx. TW8 9EW. (01 568 6441)

The handbook concentrates on facts about key markets and sources of further information in those markets. It can be sent on approval, price £25.00.

The Small Firms Service of the Department of Industry produces a free booklet *How to Start Exporting.* It is a very useful twenty-six pages, and includes a market check-list to help choose which market to tackle first. There is also a reading list and a section giving other useful organisations.

The service's counselling and information service can also provide practical advice on exporting for beginners.

Both the booklet and the counselling service can be reached on Freephone 2444.

■ SPECIALIST SERVICES FOR IMPORTING

British Importers Confederation, 69 Cannon Street, London EC4N 5AB. (01 248 4444). The confederation was founded in 1972, and represents some 3,500 importers. It is the only organisation protecting the interests of importers whatever the goods concerned.

Membership fees start at £90.00, plus VAT, and members include a significant number of one-man importers or smaller firms, as well as such companies as Shell and Unilever.

Because of its close relationship with the UK Government and the EEC Commissions, the confederation is usually aware of likely changes in import procedures long before they occur. This knowledge and other information form an important part of the service that the confederation can provide for small businesses.

Croner's Reference Book for Importers accurately spells out the regulations and procedures to import goods of any nature into the UK. It covers import controls, exchange controls, VAT, marking of goods, customs and excise, and transit and transhipment insurance. The book is in loose-leaf form, and the service includes a regular supply of amendments.

Price £21.10 from Croner Publications Ltd, Croner House, 173 Kingston Road, New Malden, Surrey KT3 3SS.

Directory of British Importers, 1983, published by the British Importers Confederation and Trade Research Publications of 6 Beech Hill Court, Berkhampstead, Herts. HP4 2PR. (04427 3951) Price £39.00. The directory gives a considerable amount of information about importing firms, and whether you simply want to find out more about your competitors or to find an alternative source of supply, this directory will give you the answers.

BOOKS AND PERIODICALS ON MARKETING

Advertising, What It Is and How to Do It, by Roderick White, published by McGraw-Hill, 34 Dover Street, London, w1x 3ra (01493 1451) 1980, in association with the Advertising Association. Price £7.50. Starting from 'Should you advertise and if so how much?' the book covers media, agencies, ad design and choice, economics and the law. It tells you what questions to ask, and whether and where the answers can be provided.

Be Your Own PR Man, a public relations guide for the small businessman, by Michael Bland, published by Kogan Page Ltd, 120 Pentonville Road, London n1, £10.95.

Campaign, Haymarket Publications Ltd, 38/42 Southampton Road, Teddington, Middx. tw11 0sw. A weekly, price 50p, mainly concentrating on advertising and agency matters.

Focus, The European Journal of Advertising and Marketing launched January 1982. More details from David Todd Associates Ltd, 117 Camberwell Road, London se5 0hb. (01 703 6207)

Introducing Marketing, by Christopher, McDonald and Wills (Pan, 18, Cavaye Place, London sw10 (01 373 6070) 1980), £1.75. Refreshing, practical and set firmly in the UK environment.

Managing for Results, Peter F. Drucker, Pan (address as above), 1964. Not strictly marketing, but a classic with many important pointers for the person running his own business.

Managing Sales Team, January 1982, by Neil Sweeney, publishers Kogan Page, 120 Pentonville Road, London n1, the price £10.95. It presents twelve management tasks and 100 management skills of use to small organisations with a sales force.

Marketing. A weekly subscription-only publication from Haymarket Publications Ltd, 12–14 Ansdell Street, London w8, price £35.00 per annum.

Marketing for Accountants and Managers by R. J. Williamson, published by Heinemann, 10 Upper Grosvenor Street, London w1x 9pa price £7.50. A very good book, despite the slightly off-putting title. It covers the ground efficiently and readably, giving very useful pointers towards additional reading at the end of each section.

Marketing for Business Growth, Theodore Levitt, published by McGraw-Hill, 34 Dover Street, London, w1x 3ra (01 493 1451) 1974. An extremely readable book on the strategic level.

Marketing, Management, Analysis, Planning and Control, by Philip Kotler, published by Prentice-Hall, 66 Wood Lane End, Hemel Hempstead, Herts, hp2 4rg 1980. The most lucid and comprehensive book on the subject. Generally accepted as the standard text, and though illustrated liberally with American examples, the theory is both readable and understandable.

The Marketing Research Process, by Margaret Crimp, published by Prentice-Hall, (address as above) 1981, price £6.50. Useful coverage of the whole area of market research in such a way that the layman will have no trouble in understanding it.

Marketing Today, by Gordon Oliver, published by Prentice-Hall, (address as above) 1980. An extremely good and comprehensive marketing book set in the UK environment. Price £8.95.

Marketing Week, 60 Kingly Street, London w1r 5lh. In most newsagents, price 50p, it provides a general review of main-current marketing topics.

Offensive Marketing, by J. H. Davidson, published by Pelican, 536 Kings Road, London sw10 1975.

Successful Retailing through Advertising, by Eric Lowe, to be published by McGraw-Hill, 34 Dover Street, London w1x 3ra (01 493 1451) in January 1983. It is a step-by-step approach to improving retailers' sales and profits, and advertising.

RAISING THE MONEY

PREPARING YOUR CASE

There does not seem to be a shortage of money to finance the launching of new business and the growth of existing ones. What are scarce are good, small company propositions. At least, that is the argument put forward by the financial institutions themselves. There is certainly an element of truth in this view, but the quality of the propositions owes much to the poor groundwork and planning of some budding entrepreneurs.

The starting point for any search for funds is to determine how much is needed, and then to demonstrate the security that the likely investor will then enjoy.

The accepted way in which proposals for funds are put forward is through a Business Plan. The Business Plan brings together the marketing and operational aspects of the business or proposed business, and expresses these actions in terms that a financial institution will understand. Not surprisingly, these institutions will expect the plan to contain financial statements both actual and projected.

The National Westminster Bank has prepared a useful 'presentation check list', which is reproduced below.

Check List

About you

☐	Very brief synopsis for your own banker, detailed for approach to others: age, education, experience.
☐	Personal means eg property, liabilities guarantees. Other business connections.
☐	For a type of business new to you, or start-up situation, outline experience, ability and factors leading up to your decision.

157

Your business

- [ ] Brief details of: when established, purpose then and now, how the business has evolved, main factors contributing to progress.

- [ ] Reputation, current structure and organisation. Internal accounting system

- [ ] Past 3 years audited accounts if available, and latest position.

- [ ] Up to date Profit and Loss figures, including details of withdrawals.

- [ ] Up to date liquid figures, ie debtors, creditors, stock, bank balance etc.

- [ ] Borrowing history and existing commitments, eg HP, leasing loans. Bankers.

- [ ] Description of major assets, and any changes.

Your key personnel

- [ ] Age, qualifications, experience, competence, of directorate/senior management. Directors' Bankers.

- [ ] Emergency situation, someone to run the business in your absence.

- [ ] List of principal shareholders/relationships.

Your purpose

- [ ] Explain fully your business plan, the use to which the money will be put, eg expansion, diversification, start-up.

- [ ] Describe the practical aspects involved and the how and when of implementation.

- [ ] Diagrams, sketches, photographs etc. are usually helpful, eg property purchase and conversion to your use.

- [ ] Consider: planning permission, legal restrictions, government policy.

- [ ] Contingency plans for setbacks: reliability of supplies/raw materials/alternative sources, other factors outside your control, eg weather.

☐ Relevance to existing operations, (if any) opportunity for shared overheads, disruption of current business.

☐ Personnel, are more staff required, availability of specialist skills/training. Management ability for expanded/different operation?

Your Market

☐ Estimated demand, short and long term. External verification of market forecasts, eg from trade associations, market research publications.

☐ Competition, who from, likely developments.

☐ Describe your competitive advantages, eg quality, uniqueness, pricing (justify) location-local/national.

☐ Marketing included in costings?

☐ If new, or technology based or highly specialised business – detail and perspective necessary.
NB A banker does not need to know how it works (though he may be interested), just that what it does, is reliable, and has good sales prospects.

Your profit

☐ Demonstrate how profits will be made, include detailed breakdown of costings, timing, projected sales, orders already held.

☐ Profit projections should attempt to cover the period of a loan, however sketchy.

☐ For capital investment – profit appraisal. Capital allowances eg new small workshop scheme.

☐ Everything included in costings? eg tax, stamp duty, legal fees, bank interest.

The amount

- [ ] State precisely the amounts and type of finance required and when it will be needed. Is type of finance correct? eg overdraft to finance working capital, term loan for capital expenditure.

- [ ] Is the amount requested sufficient? eg increased working capital requirements/margin for unforeseen circumstances.

- [ ] Detail the amount and form of your contribution to the total cost.

- [ ] Justify all figures – Cash flow forecast for next 12 months: show maximum range. All outgoings considered eg net VAT, holiday pay, bank interest and repayments, personal drawings.

Repayment

- [ ] Relate projected profitability and cash flow to expected repayments. Justify fully the term requested. Is it long enough?

- [ ] How quickly will the business generate cash? Is a repayment 'holiday' necessary and what turnover needs to be achieved to break-even?

- [ ] Consider the worst situation, feasibility of contingency plans, irretrievable losses.

- [ ] Interest rate – What is the effect of variation in base rate on plans?

Security

- [ ] What assets are/will be available as security?

- [ ] Are any assets already used for security elsewhere?

- [ ] Independent/realistic valuation of assets offered. Leasehold considerations, any unusual features/saleability. Support for guarantees.

- [ ] Agreement of other interested parties/realistic awareness of loss of asset.

- [ ] Insurance e.g. life, property, business.

If you can provide a satisfactory and comprehensive answer to most of these points, you will certainly find yourself at the head of most queues for funds.

Books that can help you with business plans are included at the end of this section.

A number of organisations can help you in putting together your case. In particular, the Enterprise Agencies, the small firms service or even an informal talk with your bank manager or other professional advisers will be helpful.

One very new organisation, New Ventures Ltd, that operates in conjunction with the City University Business School, has developed a business planning and launch package.

The first part of the package is an in-depth assessment of your business proposal. This lasts two weeks, and at the end you should have a good idea of your chances of success and a detailed plan of how to set about it. This can then form the basis of any later presentation to an outside source of finance or even a potential partner.

The second part of the launch package consists of a contract entitling clients to the full range of NVL service during the first twelve weeks of their business launch and certain services afterwards too.

The first NVL unit was launched in May 1982 at Old Loom House, Backchurch Lane, London E1 1LU (01 488 1067) and is managed by Jock Scholefield.

The service includes:

- a work space with desk, chairs and telephone, and use of conference room as needed;
- high-quality secretarial support with a competent telephonist and automatic telephone recording service;
- immediate access to office services, including copying, photo-lithographic printing, telex, computing and word processing;
- contracts with experts in various fields, such as marketing, finance, accountancy, taxation, insurance, property, law, etc;
- extensive files of up-dated information on premises, supplies and services.
- contacts with reputable sources of finance, including grant agencies of central and local government;
- a unit manager with extensive business experience;
- pyschological support in a small community of others with similar aspirations and problems.

The fee for the intensive two-week course is £700 plus VAT; two of the first participants were sponsored by a TOPs grant from the Manpower Services Commission.

The Venture Launch Contract (as the second part of the package is called) is provided for a basic fee of £1,800 plus VAT.

Neither of these fees is designed to make NVL any profit. They are set at a level to cover costs only. NVL do, however, hope to make a profit, but only if their clients are successful. With each client they negotiate a quarterly commission based on turn-over or profit before tax, before the beginning of each contract.

You should not overlook the New Enterprise Programmes run at Durham, London and Manchester business schools, or the Small Business Courses run at some twenty polytechnics and universities up and down the country. These courses, in the main supported by the MSC, can give you all the background you need to prepare a good financial case. (See Education section for more details.)

WHAT ARE THE DIFFERENT TYPES OF MONEY?

Small businesses need to borrow money for a variety of reasons: in order to start up, expand, re-locate, to start exporting or importing, to innovate or carry out research and development, or to meet the unexpected, such as the collapse of a major customer or supplier. The level of borrowing that you can secure will be related in some way to your abilities, the nature of your business and how much you have put into the business. Few lenders like to see themselves much more exposed to financial risk than the owner(s), who after all expect to make the most gain.

In the eye of most lenders, finance for the small business fits into two distinct areas: short-term, which does not necessarily mean that you only want the money for a short term, but rather the life of the asset you are buying is itself relatively short; and long-term, which is the converse of that. The table overleaf may help you get a clearer picture.

Now, of course, starting up or expanding a small business will call for a mix of short- and long-term finance. You may be able to get all this from one source; more likely, though, once you start to trade you will find that different sources are better organised to provide different types of money.

All methods of financing have important implications for your tax and financial position, and appropriate professional advice should always be taken before embarking on any financing exercise.

Term	Business need (e.g.)	Financing method
Short (up to 3 years)	For raw materials or finished goods; to finance debtors; equipment with a short life or other working capital needs; for dealing with seasonal peaks and troughs; to start exporting; or to expand overseas sales	Overdrafts Short-term loans Factoring Invoice discounting Bill finance Trade credit Export & import finance
Medium to Long (3 years plus)	Acquiring or improving premises, buying plant and machinery with a long life; buying an existing business, including a franchise; for technological innovations or developing a 'new' product or idea.	Mortgage Sale and leaseback Loan finance Long-term leasing Hire purchase Equity & venture finance Public-sector finance

Overdrafts Bank overdrafts are the most common type of short-term finance. They are simple to arrange; you just talk to your local bank manager. They are flexible with no minimum level. Sums of money can be drawn or repaid within the total amount agreed. They are relatively cheap, with interest paid only on the outstanding daily balance.

Of course, interest rates can fluctuate. So what seemed a small sum of money one year can prove crippling if interest rates jump suddenly. Normally you do not repay the 'capital'. You simply renew or alter the overdraft facility from time to time. However, overdrafts are theoretically repayable on demand, so you should not use short-term overdraft money to finance long-term needs, such as buying a lease or some plant and equipment. Overdrafts are more usually used to finance working capital needs, stocks, customers who have not paid up, bulk purchases of materials and the like.

Term Loans (Short, Medium and Long) These are rather more formal than a simple overdraft. They cover periods of 0–3, 3–10 and 10–20 years respectively. They are usually secured against an existing fixed asset or one to be acquired, or are guaranteed personally by the directors (proprietors). As such, this may involve you in a certain amount of expense with legal fees and arrangement or consultants' fees. So it may be a little more expensive than an overdraft, but unless you default on the interest charges you can be reasonably confident of having the use of the money throughout the whole term of the borrowing.

The interest rates on the loan can either be fixed for the term or variable with the prevailing interest rate. A fixed rate is to some extent a gamble, which may work in your favour, depending on how interest rates move over the term of the loan. So, if general interest rates rise you win, and if they fall you lose. However, a variable rate means that you do not take that risk. There is another benefit to a fixed rate of interest. It should make planning ahead a little easier with a fixed financial commitment, unlike a variable over-draft rate, in which a sudden rise can have disastrous consequences.

Government Loan Guarantees for Small Businesses were introduced in March 1981 for an initial period of three years. To be eligible for this loan, your proposition must have been looked at by an approved bank and considered viable, but should not be a proposition that the bank itself would normally approve. You can be a sole trader, partnership, co-operative or limited company wanting funds to start up or to expand. The bank simply passes your application on to the Department of Industry, using an approved format.

This is an elementary business plan, which asks for some details of the directors, the business, their cash needs and profit performance or projection of the business. There are no formal rules on size, number of employees or assets, but large businesses and their subsidiaries are definitely excluded from the scheme. The other main exclusions are businesses in the following fields: agriculture, horticulture, banking, commission agents, education, forestry (except tree-harvesting and saw-milling), house and estate agents, insurance, medical and veterinary, night-clubs and licensed clubs, pubs and property, and travel agencies.

The loans can be for up to £75,000 and repayable over 2 to 7 years. It may be possible to delay paying the capital element for up to two years from the start of the loan. However, monthly or quarterly repayments of interest will have to be made from the outset. The loan itself, however, is likely to be expensive. Once approved by the Department of Trade, the bank lends you the money at bank rate plus 4 or 5 per cent and the Government guarantees the bank 80 per cent of its money if you cannot pay up.

In return for this the government charge you a 2–3 per cent 'insurance' premium on the 80 per cent of the loan it has taken on risk. Borrowers would be expected to pledge all available business assets as a security for the loan, but they would not necessarily be excluded from the scheme if there are no available assets.

Also on the plus side, directors will not normally be asked to give personal guarantees on security, an undertaking they may have to make for other forms of borrowing.

There are now thirty banks operating the scheme, and by June 1982 some 4,500 loans worth £150 million had been granted. National Westminster led the field with 1,018 loans worth £33.5

million. The average loan is about £33,000.

Although there are no official figures to go on, a business failure rate of one for every thirteen loans granted was the picture emerging for the scheme's first year. The rule certainly seems to be to ask for as much as you need, plus a good margin of safety. Going back for a second bite too soon is definitely frowned upon. You do not have to take all the money at once. At the discretion of your bank manager, you can take the money in up to four lots. However each lot must be 25% or more.

Encouraging, too, is the evidence that these loans were fairly evenly split between 'start-ups' and growing young businesses.

One final point on term loans. Banks tend to lump overdraft facilities and loans together into a 'total' facility, so one is often only given at the expense of the other.

Mortgate Loans These operate in much the same way as an ordinary mortgage. The money borrowed is used to buy the freehold on the business premises. That then acts as the main security for the loan, with regular repayments made up of interest charges and principal, paid to the lender.

The main suppliers are the insurance companies and pension funds, who generally prefer to deal in sums above £50,000. Some of the smaller companies will lend as little as £5,000, particularly if the borrower is a policyholder. As well as the regular payments, a charge of about 2 per cent will be made to cover the survey, valuation and legal work in drawing up agreements.

Sale and Leaseback This involves selling the freehold of a property owned by a business to a financial institution, which agrees to grant you a lease on the premises.

The lender will want to be sure that you can afford the lease, so a profit track record will probably be needed, and all expenses involved in the negotiations are met by the borrower. The borrower then has the use of the value of the asset in immediate cash to plough into the business.

The tax aspects of sale and leaseback are complex and work more in the favour of some types of business than others, so professional advice is essential before entering into any arrangement.

As with other forms of finance, it is a competitive market and a few 'quotes' are worth getting.

Trade Credit Once you have established creditworthiness, it may be possible to take advantage of the trade credit extended by suppliers. This usually takes the form of allowing you anything from seven days to three months from receiving the goods, before having to pay for them.

You will have to weigh carefully the benefit of taking this credit against the cost of losing any cash discounts offered. For example, if you are offered a 2½ per cent discount for a cash settlement, then this is a saving of £25 for every £1,000 of purchases. If the alternative is to take six weeks' credit, then the saving is the cost of borrowing that sum from, say, your bank on overdraft. So if your bank interest is 16 per cent per annum, that is equivalent to 0.31 per cent per week. Six weeks would save you 1.85 per cent. On £1,000 of purchase you would only save £18.50 of bank interest. This means that the cash discount is more attractive. However, you may not have the cash or overdraft facility, so your choice is restricted.

Bill Financing This is rather like a post-dated cheque which can be sold to a third party for cash, but at a discount. Once you have dispatched the goods concerned to your customer, you can draw a trade bill to be accepted by him on a certain date. This, in effect, is a commitment by him to settle his account on that date, and he is not expected to pay until then. You can sell this bill to a bank or a discount house and receive immediate cash. Of course, you have to pay for this service. Payment takes the form of a discount on the face value of the bill, usually directly related to the creditworthiness of your customer. It has several advantages as a source of short-term finance.

Firstly, it is usually competitive with bank overdrafts. Secondly, you can accurately calculate the cost of financing a transaction, because the discount rate is fixed and not subject to interest rate fluctuations. This is particularly important if the time between dispatch of the goods and payment by the customer is likely to be several months. Thirdly, by using bill finance, you can free up overdraft facilities for other purposes. For example, you can get on with making up more products for other customers – something you may not have been able to do if you were waiting for the last customer to pay up.

Factoring This is an arrangement which allows you to receive up to 80 per cent of the cash due from your customers more quickly than they would normally pay. The factoring company buys your trade debts and provides a debtor accounting and administration service. In other words, it takes over the day-to-day work of invoicing and sending out reminders and statements. This can be a particularly helpful service to a small, expanding business. It can allow the management to concentrate on growing the business, with the factoring company providing expert guidance on credit control, 100 per cent protection against bad debts, and improved cash flow.

You will, of course, have to pay for factoring services. Having the cash before your customers pay will cost you a little more than normal overdraft rates. The factoring service will cost between ½ and 3½ per cent of turn-over, depending on volume of work, the number of debtors, average invoice amount and other related factors. You can get up to 80 per cent of the value of your invoice in advance, with the remainder paid when your customer settles up, less the various charges just mentioned.

If you sell direct to the public, sell complex and expensive capital equipment or expect progress payments on a long-term project, then factoring is not for you.

If you are expanding more rapidly than other sources of finance will allow, then this may be a useful service. All other things being equal, it should be possible to find a factor if your turn-over exceeds £25,000 per annum, though the larger firm will look for around £100,000 as the economic cut-off point.

Invoice Discounting This is a variation of factoring open to businesses with a net worth of £30,000. Unlike factoring, where all your debtors are sold to the factor, in this service only selected invoices are offered. This can be particularly useful if you have a few relatively large orders to reputable, 'blue-chip'-type customers in your general order book.

Up to 75 per cent of the value of the invoices can be advanced, but you remain responsible for collecting the money from your customers. This you forward to the discounting company, who in turn sends you the balance less a charge on the assigned invoices. This charge will be made up of two elements. You will pay interest on the cash advanced for the period between the date of the advance and your refunding the discount company. You will also have to pay a factoring charge of between ¼ and ¾ per cent.

The twist is that, if your customer does not pay up, you have to repay the discount house their advance. Unlike normal factoring, however, your customer will never know that you discounted his invoice.

Export Finance This is a specialist subject in itself. The range of possibilities open to the exporter is described in considerable detail in the Bank of England booklet referred to at the end of this section. The central feature of most forms of export financing is ECGD (Export Credits Guarantee Department) credit insurance. This is a government-backed credit insurance policy that gives cover against the failure of your foreign customers either to take up the goods you have dispatched or to pay for them. The cover includes loss caused by war and trade sanctions. Although the government themselves do not provide export finance, ECGD credit insurance will put you in a highly favourable position with, for example, your bank. They in turn would be able to provide finance with a greater degree of security than they could normally expect.

Some banks, notably the Midland, operate a *Smaller Exporters' Scheme* providing ECGD-backed post-shipment finance for small exporters who may find it uneconomic to take out an ECGD policy on their own. In certain cases, an *Export house* may be willing to manage your overseas business for you, acting as your agent in finding customers, or even as a merchant actually buying the goods from you for re-sale in certain overseas markets.

Import Finance This includes such elements as a produce or merchandise advance. In this case the imported goods themselves are offered as security for a loan. There are some obvious limitations on the type of goods that could be accepted. Fruit and vegetables, and other perishable goods or commodities in volatile markets are excluded. However, under the right circumstances up to 80 per cent of the value of sold goods and 50 per cent of unsold goods can be realised in cash quite quickly.

Leasing This is a way of getting the use of vehicles, plant and equipment without paying the full cost at once. *Operating leases* are taken out where you will use the equipment for less than its full economic life – for example, a car, photocopier or vending machine. The lessor takes the risk of the equipment becoming obsolete, and assumes responsibility for repairs, maintenance and insurance. As you, the lessee, are paying for this service, it is more expensive than a *Finance lease*, where you lease the equipment for most of its economic life and maintain and insure it yourself.

Leases can normally be extended, often for fairly nominal sums, in the later years.

The obvious attractions of leasing are that no deposit is needed, leaving your working capital for more profitable use elsewhere. Also, the cost of leasing is known from the start, making forward planning more simple. There may even be some tax advantages over other forms of finance.

Hire Purchase This differs from leasing in that you have the option at the start to become the owner of the equipment after a series of payments have been made. The interest is usually fixed and often more expensive than a bank loan. However, manufacturers (notably car makers) often subsidise this interest, so it pays to shop around both for sources of HP finance and manufacturers of equipment.

Equity Finance This is only relevant if your business is or is shortly to become a Limited Company, and it refers to the sale of ordinary shares to investors. Unlike other forms of 'borrowing', where interest has to be paid whether or not the business makes a profit, shares usually only attract a dividend when the business is profitable. This makes it extremely important to get as large an equity base as possible at the outset. Although it does mean giving up some control, you may gain some valuable business expertise, and your reputation can be enhanced if the investors are respected themselves.

Apart from equity finance you provide yourself, you can attract outside investment from outside sources.

Individuals: Unlike publicly quoted companies, which have a stock-exchange facility, you will have to find investors yourself. Recent tax changes – in particular, those incorporated in the Government's 'Business Start-up Scheme' (described below) – have made it attractive for high taxpayers to invest in new business. Several organisations have been established to acquire such funds and find suitable investments.

Institutions such as ICFC (see page 181), subsidiaries of the clearing banks and venture capital organisations, provide equity capital, usually for companies with exceptionally high growth potential. In general equity financing from people other than those known well by you is the most difficult money to raise.

The Business Start-up Scheme This was introduced under the 1981 Finance Act, making it attractive for most UK income taxpayers to invest in new business. It is intended to run until April 1984.

The term 'New Business' refers to businesses less than five years old. The main businesses excluded from this scheme are, banking, hiring or leasing; dealing in shares or in land; providing legal or accounting services; and financial investments in (for example) silver, gold, paintings or wine.

The investors at whom the scheme is aimed are UK taxpayers who are *not connected* with the business they are going to invest in. They cannot be paid directors or employees of the business, nor can they own more than 30 per cent of the business. They could, however, be unpaid directors or take fees for professional services. The investor gets tax relief on up to £10,000 invested in any one year. This is expected to increase to £20,000 for 1983 and 1984. There are, however, a number of other restrictions. For example, the minimum investment is normally £500, and it must be kept in the business for five years if the tax relief is to be retained.

Your solicitor, accountant or bank manager may be able to put you in touch with interested individuals.

Alternatively, a number of financial institutions are offering 'portfolio' facilities to investors. This means that investors put their funds into an approved organisation which seeks out potential investment opportunities on their behalf. This spreads their risk, and gives them the benefit of 'professional' management. The effect of this scheme is that a top-rate taxpayer could be putting as little as £2,500 of his own money into a business in return for a £10,000 share, the balance being effectively paid by the Inland Revenue.

Public-sector sources These include central and local government, certain agencies and EEC funds. There are over 111 different types of funds available, with differing types of eligibility. In the main, they are concentrated on providing regional and local assistance, encouragement for specific industries, ranging from agriculture to encouraging tourism in Wales; and assistance for specific purposes such as research and development, employment or exporting. The booklet *Financial Incentives and Assistance for Industry*, referred to at the end of this section, covers this subject comprehensively.

Venture Capital This is start-up capital usually associated with businesses involved in technological and technical innovation. The sums involved are usually up to £100,000 over periods of five years or more. With this capital usually comes management expertise, often in the form of a board member from the financial institution. So you are going to have to be able to work with him, and probably give a personal guarantee for the sums involved.

Perhaps the greatest benefit coming from the provider of venture capital is their expertise at keeping your financial structure in line with your changing needs.

Development Capital These are funds to help established firms grow and diversify. Like venture capital, the period involved is five years or so, and the investing institution expects to be able to sell its stake either to the directors or possibly through an eventual Stock Exchange quotation. Generally you will need to have a pre-tax profit of £30,000 per annum and be looking for more than £50,000 additional finance. The investor will want to put a director on your board – as much to help you and the company as to keep an eye on its investment.

Management Buy-outs This is not a type of money. It is, however, an increasingly popular activity that involves the existing managers of a business buying out the business from its owners. As both the business and the managers will have a 'track record', it may be easier to find equity finance for such ventures; an increasing number of lending organisations have moved into this field.

WHERE YOU CAN GET THE MONEY

For most of us, borrowing money usually means either a visit or a letter to our local bank manager. Although he is by no means the only source of finance for a new or small business, the local bank manager is a good starting point.

Clearing Banks This is the general name given to the high street bankers. We immediately think of the big four banks – Barclays, Lloyds, Midland and the National Westminster – when we think of 'clearers'. However, there are another dozen or so that fit within the general meaning of 'clearing and domestic deposit bank'.

The banks offer a wide range of services in their own right. Through wholly- or partially-owned subsidiaries they cover virtually every aspect of the financial market. These services include over-drafts, term loans, trade bill finance, factoring, leasing, export and import finance, the Government Loan Guarantee Scheme, and equity financing.

In addition to providing a source of funds, the clearing banks have considerable expertise in the areas of tax, insurance and financial advice generally. Very little of this expertise will rest in your local branch office. The bank's regional and main head offices are where these centralised services are provided.

As you probably already have a bank account, this may be your starting point in looking for money for business. Do not forget, however, that the banks are in competition with one another and with other lenders. So shop around if you do not get what you want first time.

The banks are becoming quite adventurous in their competition for new and small business accounts. Barclays Bank Business Start Loan is one such adventurous scheme. It is aimed exclusively at providing some, though not all, of set-up costs of a new business. The amount needed should be between £5,000 and £100,000. The period of the loan is three to five years, and the capital is to be repaid in full at the end of the fifth year. Not only do borrowers get the advantage of deferring capital repayments for up to five years, but interest charges are taken in the form of royalty on sales. In this way you pay only when you can best afford to, and so ease early cash-flow problems.

Some of the banks have a small firms specialist, one of whose tasks is to help new, small-business clients get the best out of their banking services. To get an opinion from one of these specialists would be a good way of finding the possibilities of getting finance and how best to go about it.

Clearing and Other Domestic Deposit Banks	Small Firms Adviser (if any)
Allied Irish Banks Ltd, 64/66 Coleman Street, London EC2R 5AL. (01 588 0691)	Area General Manager, Britain, Declan M. Wyley or Fergus G. Cotter
Bank of Ireland, Advances Dept. 36 Moorgate, London EC2R 6DP. (01 628 8811/9)	General Manager, Britain
Branch Administration East, Bank of Scotland, The Mound, Edinburgh EH1 1YZ. (031 229 2555)	General Manager, Britain
Barclays Bank PLC, Corporate Business Department, Bucklersbury House, 3 Queen Victoria Street, London EC4P 4AT. (01 626 1567)	Manager, Small Business Unit, P. E. J. Jackson
Clydesdale Bank Ltd, Business Development Department *or* Export Finance Department, 30 St Vincent Place, Glasgow G1 2HL. (041 248 7070)	

171

Co-operative Bank Ltd, 1 Balloon Street, Manchester M60 4EP. (061 832 3456)

Corporate Business Manager, Peter Walker ext 282 or R. A. Street ext 280

Coutts & Co (*a member of the National Westminster Bank Group*), 440 Strand, London WC2R 0QS. (01 379 6262)

David Boyce

Lloyds Bank PLC, Head Office, PO Box 215, 71 Lombard Street, London EC3P 3BS. (01 626 1500)

John Kirkwood and Mario Areste

Midland Bank PLC, Independent Business Banking Unit, Corporate Finance Division, 27/32 Poultry, London EC2P 2BX. (01 606 9911)

Norman Robson

Midland Bank PLC, International Division, Corporate Finance Department *or* Export Finance Department, 60 Gracechurch Street, London EC3P 3BN. (01 606 9944)

National Westminster Bank PLC, Corporate Finance Services Section, Domestic Banking Division, 41 Lothbury, London EC2P 2BP. (01 606 6060)

Noel Deening and Russ Wilson

Northern Bank Ltd (*a member of the Midland Bank Group*), Corporate Finance Department, PO Box 183, Donegall Square West, Belfast BT1 6JS. (0232 45277)

The Royal Bank of Scotland Ltd, PO Box 183, 42 St Andrew Square, Edinburgh EH2 2YE. (031 556 855)

Business Development Manager

Ulster Bank Ltd (*a member of National Westminster Bank Group*), Planning and marketing division 47 Donegall Place, Belfast BT1 5AU. (0232 220222)

Williams & Glyn's Bank Ltd (*a member of the Royal Bank of Scotland Group*), Marketing Department, New London Bridge House, 25 London Bridge Street, London SE1 9SX. (01 407 3121)

Yorkshire Bank Ltd, 20 Merrion Way, Leeds LS2 8NZ. (0532 441244)

Controller (Marketing)

Central Trustee Savings Bank Ltd, Corporate Lending Department, PO Box 99, St Mary's Court, 100 Lower Thames Street, London EC3R 6AQ. (01 623 5266)

Discount Houses These are the specialist institutions that provide bill financing. There are a dozen members of the London Discount Market Association, whose Honorary Secretary is Mr P. L. Shepherd, 39 Cornhill, London EC3U 3NU. (01 623 1020). Bill financing is a bit of a long shot as a source of finance for a small business. Although bills may be as little as a few thousand pounds, the average is nearer £25,000. Nevertheless, given a good proposition, discount houses will be happy to listen. Gerald Quin, Cope & Co Ltd and Page & Gwyther Ltd may be among the most responsive at the small end of the bill market.

London Discount Market Association Members

Alexanders Discount PLC, 1 St Swithin's Lane, London EC4N 8DN. (01 626 5467)

Cater Allen Ltd, 1 King William Street, London EC4N 7AU. (01 623 2070)

Clive Discount Co Ltd, 1 Royal Exchange Avenue, London EC3V 3LU. (01 283 1101)

Gerrard & National PLC, 32 Lombard Street, London EC3V 9BE. (01 623 9981)

Gillett Brothers Discount Co PLC, 65 Cornhill, London EC3V 3PP. (01 283 3022)

Jessel, Tonybee PLC, 30 Cornhill, London EC3V 3LH. (01 623 2111)

King & Shaxson PLC, 52 Cornhill, London EC3V 3PD. (01 623 5433)

Page & Gwyther Ltd, 1 Founders Court, Lothbury, London EC2R 7BD. (01 606 5681)

Gerald Quin, Cope & Co Ltd, 19/21 Moorgate, London EC2R 6BX. (01 628 2771)

Seccombe Marshall & Campion PLC, 7 Birchin Lane, London EC3V 9DE. (01 283 5031)

Smith St Aubyn & Co Ltd, White Lion Court, Cornhill, London EC3V 3PN. (01 283 7261)

The Union Discount Co. of London, PLC, 39 Cornhill, London EC3V 3NU. (01 623 1020)
and 24a Melville Street, Edinburgh EH3 7MS. (031 226 3535)

Export Houses There are some 800 export houses operating in the UK, offering almost every service possible to exporters and foreign importers. Some 230 of them belong to the British Export Houses Association, and they are actively interested in working with small firms.

Three types of company will find an export house particularly useful: firstly, those that are considering exporting for the first time; secondly, those that want to expand outside their existing overseas markets; and thirdly, those that have to extend credit to their customers to a greater extent than they are willing or able to do (this may be to meet competition or currency problems).

Export houses are specialists in financing and servicing exports and are divided into four main types.

Export agents and managers sell a manufacturer's goods in selected countries where they have expert knowledge. They work very closely with their clients, and can in effect become the manufacturer's own export department. This can save a small company money, and provide a greater level of expertise than could realistically be afforded. Payment for these services is usually by commission, but sometimes a retainer or even a profit-sharing scheme can be used.

Confirming houses, buying or independent houses and stores buyers work as follows. Confirming houses represent foreign buyers in the UK and can confirm, as a principal, an order placed by that buyer with a British supplier. Buying or independent houses buy, pay for and ship goods for their overseas principals. A stores buyer is a particular type of buying house dealing only with departmental stores. Being linked to such houses costs you nothing but can open up many new overseas markets for your products.

Merchants, as the word implies, both buy and sell as a principal. They specialise in certain products and markets. One of the largest sells in 120 different countries. Others operate in a much narrower sphere. Dealing with a merchant is little different from selling in the UK, and, even better, there is no credit risk.

Finance houses can provide you with non-resource finance and allow your foreign buyer time to pay. This gives the exporter absolute security and makes the deal attractive to an overseas buyer. Normally only the foreign buyer pays a commission for the service.

The British Export Houses Association, 69 Cannon Street, London EC4N 5AB. (01 248 4444) is the best starting point for contacting an export house. The association secretary is Mr H. W. Bailey. They produce a *Directory of British Export Houses*, which tells you all about each house and its particular expertise. Alternatively, you can include full details of your requirements in the association's monthly *Export Enquiry* circular. This will cost £25.00 plus VAT for the first insertion, and £10.00 plus VAT for each repeat. The circular goes to all members and is considered to be a very effective way of communicating quickly in a rapidly changing environment.

Some Leading Export Houses

Adam & Harvey Ltd, 15/16 Bonhill Street, London EC2P 2EA. (01 628 7711)

Balfour Williamson & Co Ltd, Roman House, Wood Street, London EC2Y 5BP. (01 638 6191)

Booker Merchants International Ltd, 63–69 New Oxford Street, W1 London WC2 6DN. (01 836 4994)

British Markitex Ltd, PO Box 52, Deneway House, Potters Bar, Herts. EN5 1AH. (0707 57281)

Coutinho Caro & Co Ltd, Walker House, 87 Queen Victoria Street, London EC4V 4AL. (01 236 1505)

Dalgety Ltd, Dalgety Export Service Division, Corn Exchange Building, 52/57 Mark Lane, London EC3R 7SR. (01 488 3100)

Dominion Shippers Ltd, 17 Stamford Street, London SE1 9NG. (01 633 0066)

Gellatly Hankey & Co Ltd, International House, Mitre Spire, London EC3A 5ED. (01 621 0388)

Gillespie Brothers & Co Ltd, Ling House, Dominion Street, London EC2M 2RT. (01 606 6431)

Inchcape Exports Ltd, Dugard House, Peartree Road, Stanway, Colchester, Essex CO3 5UL. (0206 44166)

W. H. Jones & Co (London) Ltd, Tower House, 17 Oakleigh Park North, London N20 9AP. (01 445 5006)

Keep Brothers Ltd, The Rotunda, New Street, Birmingham B2 4NQ. (021 643 6851)

Lewis & Peat (Merchanting) Ltd, 32 St Mary at Hill, Eastcheap,, EC3P 3HA (01 623 9333)

Matheson & Co Ltd, 142 Minories, London EC3N 1QL. (01 480 6633)

Rabone Petersen & Co Ltd, PO Box 326, 42 Hagley Road, Birmingham B16 8PU. (021 454 5843)

Saltraco Ltd, Maridian House, 42 Upper Berkeley Street, London W1H 7PL. (01 723 1222)

Scholefield Goodman & Sons Ltd, 135 Edmund Street, Birmingham B3 2HS. (021 236 7471)

UAC International Ltd, UAC House, Blackfriars Road, London SE1 9UG. (01 928 2070)

United City Merchants Ltd, UCM House, 3/5 Swallow Place, London W1A 1BB. (01 629 8424)

Some Finance Houses

British Overseas Engineering & Credit Co Ltd, Walker House, 87 Queen Victoria Street, London EC4V 1AP. (01 236 6544)

Charterhouse Japhet Export Finance PLC, 1 Paternoster Row, St Paul's, London EC4M 7DH. (01 248 3999)

Grindlay Brandts Export Finance PLC, 23 Fenchurch Street, London EC3P 3ED. (01 626 0545)

Manufacturers Hanover Export Finance Ltd, 7 Princes Street, London EC2P 2EN. (01 606 8461)

Tennant Guaranty Ltd, 1 Seething Lane, London EC3N 4BP. (01 488 1309)

Tozer Kemsley & Millbourn (Holdings) Ltd, 28 Great Tower Street, London EC3R 5DE. (01 283 3122)

UDT International Finance Ltd, 51 Eastcheap, London EC3P 3BU. (01 623 3020)

Factoring Companies These financial institutions provide a full sales accounting service, often including credit management and insurance against bad debts. The Association of British Factors is at Moor House, London Wall, London EC2, Secretary, Mr Michael Burke.

ABF members charge between $3/4$ and $2\frac{1}{2}$ per cent of gross turnover for the sales ledger package and around bank overdraft rate for finance charges. They will advance about 80 per cent of invoice price almost immediately the invoice is raised. They generally only consider customers with £100,000 per annum turn-over, but may consider good cases from £50,000.

Members of the Association of British Factors

Alex. Lawrie Factors Ltd, Beaumont House, Beaumont Road, Banbury, Oxon. OX16 7RN. (0295 4491) (*Lloyds & Scottish Group*)
Branches: Bristol, Coventry, Edinburgh, London, Manchester, Newcastle and Stockport.

Arbuthnot Factors Ltd, Arbuthnot House, Breeds Place, Hastings, Sussex TN34 3DG. (0424 430824) (*Arbuthnot Lathams & Yorkshire Bank*)

Barclays Factoring Ltd, PO Box 9, Paddington House, Basingstoke RG21 1BE. (0256 56161) (*Barclays Bank Group*)

Credit Factoring International Ltd, Smith House, PO Box 50, Elmwood Avenue, Feltham, Middx. TW13 7QD. (01 890 1390) (*National Westminster Bank Group*)

Griffin Factors, Forward Trust Group Ltd, Griffin House, 21 Farncombe Road, Worthing, Sussex BN11 2BW. (0903 205181) (*Midland Bank Group*)

H and H Factors Ltd, Randolph House, 46–48 Wellesley Road, Croydon, Surrey CR9 3PS. (01 681 2641) (*Walter E. Heller Overseas Corporation & Hambro Bank*)

Independent Factors Ltd, International Factors Ltd, Sovereign House, 98–99 Queen's Road, Brighton BN1 3WZ. (0273 21211) (*Lloyds & Scottish Group*)

Anglo Factoring Services Ltd, 44 Old Steine, Brighton, Sussex BN1 1NH. (0273 722532) (*J. Rothschild & Co.*)

Invoice Factors

The Association of Invoice Factors, 109/113 Royal Avenue, Belfast BT1 1FF. (0232 24522). Mr A. M. Selig.

This may be a better bet for a small business. Their members' average client has a turn-over of £100,000 per annum, and they would be prepared to look at propositions from £1,000 per month gross sales value. They advance 70 to 80 per cent of the value of the invoice, and charge between ½ and 3½ per cent for maintaining the sales ledger. Between advancing you the money and getting it in from your client, their financing rate charges are similar to overdraft rates.

Members of the Association of Invoice Factors

Anpal Finance Ltd, PO Box 37 Kimberly House, Vaughn Way, Leicester LE1 9AX. (0533 56066)

Century Factors Ltd, Vincent Chambers, 60 Princes Street, Yeovil, Somerset BA20 1HL. (0935 6051)

Gaelic Invoice Factors Ltd, 117 Douglas Street, Glasgow G2 4JX. (041 248 4901)

Larostra Ltd, 69 King William Street, London EC4P 4DA. (01 623 8462)

London Wall Factors Ltd, 15 South Moulton Street, London W1Y 1DE. (01 629 9891 and 01 573 3783)

Ulster Factors Ltd, Northern Bank House, 109–113 Royal Avenue, Belfast BT1 1FF. (0232 24522)

Alternatively, arrangements can be made through a factoring broker, who will charge the factor rather than the client.

Expansion Finance & Investments Co, 3 Tudor House, Heath Road, Weybridge, Surrey KT13 8TZ. (0932 47682), J. L. A. Ormisten.

Leasing Companies These may be a little more adventurous in dealing with new and small businesses than other sources of finance. In the last resort, they do own the assets they are financing. The Equipment Leasing Association, with some sixty members, is the main organisation in this field. It is located at 18 Upper Grosvenor Street, London W1X 6PD. (01 491 2783)

Most leasing companies are subsidiaries of much larger financial institutions, including the clearing banks. Some of them operate in specialist markets such as aircraft or agriculture, as their names imply. Many would not look at anything under £1 million. A phone call to the association will put you in touch with a selection of appropriate companies. Four companies that have a spread of business between a few hundred pounds and £50,000 are Anglo Leasing Ltd, FC Finance Ltd, Hamilton Leasing Ltd, and Schroder Leasing Ltd.

Airlease International Management Ltd, 24–28 St Mary Axe, London EC3A 8DE. (01 626 9393)
Allied Irish Finance Co Ltd, 10–12 Neeld Parade, Wembley Hill Road, Wembley HA9 6QU. (01 903 1383)
American Express Equipment Finance (UK) Ltd, 120 Moorgate, London EC2P 2JY. (01 588 6480)
Anglo Leasing International Ltd, 37 Queen Street, London EC4R 1BY. (01 236 5281)
Bank America Finance Ltd, Eldon Lodge, 196–200 King's Road, Reading, Berks. RG1 4NJ. (0734 55891)
Barclays Mercantile Industrial Finance Ltd, Elizabethan House, Great Queen Street, London WC2B 5DX. (01 242 1234) (*A member of the Barclays Bank Group*)
Baring Brothers Co Ltd, 8 Bishopsgate, London EC2N 4AE. (01 283 8833)
Robert Benson Lonsdale & Co Ltd, 20 Fenchurch Street, London EC3P 3DB. (01 623 8000)
Bowmaker Leasing Ltd, Bowmaker House, 17 Christchurch Road, Bournemouth BH1 3LG. (0202 22077)
British Credit Trust Ltd, 26 High Street, Slough SL1 1ED. (0753 73211)
British Industrial Corporation (Leasing) Ltd, PO Box 243, 30 Gresham Street, London EC2P 2EB. (01 600 4555)
Capital Leasing Ltd, 4 Melville Street, Edinburgh EH3 7NZ (031 226 4071) (*A member of the Bank of Scotland Group*)
Carolina Leasing Ltd, 14 Austin Friars, London EC2N 2EH. (01 588 9133)
Chartered Trust PLC, 24–26 Newport Road, Cardiff CF2 1SR. (0222 484484)
Chase Manhattan Ltd, PO Box 16, Woolgate House, Coleman Street, London EC2P 2HD. (01 638 6999)
Citicorp International Bank Ltd, 336 Strand, London WC20 1HB. (01 836 1230)
City Leasing Ltd, 23 Great Winchester Street, London EC2P 2AX. (01 588 4545)

Commercial Credit Leasing Ltd, 125 High Street, Croydon, Surrey CR9 1PU. (01 686 3466)

CTSB Leasing Ltd, PO Box 99, St Mary's Court, 100 Lower Thames Street, London EC3R 6AQ. (01 623 5266) (*A member of the Trustee Savings Bank Group*)

Eastlease Ltd, 8 Surrey Street, Norwich, Norfolk NR1 3ST. (0603 22200 ext. 2555)

ELCO Leasing Ltd, 107 Station Street, Burton–on–Trent, Staffordshire, (0283 45320)

European Banking Co Ltd, 150 Leadenhall Street, London EC3V 4PP. (01 638 3654)

First Cooperative Finance Ltd, 1 Balloon Street, Manchester, M60 4EP (061 832 3300)

Forward Trust Group Ltd, Broad Street House, 55 Old Broad Street, London EC2M 1RX. (01 920 0141) (*A member of the Midland Bank Group*)

Gray Dawes Leasing Ltd, 22 Bevis Marks, London EC3A 7DY. (01 283 8765)

Grindlays Bank Group, Leasing Department, 13 St James Square, London, SW1Y 4LF (930 5395)

Guinness Mahon Leasing PLC, PO Box 442, 32 St Mary At Hill, London EC3P 3HA. (01 623 9333)

Hambros Bank PLC, Equipment Leasing Department, 41 Bishopsgate, London EC2P 2AA. (01 588 2851)

Hamilton Leasing Ltd, Hamilton House, 80 Stokes Croft, Bristol BS1 3QW. (0272 48080)

Hill Samuel Leasing Co Ltd, 100 Wood Street, London EC2P 8AJ. (01 628 8011)

ICFC Leasing Ltd, 91 Waterloo Road, London SE1 8XP. (01 928 7822)

Lloyds Leasing Ltd, 57 Southwark Street, London SE1 1SH. (01 403 1600) (*A member of the Lloyds Bank Group*)

Lloyds & Scottish (Leasing) Ltd, Finance House, Orchard Brae, Edinburgh EH4 1PF. (031 332 2451)

Lombard & Ulster Leasing Ltd, Canada House, 22 North Street, Belfast BT1 1JX. (0232 29261) (*A member of the National Westminster Bank Group*)

Lombard North Central PLC, Lombard House, Curzon Street, Park Lane London W1A 1EU. (01 409 3434) (*A member of the National Westminster Bank Group*)

Lynn Regis Finance Ltd, 10 Tuesday Market Place, King's Lynn, Norfolk PE30 1JL. (0553 3465)

Maidenhead Finance Ltd, Carrier House, Warwick Row, London SW1E 5ER. (01 828 5656)

Nordic Leasing Ltd, Nordic Bank House, 20 St Dunstans Hill, London EC3R 8HY. (01 621 1111)

North West Securities Ltd, North West House, City Road, Chester CH1 3AN. (0244 315351) (*A member of the Bank of Scotland Group*)

Orient Leasing Co Ltd, London Representative Office, 14 Curzon Street, London W1Y 7FH. (01 499 7121/2)

Orion Leasing Ltd, 1 London Wall, London EC2Y 5JX. (01 600 6222)

Premier Computers Ltd, 3 Union Court, Richmond, Surrey TW9 1AA. (01 940 1134)

Rea Brothers Leasing PLC, King's House, 36–37 King Street, London EC2V 8DR. (01 606 4033)

Royal Bank Leasing Ltd, PO Box 31, 42 St Andrew Square, Edinburgh EH2 2YE. (031 556 8555) (*A member of the Royal Bank of Scotland Group*)

St Michael Finance Ltd, 47/67 Michael House, Baker Street, London W1A 1DN. (01 935 4422)

Scandinavian Leasing Ltd, Scandinavian House, 2–6 Cannon Street, London EC4M 6XX. (01 236 6090), ext 541.

Schroder Leasing Ltd, PO Box 99, Harrow, Middx. HA1 2HP. (01 863 7711)

Shawlands Securities Ltd, 8 Christchurch Road, Bournemouth BH1 3NQ. (0202 295544)

Standard Chartered Merchant Bank Ltd, 33–36 Gracechurch Street, London EC3V 0AX. (01 623 8711)

Tiger Leasing (UK) Ltd, 173 Sloane Street, London SW1X 9QG. (01 235 9285)

United Dominions Leasing Ltd, 51 Eastcheap, London EC3P 3BU. (01 623 3020) (*A member of the Trustee Savings Bank Group*)

United Leasing Ltd, 14 Welbeck Street, London W1M 7PF. (01 935 7104)

Williams & Glyn's Leasing Co Ltd, 29 Birchin Lane, London EC3P 3DP. (01 623 4356) (*A member of the Royal Bank of Scotland Group*)

Yorkshire Bank Leasing PLC, 2 Infirmary Street, Leeds LS1 2UL. (0532 442511)

Finance Houses These provide instalment credit for short-term credit facilities such as hire purchase. Their association is at 18 Upper Grosvenor Street, London W1X 9PB. (01 491 2783)

Finance Houses Association Members, Hire Purchase

Allied Irish Finance Co Ltd, Wembley Hill House, 10/12 Neeld Parade, Wembley Hill Road, Wembley HA9 6QU. (01 903 1383)

Associates Capital Corporation Ltd, Associates House, PO Box 200, Windsor, Berks. SL4 1SW. (Windsor 57100)

AVCO Financial Services Ltd, 66–68 St Marys Butts, Reading, Berks. RG1 2PE. (0734 584241)

Bank America Finance Ltd, Eldon Lodge, 196–200 Kings Road, Reading, Berks. RG1 4NJ. (0734 55891)

Beneficial Trust Ltd, Prudential House, Wellesley Road, Croydon, Surrey CR0 9XY. (01 681 1133)

Boston Trust & Savings Ltd, Boston House, Lower Dagnall Street, St Albans, Herts. AL3 4PG. (0727 32241)

Bowmaker Ltd, Bowmaker House, Christchurch Road, Bournemouth BH1 3LG. (0202 22077)

British Credit Trust Ltd, 26 High Street, Slough SL1 1ED. (0753 73211)

Cattle's Holdings Finance PLC, 6 Wolfreton Drive, Springfield Way, Anlaby, Hull HU10 7BZ. (0482 659371)

Chartered Trust PLC, 24–26 Newport Road, Cardiff CF2 1SR. (0222 484484)

Citibank Trust Ltd, St Martin's House, 1 Hammersmith Grove, London W6 9HW. (01 741 8000)

Commercial Credit Services Ltd, Grosvenor House, 125 High Street, Croydon, Surrey CR9 1PU. (01 686 3466)

First Co-operative Finance PLC, 1 Balloon Street, Manchester M60 4EP. (061 832 3300)

First National Securities Ltd, First National House, College Road, Harrow, Middx. HA1 1FB. (01 861 1313)

Forthright Finance PLC, 114/116 St Mary Street, Cardiff CF1 1XJ. (0222 396131)

Forward Trust Group PLC, Broad Street House, 55 Old Broad Street, London EC2M 1RX. (01 920 0141)

HFC Trust Ltd, Cory House, The Ring, Bracknell, Berks. RG12 1BL. (0344 24727)

ICFC Leasing Ltd, 91 Waterloo Road, London SE1 8XP. (01 928 7822)

Industrial Funding Trust Ltd, 1/3 Worship Street, London EC2A 2HQ (01 638 6070)

KDB Finance Ltd, Oakvale House, Chatham Road, Sandling, Maidstone, Kent ME14 3BQ. (0622 57294)

Lloyds & Scottish Finance Group, Finance House, Orchard Brae, Edinburgh EH4 1PF. (031 332 2451)

Lombard North Central PLC, Lombard House, Curzon Street, London W1A 1EU. (01 409 3434)

London Scottish Finance Corporation PLC, Speaker's House, 39 Deansgate, Manchester M3 2BE. (061 834 2861)

Lynn Regis Finance Ltd, 10 Tuesday Market Place, King's Lynn, Norfolk PE30 1JL. (0553 3465)

Medens Ltd, 46/50 Southwick Square, Southwick, Brighton BN4 4UA. (0273 593358)

Mercantile Credit Co Ltd, Elizabethan House, Great Queen Street, London WC2B 5DP. (01 242 1234)

Milford Mutual Facilities Ltd, Milford House, 29 Ardwick Green North, Manchester M12 6HB. (061 273 2531)

North British Securities Ltd, King William House, Market Place, Hull HU1 1RB. (0482 224181)

North West Securities Ltd, North West House, City Road, Chester CH1 3AN. (0244 315351)

RIGP Finance Ltd, 65 Triumph Road, Nottingham NG7 2FY. (0602 781841)

St Margaret's Trust Ltd, The Quadrangle, Imperial Square, Cheltenham GL50 1PZ. (0242 36141)

Security Pacific Finance Ltd, Security Pacific House, 308–314 Kings Road, Reading, Berks. RG1 4PA. (0734 61022)

Shawlands Securities Ltd, 8 Christchurch Road, Lansdowne, Bournemouth BH1 3NQ. (0202 2955441)

United Dominions Trust Ltd, 51 Eastcheap, London EC3P 3BU. (01 623 3020)

Vernons Finance Corporation, Vernons Building, Mile End, Liverpool L5 5AF. (051 207 3181)

The Wagon Finance Corporation PLC, 3 Endcliffe Crescent, Sheffield S10 3EE. (0742 665094)

Wrenwood Finance Co Ltd, Lancaster House, Blackburn Street, Radcliffe, Manchester M26 9TS. (061 723 1628)

Yorkshire Bank Finance Ltd, 2 Infirmary Street, Leeds LS1 2UL. (0532 442551)

Public-Sector Finance There are over 111 different incentive schemes operating at central and local government level, offering a wide range of assistance to new and existing businesses. Two of the more authoritative publications on the subject are over sixty pages long, and a further booklet devotes sixty-one pages to one section of incentives alone. (See page 196/8.)

New schemes are coming in all the time. The latest to arrive is the Small Engineering Firms Investment Scheme, which is open to engineering companies with fewer than 200 employees. It can provide a grant of one-third of the cost of new capital equipment worth between £15,000 and £200,000.

For the period April 1982/1983, £20 million has been made available, and will be handed out on a first-come, first-served basis. Guidance notes for this scheme are available from the Department of Industry, West Midlands Regional Office, Ladywood House, Stephenson Street, Birmingham B2 4DT. (021 632 4111).

In addition, the Enterprise Allowance Scheme is currently on trial in five areas. Under this scheme the Manpower Services Commission can pay Entrepreneurs an allowance of £40.00 per week for up to fifty-two weeks, to supplement the receipts of their business.

In order to find out if you are eligible, your first port of call should be your nearest Small Firms Information Centre at the Department of Industry.

Your local authority Employment Development Officer will be well up on schemes that particularly apply to your area, and on schemes in general.

If you have an Enterprise Agency nearby, they too will have access to up-to-date information on appropriate incentive schemes.

All of these organisations are listed in the first section of this book. A number of publications explaining the types of public-sector finance are listed at the end of this section.

Development and Venture Loans and Capital Financial Institutions There are now a considerable number of financial institutions under this heading. Many are subsidiaries of the clearing banks, insurance companies, pension funds, overseas banks; and even the Bank of England and the Government. Some of them can provide a range of services beyond equity and loan finance, although in general that is their speciality. A brief description of some of these institutions and their activities will give a flavour of the whole sector.

Industrial & Commercial Finance Corporation Ltd (ICFC) is part of Finance for Industry, was formed in 1945 and now claims to be the major source of long-term finance for new and small businesses.

ICFC's shareholders are the Bank of England (15 per cent) and the English and Scottish clearing banks (85 per cent). It operates as a private-sector organisation concerned exclusively with private-sector business. However, it also administers funds with low interest rates from the European Investment Bank (EIB), the European Coal and Steel Community (ECSC), and participates in the Government's loan guarantee scheme.

The corporation currently has over £400 million invested in some 3,500 companies, £100 million of which was advanced to just over 1,000 businesses in the year 1981/1982.

Funds for individual investments range from £5,000 up to £2 million. About 70 per cent of these were for £100,000. Indeed about half of all ICFC loans are far less than £50,000.

Finance is provided through long-term loans, or in the form of ordinary or preference shares, or in any combination of these. ICFC takes an equity stake in about a third of cases, the balance being term loans.

ICFC's close relationship with the clearing banks makes the negotiation of security cover easier. This is particularly true when, for example, the clearer already has a charge on the business's assets.

ICFC's main areas of activity are financing new business, providing funds for expansion, and arranging management buy-outs. ICFC have completed over 200 buy-outs, and claim to be the pioneers of the technique. More recently they have moved into the leasing and hire-purchase fields, with over £24 million provided in 1981/1982. This spread of facilities allows ICFC to propose the best financial package for the company's current needs.

Midland Bank Venture Capital Ltd, is, as the name implies, the venture capital area of the Midland Bank. Their operation is similar to the **National Westminster Bank's** Capital Loan Scheme. The starting threshold for the schemes are £5,000 and £10,000 respectively, and both go up to £50,000.

Whilst the Midland Bank take equity and are rewarded with a dividend, the National Westminster Bank offers a loan on which interest is due. It is, however, a loan with a difference: when the loan is taken out, the National Westminster expect to take an option to buy the shares in the company at some future date. The loan itself then ranks next to the shareholders' equity and behind that of the other creditors.

Ranking closer to the shareholders' equity increases the riskiness, as they are paid last. If the money runs out, the shareholders get nothing, then the next in line lose out and so on. So, by placing their loan in this way, the bank has made it virtually capital – hence the term 'capital loan'.

There are other specialist investment schemes. The British Technology Group has two established schemes, Oakwood Loan Finance and the Small Company Innovation Fund. These make an active contribution to high technology and innovative businesses, as well as in more traditionally based industries.

The Creative Capital Fund of the British Linen Bank is one of the latest venture funds designed to make use of the provisions of the 1981 Finance Act. Rather than have individual investors trying to find small new companies to invest in, it was thought advisable to put their money into a professionally managed fund. The fund managers then search for suitable business opportunities and monitor the performance of those companies on behalf of investors. In this way, as well as having the advantage of professional advice, investors can have their funds invested in a portfolio of small businesses, spreading both the risk and cost of the investment.

Creative Capital is now actively looking for companies with good prospects of growth and entrepreneurs with either good experience or potential for success. Initially, the fund will be investing £500,000, spread over some five businesses.

The whole investment and lending field is extremely dynamic, so you would be well advised to look around carefully. Once you find the institution that has a package you like, find its competitor(s), and then you can negotiate the best deal for your needs.

The following list of institutions is not quite exhaustive, but should give you a good cross-section from which to find a source of long-term finance. The guide to their services is simply intended to give you a clue to their policies. The £20,000 threshold was selected because a vast majority of new businesses are not looking for a greater level of external long-term financing.

Some institutions service only existing businesses with a proven track record. Others insist on an equity stake or board participation, either or both of which may be unacceptable. The mark against each institution in the list will give you answers to some of these questions.

	Loans less than £20,000	Start-up loans provided	Equity stake not required	May not put a director on your board	No special restrictions
Abingworth (various City Institutions, including Barclays Bank) 26 St James's Street, London SW1A 1HA. (01 839 6745)		•			
Advent Technology PLC (Advent Management Ltd), Secretary, 48 Manor Place, Edinburgh EH3 7EH (031 225 5784).		•			
Alan Patricof Associates Ltd, 37 Upper Grosvenor Street, London W1X 9PE. (01 493 3633)		•		•	
Allied Combined Trust Ltd (Allied Irish Bank Group), Pinners Hall, 8/9 Boston Friars, London EC2N 2AE (01 920 9155)					
A P Bank (Norwich Union), 21 Great Winchester Street, London EC2N 2HH (01 638 4711)					
Arbuthnot Industrial Investments Ltd (Arbuthnot Latham), 37 Queen Street, London EC4. (01 236 5281)	•	•	•	•	•
Barclays Development Capital (Barclays Bank), Dashwood House, Old Broad Street, London EC2. (01 600 9234)					•
British Steel Corporation (Industry) Ltd (BSC), NLA Tower, 12 Addiscombe Road, Croydon CR9 3JH. (01 686 0366)	•	•	•		
British Technology Group (Government-financed organisation), 12–18 Grosvenor Gardens, London SW71W ODW. (01 730 9600) *and* Kingsgate House, 66 Victoria Street, London. (01 828 3400)	•	•	•	•	
Regional offices: **North East Regional Enterprise Office,** Centro House, 3 Cloth Market, Newcastle upon Tyne NE1 1EH. (0632 327068)	•	•	•	•	
North West Regional Enterprise Office, 8th Floor, Bank House, Charlotte Street, Manchester M1 4ET. (061 236 9800)	•	•	•	•	
Merseyside Regional Enterprise Office, Richmond House, 1 Rumford Place, Liverpool L3 9QY. (051 227 1366)	•	•	•	•	

	Loans less than £20,000	Start-up loans provided	Equity stake not required	May not put a director…	No special restrictions
Yorkshire & Humberside Regional Enterprise Office, 9 Bond Court, Leeds LS1 2SN. (0532 459858)	●	●	●	●	
South West Regional Enterprise Office, Phoenix House, Notte Street, Plymouth PL1 2HF. (0752 665262)	●	●	●	●	
BTG in Scotland, 87 St Vincent Street, Glasgow G2 5TF. (041 221 1820)	●	●	●	●	
Anglo American Venture Management Ltd, 8th Floor, Bank House, Charlotte Street, Manchester M1 4ET. (061 236 7302)	●	●	●	●	
Merseyside Enterprise Fund Ltd, Richmond House, 1 Rumford Place, Liverpool L3 9QY. (051 227 1366)	●	●	●	●	
Western Enterprise Fund Ltd, Shinners Bridge, Dartington, Totnes TQ9 6JE. (0803 862271)	●	●	●	●	
Brown Shipley Developments (BS & Co), Founders Court, Lothbury, London EC2R YHE. (01 606 9833)		●			
Business Mortgages and Investment Trust PLC, Manager, 1 Marlborough Road, Sherwell, Plymouth PL4 8LP. (0752 669286)	●	●			
Candover Investments, 4/7 Red Lion Court, London, EC4A 3EB (583 5090).			●		
Capital Partners International Ltd (private European investors), 40 Edgerton Crescent, London SW3 2EB. (01 584 7209)	●	●			●
Castle Finance (Norwich Union), Norwich Union Insurance Group, Surrey Street, Norwich NR1 3NL. (0603 22200)				●	
Charterhouse Development Capital (Charterhouse Group) 25 Milk Street, London EC2V 8JE. (01 606 7070)					●
CIN Industrial Finance (National Coal Board Pensions Funds), 10 Bouverie Street, London EC4Y 8DA. (01 353 1500)		●		●	
Citicorp Development Capital Ltd, Melbourne House, Melbourne Place, Aldwych, London WC2B 4ND, (01 438 1266).				●	
Clydesdale Bank Industrial Finance Ltd (a member of the Midland Bank Group), 24 St Vincent Place, Glasgow G1 2HL. 041 221 5570.		●			●
Commercial Bank of the Near East (private shareholders, mainly Greek), 107/112 Leadenhall Street, London EC3A 4PE. (01 283 4041)	●	●	●	●	●

	Loans less than £20,000	Start-up loans provided	Equity stake not required	May not put a director ...	No special restrictions
Commonwealth Development Finance Co (several Commonwealth central banks and 160 major UK companies), Colechurch House, London Bridge Walk, SE1 2SS. (01 407 9711) (Mostly overseas, equity-oriented)					●
Corinthian Securities Ltd (ARMCO), 20 Welbeck Street, London W1M 7PS. (01 486 2234)	●		●	●	●
Council for Small Industries in Rural Areas (HM Government and other financial institutions), 141 Castle Street, Salisbury, Wilts. SP1 3TP. (0722 6255) (CoSIRA)	●	●	●	●	
County Bank (NatWest), 11 Old Broad Street, London EC2N 1BB. (01 638 6000)		●	●	●	
Creative Capital Fund (British Linen Bank), c/o The British Linen Bank Ltd, 4 Melville Street, Edinburgh EH3 7NZ (0271 763324).		●			●
Dartington & Co Ltd, Shinners Bridge, Dartington, Totnes, Devon TQ9 6JE. (0271 76324)	●				
Dawnay, Day & Co Ltd, Managing Director, Corporate Finance, Garrard House, 31 Gresham Street, London EC2V 7DT. (01 600 7533)	●	●			
Development Capital Investments (Electra Investment Trust and others), 88 Baker Street, London W1M 1DL. (01 486 5021)		●			
Development Capital (Services) Ltd, 88 Baker Street, London W1M 1DL. (01 486 5021)		●			
East of Scotland Onshore Ltd (ESO Ltd), 3 Albyn Place, Edinburgh EH2 4NQ. (031 225 7515)		●			
Electra Risk Capital (Electra Investments), Electra House, Temple Place, Victoria Embankment, London WC2R 3HP. (01 836 7766)		●			
English and Caledonian Investment PLC, Cayzer House, 2–4 St Mary Axe, London EC3A 8BP.			●		
Estate Duties Investment Trust (see ICFC)					
Equity Capital for Industry (City Institutes), Leith House, 47/57 Gresham Street, London EC2B 7EH. (01 606 8513)			●		
European Investment Bank (EEC's long-term bank), 23 Queen Anne's Gate, London SW1H 9BU. (01 222 2933)	●	●	●	●	
Exeter Trust Ltd (ET Ltd), Sanderson House, Blackboy Road, Exeter, Devon, EX4 6SE. (0392 50635)	●	●	●	●	●

	Loans less than £20,000	Start-up loans provided	Equity stake not required	May not put a director …	No special restrictions
F & C Management Ltd, Secretary, 1 Laurence Pountney Hill, London EC4R 0BA. (01 623 4680)		•			•
Federation Pension Funds (National Federation of Self-employed & Others), 45 Russell Square, London WC1B 4JF. (01 636 3828)		•		•	•
Finance Corporation for Industry Ltd, General Manager, 91 Waterloo Road, London SE1 8XP. (01 928 7822)					
Gresham Trust (Gresham), Barrington House, Gresham Street, London EC2Z 7HE. (01 606 6474)		•			•
Grainger & Co Ltd, Managing Director, 18 Woodside Terrace, Glasgow G3 7NY. (041 332 8751)	•	•			
Growth Options Ltd, (Member of Nat West Bank Group) Business Development Division, National Westminster Bank Ltd. 161 Fenchurch Street, London EC4. (01 726 1000)	•	•		•	
Guidehouse Ltd, 1 Love Lane, London EC2 7JJ.	•	•	•	•	•
Halfren Investment Finance Ltd (Welsh Development Agency), Treforest Industrial Estate, Pontypridd, Mid Glamorgan CF37 5UT. (044 385 2666)	•	•	•	•	
Highlands & Islands Development (HM Government & Scottish Office), 27 Bridge House, Bank Street, Inverness IV1 1QR. (0463 34171)	•	•	•	•	
Industrial & Commercial Finance Corporation (ICFC) (Bank of England and clearing banks), 91 Waterloo Road, London SE1 8XP. (01 928 7822)	•	•	•	•	•
Regional Offices: **Aberdeen,** 38 Carden Place, Aberdeen AB1 1UP. (0224 638666) Contact: A. K. Mair	•	•	•	•	•
Birmingham, Colemore Centre, 115 Colemore Row, Birmingham B3 3SA. (021 236 9531) Contact: D. S. Sach	•	•	•	•	•
Brighton, 47 Middle Street, Brighton BN1 1AL. (0273 23164) Contact: P. B. G. Williams	•	•	•	•	•
Bristol, Pearl Assurance House, Queen Square, Bristol BS1 4LE. (0272 277412) Contact: J. G. Kingston	•	•	•	•	•
Cambridge, Jupiter House, Station Road, Cambridge CB1 2HZ. (0223 316568) Contact: R. D. M. J. Summers	•	•	•	•	•
Cardiff, Alliance House, 18/19 High Street, Cardiff CF1 3TS. (0222 34021) Contact: R. Braddick	•	•	•	•	•
Edinburgh, 8 Charlotte Square, Edinburgh EH2 4DR. (031 226 7092) Contact: J. J. U. Hayward	•	•	•	•	•

	Loans less than £20,000	Start-up loans provided	Equity stake not required	May not put a director ...	No special restrictions
Glasgow, 20 Blythswood Square, Glasgow G2 4AR. (041 221 4456) Contact: A. M. Walker	●	●	●	●	●
Leeds, Headrow House, The Headrow, Leeds LS1 8ES. (0532 430511) Contacts: D. Thorpe, B. A. Anysz	●	●	●	●	●
Leicester, Abacus House, 32 Friar Lane, Leicester LE1 5QU. (0533 25223) Contact: T. M. Moulds	●	●	●	●	●
Liverpool, Silkhouse Court, Tithebarn Street, Liverpool L2 2LZ. (051 236 2944) Contact: J. C. Platt	●	●	●	●	●
Manchester, Virginia House, 5 Cheapside, Manchester M2 4WG. (061 833 9511) Contact: P. J. Folkman	●	●	●	●	●
Newcastle, Scottish Life House, Archbold Terrace, Jesmond, Newcastle upon Tyne NE12 1DB. (0632 815221) Contact: D. H. Wilson	●	●	●	●	●
Nottingham, 38 The Ropewalk, Nottingham NG1 5DW. (0602 412766) Contact: P. Brooks	●	●	●	●	●
Reading, 43/47 Crown Street, Reading RG1 2SN. (0734 861943) Contact: R. L. Cottrell	●	●	●	●	●
Sheffield, 11 Westbourne Road, Sheffield S10 2QQ. (0742 680571) Contact: P. A. L. Gilmartin	●	●	●	●	●
Southampton, Capital House, 1 Houndwell Place, Southampton SO1 1HU. (0703 32044) Contact: R. M. Scrase	●	●	●	●	●
Industrial Common Ownership Finance Ltd, 4 St Giles Street, Northampton NN1 1AA. (0604 37563)	●	●	●	●	
James Finlay Corporation (James Finlay Group), 10/14, West Nile Street, Glasgow G1 2PP. (041 204 1321)				●	
Local Enterprise Development Unit (Department of Commerce Northern Ireland), Lamont House, Purdys Lane, New Town Breda, Belfast BT8 4TB. (0230 691031)	●	●	●	●	
London Wall Industrial Consultants Ltd (Smithdown Investments Ltd), Managing Director, 15 South Molton Street, London W1Y 1DE. (01 629 9891)	●	●			
Lovat Enterprise Fund (National Coal Board Pension Fund & others), 27/28 Lovat Lane, London EC3R 8EB. (01 621 1212)				●	
Melville Street Investments (Edinburgh) Ltd (British Linen Bank), 4 Melville Street, Edinburgh EH3 7NZ. (031 226 4071)		●		●	●
Meritor Investment Ltd (Midland Bank and Rolls Royce Pension Fund), 36 Poultry, London EC2R 98AJ. (01 606 2179)				●	●

	Loans less than £20,000	Start-up loans provided	Equity stake not required	May not put a director ...	No special restrictions
Midland Bank Industrial Finance (Midland Bank), 36 Poultry, London EC2R BAJ. (01 623 8861)	•	•			•
Midland Bank Venture Capital Ltd, 36 Poultry, London EC2P 2BX. (01 638 8861)	•	•	•	•	•
Minster Trust (Minster Assets), Minster House, Arthur Street, London EC4R 9BH. (01 623 1050)	•	•		•	•
Moracrest Investments (Midland Bank, Prudential and British Gas Pension Fund), Scottish Life House, Poultry, London EC2R 8AJ. (01 628 8409)		•		•	•
National Coal Board Pension Fund (NCB), Hobart House, Grosvenor Place, London SW1. (01 235 2020)	•	•		•	•
National & Commercial Development Capital (National & Commercial Banking Group), 88 Baker Street, London W1M 1DL (01 486 5021)					
Newtown Securities (Northern) Ltd (NEB and Midland Bank), c/o Midland Bank, 25 Mosley Street, Newcastle upon Tyne, (0632 28351)					
Noble Grossart Investments (Scottish Investment Institute), 48 Queen Street, Edinburgh EH2 3NR. (031 226 7011)	•				•
Norwich General Trust (Norwich Union Insurance), Nuffield House, 41–46 Piccadilly, London W1V 9AJ. (sister organisation: Castle Finance) (01 493 8030)	•	•	•	•	•
Oakwood Loan Finance Ltd (British Technology Group), 12–18 Grosvenor Gardens, London SW1W 0DW. (01 730 7600)	•	•	•	•	•
P. A. Developments Ltd (P. A. Ltd), Managing Director, Bowater House East, 68 Knightsbridge, London SW1X. (01 589 7050)					
Pegasus Holdings Ltd (a member of the Lloyds Bank Group), General Manager, 11–15 Monument Street, London EC3R 8JU. (01 626 1500 ext. 2036)				•	•
Prutec Ltd, Chief Executive, 33 Davies Street, London W1Y 2EA. (01 491 7000)	•	•			•
Rainsford Venture Capital (Pilkington Brothers, Prudential Assurance, Community of St Helen's Trust and others), Prescott Road, St Helen's, Merseyside, WA10 3TT. (0744 28882)			•		
Royal Bank Development Ltd (Royal Bank of Scotland), Edinburgh House, 3–11 North St Andrews Street, Edinburgh EH2 1HW. (031 556 8555)			•	•	•

	Loans less than £20,000	Start-up loans provided	Equity stake not required	May not put a director...	No special restrictions
Safeguard Industrial Investments (major insurance companies and pension funds), 2a Pond Place, London SW3 6QJ (01 581 4455)		•		•	•
Scottish Allied Investors (James Finlay Royal Bank Development Ltd, Scottish Western Trust Ltd, James Finlay & Co, Allied Investors), James Finlay PLC, 10/14 West Nile Street, Glasgow G2 2PT. (041 204 1321)				•	•
Scottish Offshore Investors (James Finlay & others), 10/14 West Nile Street, Glasgow G2 1PP. (041 204 1321)					•
Scottish Development Agency (UK Government), 120 Bothwell Street, Glasgow G2 7JP. (041 248 2700)	•	•	•	•	
Shandwick Consultants Ltd, Wamford Court, 29 Throgmorton Street, London EC2N 2AT. (01 588 4278)	•	•	•	•	•
Sharp Unquoted Midland Investment (Legal & General, Royal Insurance, Sun Life Assurance and others), Edmund House, 12 Newall Street, Birmingham B3 3ER. (021 236 5801)				•	•
Small Company Innovation Fund (British Technology Group), Kingsgate House, 66–74 Victoria Street, London SW1E 6SL. (01 828 3400)	•	•	•	•	•
Smithdown Investments (private individuals), 141 North Hyde Road, Hayes, Middx. (01 573 3783) *Also at* 15 South Moulton Street, London W1Y 1DE.	•	•	•	•	•
Technical Development Capital (ICFC), 91 Waterloo Road, London SE1 8XP. (01 928 7822)		•			
Thamesdale Investment & Finance Co Ltd, Manager, 43 Museum Street, London WC1A 1LY. (01 405 9875)		•	•		
Thomson Clive & Partners Ltd (TCP Ltd), 24 Old Bond Street, London W1X 3DA. (01 491 4809)		•			
Trust of Property Shares Ltd Managing Director, 6 Welbeck Street, London W1M 8BS. (01 486 4684)		•			
Venture Founders Ltd, (British Investment Trust), 39 The Green, South Bar Street, Banbury, Oxon, LS16 9AE. (0295 65881)	•	•	•	•	
Welsh Development Agency (UK Government), Treforest Industrial Estate, Pontypridd, Wales. (044 385 2666)	•	•	•	•	
Western Enterprise Fund Ltd (British Technology Group), Shinners Bridge, Dartington, Totnes TQ9 6JE. (0803 862271)	•	•	•	•	
Woodside Securities Ltd (See under Grainer & Co Ltd)	•	•			

CONTROLLING THE MONEY

Even with a good business plan and a reasonably willing provider of funds, your financial problems are not over. Indeed, in one sense they are just about to begin. Before you take on outside investors or lenders you only have your own money to lose. With other people's funds you will have to give an account of 'stewardship', as well as keep records to meet the needs of the Inland Revenue and the Customs and Excise.

In fact, you will probably have to show how you propose to control the finances of the business before anyone will part with any funds. They will want to know how you will keep track of the business.

There are four elements to successful financial control. Firstly, you should plan ahead. Have a budget that sets out clearly what you expect to happen over the next twelve months, month by month. This should be expressed in terms of money out and money in.

Secondly, you need management information that shows you what has actually happened at each stage in your plan.

Thirdly, you need to compare your budget or plan with the actual position.

Fourthly, you need to be able to use this comparison to take action – to control the business.

The single greatest reason that new and small businesses go out of business is lack of good financial control. They simply do not know what is happening from day to day, week to week and month to month.

Choosing a Bookkeeping and Accounting System

Peter Saunders, ACCA, of Thames Polytechnic, carried out the following survey of bookkeeping and accounting systems in March 1982.

In order to get financial control you need a bookkeeping system. This should provide you with the knowledge of how much you have in your bank, how much you are owed and how much you owe (the bare minimum). The majority of the following systems can provide you with this, but none of them provides you with equally important information, such as profit and loss or cash-flow forecasts.

The majority of small businesses begin with handwritten (manual) systems. These fit into one of five categories: 'shoe-boxes'; do-it-yourself books: halfway houses; accountants only; and computer-based systems.

'Shoe-box' systems. This is for the simplest businesses, which need relatively little financial control beyond cash, bank accounts, accounts payable and accounts receivable.

At its simplest you need four shoe boxes, a bank paying-in book and a cheque book (the last two can tell you how much you have in the bank). You keep two boxes for unpaid invoices (one for sales, one for purchases, services and so on). You transfer the invoices into the other two boxes (one for sales, one for purchases, etc.) when each invoice is paid. By adding all the invoices in one box (sales, unpaid invoices) you can find out how much you are owed, and by adding another (purchases, unpaid) you find out how much you owe.

You keep every record relating to the business, too.

This is a perfectly adequate system unless you need some form of cash control or some profit information and you need it fast. It is, however, not too good on credit control.

Essentially, this system is only for the smallest firms.

The DIY System These are normally hardback, bound books with several sections to them, each part ruled and already laid out for the entries. Each one has a set of instructions and examples for each section.

All the systems mentioned here have some advantages and disadvantages in common:

Advantages: each one tries to assist the small business person by allowing some measures of financial control, especially over cash and bank balances. They almost always include VAT sections and Profit and Loss sections. They aim, in the large part, to make an accountant unnecessary, or at least to minimise your expense in that area.

Disadvantages: none of these systems will work unless it is kept up regularly – which means weekly at a minimum, and preferably daily. As a drawback this cannot be overemphasised. Unless you currently regularly keep a diary, these books are probably not for you. If not kept properly, they can cost you more in accountacy fees rather than less. Other disadvantages are that they often assume some prior knowledge from the user, even though they give instructions. Their instructions sometimes leave much to be desired, relying largely on worked examples that are difficult to follow. They compartmentalise people and business, and they tend to ignore such expenses as 'use of home as office' (for example, home telephone bills) many of which may be tax allowable. Finally, many people also find that they would rather not use these books as the basis for dealing with their Inspectors of Taxes, and would rather have their accountants do this. In these circumstances you are going to need an accountant anyway, and your inspector is much more likely to pay attention to him in any case.

The following tables show the basic information for some of the most common systems, and the conclusions as to their relative usefulness.

Finco Small Business Bookkeeping System at £30. This system may seem dear, but it has two years' supply of forms (compared to others which provide only one), and gives a large amount of financial control for a relatively small sum. This is first choice.

The Kalamazoo Set Up is the second choice. It would have been first choice had it not cost £75. You probably also need training to be able to use it, even with their book as support. It has been chosen because it can give the best financial control, if used properly. In addition, it can save time through being a single-write system (entering up to three records simultaneously).

DIY Accounting Books, Comparison Table

Name and availability	Approximate cost	Financial control provided	Records provided
Ataglance Ataglance Publications, 16 Sawley Avenue, Lytham St Annes, Lancs. FY8 3QL. (0253 727107)	£4	Bank	Payments, Receipts, VAT
Collins Self Employed Account Book W. H. Smith and other stationers	£8	Bank, debtors, creditors	Payments, receipts, VAT subcontract
Collins Complete Traders Account Book W. H. Smith and other stationers	£8	Bank	Payments, receipts, VAT
Evrite Traders Account Book Commercial stationers *or* Evrite Publishing Co Ltd, Hill Street Chambers, St Helier, Jersey, Channel Islands	£8	Bank, debtors	Payments, receipts, VAT
Finco Small Business Bookkeeping System Casdec Ltd, 11 Windermere Avenue, Garden Farm Estate, Chester-le-Street, Co. Durham DH2 3DU. (0385 882906)	£30	Bank, cash, debtors, creditors, wages	Receipts, payments, sales, purchases; payroll, VAT
Kalamazoo Set Up Kalamazoo Business Systems, Mill Lane, Northfield, Birmingham B31 2RW. (021 475 2191)	£75	Bank, cash, debtors, creditors	Receipts
Simplex 'D' Cash Book Commercial stationers *or* George Viner (Dist. Ltd), Simplex House, Mytholmbridge Mills, Mytholmbridge, Holmfirth, Huddersfield HD7 2TA.	£3.03	Bank, cash	Receipts, payments, profit & loss

Ataglance: Few instructions, mostly related to VAT.

Collins Self Employed Accounts Book: This seems to be aimed at sub-contractors and is reasonably comprehensive, but the instructions are a little limited and hence needs prior knowledge.

Collins Complete Traders Account Book: For retail outlets only. The instructions are somewhat limited.

Evrite Traders Account Book: Short, unclear instructions. Relies on worked examples. Assumes prior knowledge. Debtor control in total only (not by individual customers).

Finco Small Business Bookkeeping System: Simple instructions, two years' supply of record sheets, loose-leaf. This is more easily adaptable to any business (there is less compartmentalisation), and gives detailed control over individual amounts outstanding, both receivable and payable. Because it is loose-leaf, your accountant can take the relevant records without depriving you of your control. It can also be used in conjunction with your accountant's minicomputer.

Kalamazoo Set Up: This is the most comprehensive system (as well as the most expensive). It provides everything that all other systems give you, two years' supply of records (loose-leaf) and a debtors/creditors ledger. Your £75 also buys you a basic bookkeeping book which gives information on how to keep it up (and why you need to). The book is by John Kellock *A Practical Guide to Good Bookkeeping and Business Systems*, and is available separately.

Simplex 'D' Cash Book: This is the best known of this type of book – and the most misused. Its instructions are short, and it relies heavily on worked examples. It would be a brave person who used the profit and loss account in the back of this book for negotiations with HM Inspector of Taxes. There are separate books for VAT and wages, as well as a separate book, *Simplified Bookkeeping for Small Business* at £3.00.

Halfway House Systems The halfway-house systems combine both the other two. Pre-printed stationery tends to be used, but in loose-leaf form. These systems are more flexible than the DIY, and tend to be cheaper than using an accountant only. However, they do require some knowledge on the part of the person who keeps the books. Again, this need not be daunting, as your accountant can probably train you (or your office girl or boy) to keep them up. The major problem is that you need your accountant before you can use your records for more advanced financial control.

There are two common half-way house systems on the market: Twinlock and Kalamazoo.

Twinlock available at commercial stationers or the publishers at Twinlock Ltd, 36 Croydon Road, Beckenham, Kent BR3 4BH. (01 650 4818)

Kalamazoo only from the publishers at Kalamazoo Ltd, Northfield, Birmingham B31 2WR. (021 475 2191)

At the basic level the two systems seem remarkably similar, both in cost and financial control. The minimum systems will cost £200 to £400. Kalamazoo offer training with their product. Both are single-write systems (where one writing can enter up to three records). You should see your accountant before installing one.

Accountant Only Systems The accountant only systems are those for the more complex (possibly larger) small businesses, and will be designed by your accountant. They often need trained bookkeepers to run them. However, the training period can be relatively short (anything from one day upwards). The bookkeeper handles the routine matters, and your accountant the non-routine. The accountant can be employed by you permanently or may be a member of the firm you have hired.

Obviously, the small business should be of a reasonable size before the expense of a full-time accountant can be justified.

Computer Systems There are many small computer systems that will carry out the bookkeeping and accountancy functions needed by a small business. But, like all systems, they are only as good as the quality of information put in. The other major problems with computer systems are these: selecting the equipment in a market with many models with claimed advantages; making sure that you have the necessary extra equipment; making sure that you have the software (programmes) capable of handling your information and record needs; and, finally, ensuring that you can use the machine efficiently. This is fine for the enthusiast, but others tend to get lost in the jungle. The part of Section 4 on using a computer will help here.

ORGANISATIONS AND PUBLICATIONS FOR FINANCE

Organisations

The Association of Authorised Public Accountants, 10 Cornfield Road, Eastbourne, East Sussex BN21 4QE. (0323 641514/5)
The Association of British Factors, Moor House, London Wall, London EC2Y 5HE. (01 638 4090)
The Association of Certified Accountants, 29 Lincoln's Inn Fields, London WC2A 3EE. (01 242 6855)
The Association of Invoice Factors, 109/113 Royal Avenue, Belfast BT1 1FF. (0232 24522)
The British Export House Association, 69 Cannon Street, London EC4N 5AB. (01 248 4444)
Corporation of Mortgate, Finance & Life Assurance Brokers Ltd, PO Box 101, Guilford, Surrey, GU1 2HZ (0483 35786/39126
The Equipment Leasing Association, 18 Upper Grosvenor Street, London W1X 9PB. (01 491 2783)

Export Credits Guarantee Department (ECGD), (Headquarters at) Aldermanbury House, Aldermanbury, London EC2P 2EL. (01 606 6699)

Regional Offices

City of London, PO Box 46, Clements House, 14–18 Gresham Street, London EC2V 7JE. (01 726 4050)

Belfast, River House, High Street, Belfast BT1 2BE. (0232 31743)

Birmingham, Colmore Centre, 115 Colmore Row, Birmingham B3 3SB. (021 233 1771)

Bristol, 1 Redcliffe Street, Bristol BS1 6NP. (0272 299971)

Cambridge, Three Crowns House, 72–80 Hills Road, Cambridge CB2 1NJ. (0223 68801)

Croydon, Sunley House, Bedford Park, Croydon, Surrey CR9 4HL. (01 686 8833)

Glasgow, Fleming House, 134 Renfrew Street, Glasgow G3 6TL. (041 332 8707)

Leeds, West Riding House, 67 Albion Street, Leeds LS1 5AA. (0532 450631)

Manchester, Elisabeth House, St Peter's Square, Manchester M2 4AJ. (061 228 3621)

Institute of Chartered Accountants in England & Wales, PO Box 433, Chartered Accountants Hall, Moorgate Place, London EC2P 2BJ. (01 628 7060)

The Institute of Chartered Accountants of Scotland, 27 Queen Street, Edinburgh EH2 1LA. (031 225 5673)

The Institute of Cost and Management Accountants, 63 Portland Place, London W1N 6AB. (01 580 6542)

London Discount Market Association, Hon. Sec., Mr P. L. Shepherd, 39 Cornhill, London EC3L 3NU. (01 623 1020)

The London Society of Chartered Accountants, 38 Finsbury Square, London EC2A 1PX. (01 628 2467)
The society provides a free booklet, *You Need a Chartered Accountant,* and will put you in touch with an accountant if you ring its client information service.

The Society of Company & Commercial Accountants, 11 Portland Road, Edgbaston, Birmingham B16 9HW. (021 454 8791/2)

Publications

The Balance Sheet Barrier, by Antony Jay, published by Video Arts, Dumbarton House, 68 Oxford Street, London W1N 9LA. (01 637 7288) It costs £2.00, and is intended to accompany the film of the same name. However it can and does stand up on its own as a very simple introduction to profit and loss accounts, balance sheets and cash flow. It is extremely clear and readable.

Blays Guide to Regional Finance for Industry & Commerce provides a guide to financial assistance available in Assisted Areas, Enterprise Zones, Inner Urban Areas, New Towns and EEC Assistance, throughout the UK. The guide was published in March 1982, costs £45.00, which includes a twelve-month subscription to their up-dating service. Blays Guides Ltd, Churchfield Road, Chalfont St Peter, Bucks SL9 9EW. (02813 84417)

Cash Flow – The Key to Business Survival published in November 1981 by Dun and Bradstreet Ltd, 26/32 Clifton Street, London EC2P 2LY. (01 247 4377) It has a foreword by Sir Kenneth Cork, who should know the answers if anyone does.

Cost Accounting, by A. J. Tubb, first edition, 1977, published by Teach Yourself Books 47 Bedford Square, London WC1B 3DP at £2.95. A very useful book for anyone starting up a manufacturing business who wants to see how to set prices at a level that will not lose money.

Directory of Grant Making Trusts, 1981 (new edition, 1983) CAF Publications Ltd, 48 Pembury Road, Tonbridge, Kent TN9 2JD. Price £32.00. Lists over 2,200 grant-making bodies, their objectives, policies and criteria.

Financial Incentives and Assistance for Industry – a Comprehensive Guide, published by Arthur Young, McClelland Moore & Co, Rolls House, 7 Rolls Buildings, Fetter Lane, London EC4A 1NL. (01 831 7131) Published June 1982 (free).

Finding Money for your Business, a Guide to Finance for the Smaller Firm, published in March 1982, price £3.50. From Confederation of British Industry, Centre Point, 103 New Oxford Street, London WC1A 1DU. (01 379 7400)

Grants and Loans from the European Community, Press Office, European Community, 20 Kensington Palace Gardens, London W8 4QQ, and from HMSO. Price, 60p.

Guide to Running a Small Business, (The Guardian), published by Kogan Page Ltd.

How to Collect Money That Is Owed to You, by Mel Lewis; published by McGraw-Hill, 34 Dover Street, London, W1X 3RA (01 493 1451). April 1982, price £8.95. This is a lively short book on the techniques which any business person can use to achieve prompt payment of money owed to him or her. It has a guide to credit insurance and factoring, examples of contracts, invoices and collection letters, lists of useful addresses and organisations and a guide to telephone collection techniques. It will be of great interest to the smaller trader.

How to Survive the Recession, by Jeremy Prescott, published by the Institute of Chartered Accountants, 1982, price £4.95. Despite the slightly off-putting title, this book sets out in clear, simple and concise terms what basic business controls you need, how to get them and how to use them. It is written by someone at ICFC who has seen many companies experiencing financial problems that came directly from lack of financial control.

Incentives for Industry in the Area of Expansion, Department of Industry, Room 219, Ashdown House, 123 Victoria Street, London SW1 6RB (01 212 0629)
Published March 1981 (free).

Industrial Aids in the UK: 1982, a Businessman's Guide, by Lisa Walker and Kevin Allen, price £8.95 available from Centre for study of Public Policy, McLance Building, University of Strathclyde, Glasgow G1 1XQ. Describes 134 different industrial aids in a 'user orientated' manner.

Institute of Directors, 116 Pall Mall London SW1Y 5ED. (01 839 1233) produce a monthly magazine called *BID (Business Investment Digest)* that puts people with funds in contact with people with business ideas.

Leasing, McGraw Hill at £15.00, T. M. Clark. This is a comprehensive guide to all aspects of leasing as a means of financing capital equipment. It traces the development of leasing to its present importance in finance for industry. It also deals with the principles of finance leasing, taxation, government policy, aspects of law and insurance, and with risks and problems involved, offering suggestions for evaluating and accounting for leasing transactions. Price £7.95.

London Enterprise Agency, 'The Marriage Bureau', 69 Cannon Street, London EC4 5AB. (01 236 2676). The agency publishes a newsletter putting people with funds (amongst other resources) in contact with people with business ideas.

Management Accounting, by Brian Murphy, second edition 1978, published by Teach Yourself Books, 47 Bedford Square, London, WC1B 3DP price £2.25. A good book for beginners, it covers all the essential stages of the business plan, together with the elements of financial control systems.

Management Buy Outs, special report no. 115, January. Published by *the Economist,* 25 St James Street, London SW1 (01 839 7000). It covers the commercial, financial, legal and tax aspects of completing a management buy-out.

Money for Business, October 1981 edition, £2.00. Published by the Bank of England, Economic Intelligence Department, London EC2R 8AW. A first-class and comprehensive guide.

Official Sources of Finance and Aid for Industry in the UK, by the National Westminster Bank Ltd, April 1981, available from Market Intelligence Unit, 41 Lothbury, London EC2P 2BP. Price £4.95.

Sources of Finance for Small Business, The Guardian, 119 Farringdon Road, London EC1. Price 75p.

Sources of Finance for Small Co-operatives, by John Pearce, Beechwood College, Elmete Lane, Roundhay, Leeds LS8 2LQ. (0532 720205)

Sources of Finance for Small Firms, published by the London Enterprise Agency, 69 Cannon Street, London EC4N 5AB. (01 236 2676) Written and compiled by David C. Bloomfield AIB, on secondment from Midland Bank PLC. Price £5.00.

Tolley's Survival Kit for Small Businesses, June 1981, from Tolley Publishing Company Ltd, 102/104 High Street, Croydon, Surrey CRO 1ND. Price £2.95. A very useful book. Part I has questionnaires and check-lists covering fixed and working capital, and taxation. Part II covers business planning and budgeting. It is a 'must' for all who have started up.

Understanding Company Financial Statements, January 1982, by R. H. Parker, published by Penguin, 530 Kings Road, London, SW10 (01 351 2393). Price £2.50. It is an excellent, simple guide to the balance sheet and other important financial statements.

Understanding Your Accounts, revised edition 1979, from Kogan Page Ltd, 120 Pentonville Road, London N1. Author A. St. J. Price, FCA. A practical and inexpensive book that concentrates on using worked examples. Price £1.95.

Venture Capital Report, 2 The Mall, Clifton, Bristol BS8 4DR. (0272 737222) The report puts people with funds in touch with people with business proposals.

Working for Yourself (Daily Telegraph), by Godfrey Golzen, Chapter 3. Published by Kogan Page Ltd, 120 Pentonville Road, London N1 9JN.

Zoning in on Enterprise, a Businessman's Guide to the Enterprise Zones, by David Rodrigues and Peter Bruinvels, published by Kogan Page, 120 Pentonville Road, London N1 9JN. 1982. Price £11.95.

Most banks produce a range of useful booklets that describe the financial functions and reports quite well.

BUSINESS AND THE LAW

Everyone is affected in some way or another by the law, and ignorance does not form the basis of a satisfactory defence. Businesses are also subject to specific laws, and a particular responsibility rests on those who own or manage them. Although an indication of some of the main legal implications is given here, there is no substitute for specific professional advice.

A lawyer will probably know the way in which your particular business will be affected by the laws mentioned here and other laws. In the area of taxation an accountant can earn his fee several times over. Other organisations and professionals who can advise you are listed at the end of each sub-section. Most of the organisations in the first section of this book will be able to give you some guidance in this field.

This section identifies and outlines some sixty of the services or publications that can help you get a better understanding of business and the law. These include a number of relatively inexpensive advisory services. One, for example, will provide, for as little as £18 per annum, on-the-spot advice, back-up research and information, as well as insurance cover to provide professional accounting or legal advice to defend yourself if you are prosecuted under one of the many relevant business laws.

Four comprehensive books that cover most of the field are listed below. Start with *The Consumer, Society and the Law*; that should meet most needs.

The Business and Professional Man's Lawyer, by Ewan Mitchell, published by Business Books Ltd., 25 Highbury Crescent, London, N5 1RX. An extremely readable 550 pages. Price £12.50.

Principles of Business Law, by Brian Ball and Frank Rose, published by Sweet and Maxwell, 11 New Fetter Lane, London EC4 (01 583 9855). A rather more technical 550 pages. Price £9.85.

The Consumer, Society and the Law, by Gordon Borne and Aubrey L. Diamond, fourth edition, 1981, Penguin, 536 King's Road, London, SW10 (01 351 2393), £2.95.

Commercial Law, by R. M. Goode, August 1982, Penguin (address as above), £10.95.

CHOOSING THE FORM OF THE BUSINESS

At the outset of your business venture you will have to decide what legal form your business will take. There are four main forms that a business can take, with a number of variations on two of these. The form that you choose will depend on a number of factors: commercial needs, financial risk and your tax position. All play an important part. The tax position is looked at in more detail later, but a summary of the main pros and cons is set out on page 204.

Sole Trader If you have the facilities, cash and customers, you can start trading under your own name immediately. Unless you intend to register for VAT, there are no rules about the records you have to keep. There is no requirement for an external audit, or for financial information on your business to be filed at Companies House. You would be prudent to keep good books and to get professional advice, as you will have to declare your income to the Inland Revenue. Without good records you will lose in any dispute over tax. You are personally liable for the debts of your business, and in the event of your business failing your personal possessions can be sold to meet the debts.

A sole trader does not have access to equity capital, which has the attraction of being risk-free to the business. He must rely on loans from banks or individuals and any other non-equity source of finance.

Partnership There are very few restrictions to setting up in business with another person (or persons) in partnership. Many partnerships are entered into without legal formalities, and sometimes without the parties themselves being aware that they have entered a partnership.

All that is needed is for two or more people to agree to carry on a business together intending to share the profits. The law will then recognise the existence of a partnership.

Most of the points raised when considering sole tradership apply to partnerships. All the partners are personally liable for the debts of the partnership, even if those debts were incurred by one partner's mismanagement or dishonesty without the other partner's knowledge. Even death may not release a partner from his obligations, and in some circumstances his estate can remain liable. Unless you take 'public' leave of your partnership by notifying your business contacts, and advertising retirement in *The London Gazette*, you will remain liable indefinitely. So it is vital *before* entering a partnership to be absolutely sure of your partner and to take legal advice in drawing up a partnership contract.

The contract should cover the following points.

Profit Sharing, Responsibilities and Duration This should specify how profit and losses are to be shared, and who is to carry out which tasks. It should also set limits on partner's monthly drawings, and on how long the partnership itself is to last (either a specific period of years or indefinitely, with a cancellation period of, say, three months).

Voting Rights and Policy Decision Unless otherwise stated, all the partners have equal voting rights. It is advisable to get a definition of what is a policy or voting decision, and how such decisions are to be made. You must also decide how to expel or admit a new partner.

Time off Every partner is entitled to his share of the profits, even when ill or on holiday. You will need some guidelines on the length and frequency of holidays, and on what to do if someone is absent for a long period for any other reason.

Withdrawing Capital You have to decide how each partner's share of the capital of the business will be valued in the event of either partner leaving or the partnership being dissolved.

Accountancy Procedures You do not have either to file accounts or to have accounts audited. However, it may be prudent to agree a satisfactory standard of accounting and have a firm of accountants to carry out that work. Sleeping partners may well insist on it.

Sleeping Partners A partner who has put up capital but does not intend to take an active part in running the business can protect himself against risk by having his partnership registered as a limited partnership.

Limited Company The main distinction between a limited company and either of the two forms of business already discussed is that it has a legal identity of its own separate from the people who own it. This means that, in the event of liquidation, creditors' claims are restricted to the assets of the company. The shareholders are not liable as individuals for the business debts beyond the paid-up value of their shares. This applies even if the shareholders are working directors, unless the company has been trading fraudulently.

Other advantages include the freedom to raise capital by selling shares and certain tax advantages.

The disadvantages include the legal requirement for the company's accounts to be audited by a chartered or certified accountant, and for certain records of the business trading activities to be filed annually at Companies House.

In practice, the ability to limit liability is severely restricted by the requirements of potential lenders. They often insist on personal guarantees from directors when small, new or troubled companies look for loans or credits. The personal guarantee usually takes the form of a charge on the family home. Since the Boland case, in 1980, unless a wife has specifically agreed to a charge on the house, by signing a Deed of Postponement, then no lender can take possession in the case of default.

A limited company can be formed by two shareholders, one of whom must be a director. A company secretary must also be appointed, who can be a shareholder, director, or an outside person such as an accountant.

The company can be bought 'off the shelf' from a registration agent, then adapted to suit your own purposes. This will involve changing the name, shareholders and articles of association. Alternatively, you can form your own company, using your solicitor or accountant.

Co-operative There is an alternative form of business for people whose primary concern is to create a democratic work environment, sharing profits and control. If you want to control or substantially influence your own destiny, and make as large a capital gain out of your life's work as possible, then a co-operative is not for you.

The membership of the co-operative is the legal body that control the business, and members must work in the business. Each member has one vote, and the co-operative must be registered under the Industrial and Provident Societies Act, 1965, with the Chief Registrar of Friendly Societies.

Forms of business: pros and cons	Advantages	Disadvantages
Form		
Sole trader	Start trading immediately; Minimum formalities; No set-up costs; No audit fees; No public disclosure of trading information; Pay Schedule 'D' Tax; Profits or losses in one trade can be set off against profits or losses in any other area. Past PAYE can be clawed back to help with trading losses.	Unlimited personal liability for trading debts; No access to equity capital; Low status public image; When you die, so does the business.
Partnership	No audit required, though your partner may insist on one; No public disclosure of trading information; Pay Schedule 'D' tax.	Unlimited personal liability for your own and your partners' trading debts (except sleeping partners); Partnership contracts can be complex and costly to prepare. Limited access to equity capital; Death of a partner usually causes partnership to be dissolved.
Limited company	Shareholders' liabilities restricted to nominal value of shares; It is possible to raise equity capital; High status public image; If income is substantial, corporation tax for small business is lower than equivalent income-tax rate; The business has a life of its own and continues with or without the founder.	Directors are on PAYE; Audit required; Trading information must be disclosed; Suppliers, landlords and banks will probably insist on personal guarantees from directors (except for government loan guarantee scheme); You cannot start trading until you have a certificate of incorporation.

Useful Organisations and Publications

Accountancy bodies are listed, together with their services, on page 195.

Organisations

The Chief Registrar of Friendly Societies, 17 North Audley Street, London W1Y 2AP. (01 629 7001)

The Companies Registration Office, Crown Way, Maindy, Cardiff CF43. (0222 388588) and for Scotland: 102 George Street, Edinburgh 2. (031 225 5774). Both provide information and guidance on registering a limited company.

The Law Society, 113 Chancery Lane, London WC2. (01 242 1222) Their Legal Aid Department publishes a list in twenty-eight separate booklets which give the name, address and telephone number of solicitors in each area, indicating their area(s) of specialisation. For example, it is possible to see if they have experience in consumer law, landlord–tenant problems, employment and industrial relations or business problems generally, including tax and insolvency. This book is available only at your local library or Citizens' Advice Bureau, and is solely concerned with solicitors willing to undertake legal aid work.

Alternatively the society will simply give you the names of some firms of solicitors in your area.

Publication

How to Form a Private Company, by Alec Just, 19th Edition published by Jordans, Jordan House, 47 Brunswick Place, N1 (01 253 3030) £3.00.

THE BUSINESS NAME

The main consideration in choosing a business name is its commercial usefulness. You want one that will let people know as much about your business, its products and services as possible. Since 26 February 1982, when the provisions of the Companies Act, 1981, came into effect, there have been some new rules that could influence your choice of name.

Firstly, anyone wanting to use a 'controlled' name will have to get permission. There are some eighty or ninety controlled names that include words such as 'International', 'Bank' and 'Royal'. This is simply to prevent a business implying that it is something that it is not.

Secondly, all businesses that intend to trade under names other than those of their owner(s) must state who does own the business and how the owner can be contacted. So, if you are a sole trader or partnership and you only use surnames with or without forenames or initials, you are not affected. Companies are also not affected if they simply use their full corporate name.

If any name other than the 'true' name is to be used, then you must disclose the name of the owner(s) and an address in the UK to which business documents can be sent. This information has to be shown on all business letters, on orders for goods and services, invoices and receipts, and statements and demands for business debts. Also, a copy has to be displayed prominently on all business premises. The purpose of the Act is simply to make it easier to 'see' who you are doing business with.

Useful Organisations and Publications

Department of Trade, Guidance Notes Section, 55 City Road, London EC1Y 1BB produce two useful free publications, notes for guidance on *Disclosure of Business Ownership* and *Control of Business Names.*

Jordan's Business Information Service, Jordan House, Brunswick Place, London N1 6EE. (01 253 3030) Under the 1982 Company Rules, the onus is on you to object within twelve months to someone else using your business name. For around £25 per annum, Jordans will alert you if anyone tries to register a company using your trading name.

PROTECTING YOUR IDEAS

Patent law can give you temporary protection for technological inventions. The registration of a design can protect the appearance or shape of a commercial product; copyright protects literary, artistic or musical creations and, more recently, computer programmes; trade marks protect symbols, logos and pictures.

The period of the protection which these laws can give vary from five years, for the initial registration of the design, to fifty years after your death, for the copyright on an 'artistic' work. The level and scope of protection varies considerably, and is in the process of change. A flurry of activity in the late seventies set UK patent law on a course to harmonise it with EEC law. So, for example, it is now possible with a single patent application made in the UK to secure a whole series of protections throughout Europe. The Patent Co-operation Treaty will eventually extend that protection to the USA, USSR and Japan.

In practice, however, defending 'intellectual' property is an expensive and complex process for a new or small business.

Patent Protection This covers inventions which are 'truly' novel and are capable of industrial application. Scientific or mathematical theories and mental processes are included in the long lists of unpatentable items. Ideas that may encourage offensive, immoral or anti-social behaviour are also excluded.

Obviously, it is important to establish first whether or not your idea is really new. With 20 million or so registered patents it is possible that the idea belongs to someone else, even if it is not being used. A search of patents granted and applied for will give you some idea of the activity in your area of interest. This can be done by studying abstracts of published specifications. These are classified under 400 main headings, with 6,000 'catch' words to guide you. You can get details of the classification key free of charge from the Patent Office. You can then either subscribe to a weekly service that selects and supplies patent specifications under the classification that interests you, or you can carry out a search yourself at the Science Reference Library. Otherwise, you could get a Patent Agent both to investigate your claim and look after your interests.

If the patent is good, then you may be able to sell a 'licence' to manufacture under that patent, or even sell the patent rights. This may not be as profitable as setting up a business to exploit the patent yourself, but that task may be beyond your means anyway. It would be unwise to discuss your patent in any detail with any other person until you have either registered it or got him to sign a non-disclosure agreement. This will prevent him from making use of your idea, if you do not reach an agreement with him.

Registering Designs The shape, design or decorative features of a commercial product may be protectable by registering the design. The laws exclude any shape or appearance which is dictated solely by the production function. Thus, in order to be registerable, a design must be new or original, never published before or, if already known, never applied to the type of product you have in mind.

Unlike patent searches, which you can do yourself, as a design application you have to entrust this work to the officials at the Design Registry.

Copyright The copyright laws protect you from the unlicensed copying of 'original' creative works. Some skill and judgement are required to qualify a work for protection, but the 'originality' itself may be of quite a low order.

The categories protected by copyright include literary works (including not just the obvious, but such items as rules for games, catalogues, advertising copy, etc); dramatic and musical works; artistic works, including maps, graphs, photographs; films, TVs and radio programmes, records, tapes and so on.

While the work remains unpublished no legal steps need be taken to protect it. Once it is published, all you need do is to add a copyright line to each copy of the work. This *must* take the form © BAR-

BARA UPCHURCH 1983. If you want to record the date on which a work was completed this can be registered for a fee with The Registrar, Stationers Hall. It is a fairly unusual thing to do, only important if you expect an action for infringement.

It is generally illegal to reproduce copyright work, but less than a substantial part may be used without infringement. The use of the word 'substantial' is more likely to mean important rather than large, though it is up to the courts to interpret.

Trade Marks A trade mark is a symbol by which the goods of a particular manufacturer, merchant or trader can be identified by customers. This can take the form of a word, a signature, a monogram, a picture or logo – or any combination of these. If you have been using an unregistered trade mark so extensively that it is clearly associated in your customers' minds with your brand or product, then you may have acquired a 'reputation' in that mark, which gives you rights under common law.

Otherwise the process of registration is similar to that of patents. First, a search must be carried out either in person or having a Trade Mark Agent to act for you. Then, using forms from the Trade Marks Registry, you can apply for registration. Once your application has been accepted by the registry it is advertised in a weekly journal, *The Trade Marks Journal*. If this raises no objections the mark is officially registered. Once your mark is registered you have the right to bring an 'infringement' action if anyone else uses your trade mark. The courts also recognise that a trade mark acts as a protection to your customers. When they ask for a branded product by its trade mark, they can be confident of getting your product and not a 'pirate' product.

Organisations

The British Technology Group, PO Box 236, Kingsgate House, 66–74 Victoria Street, London SW1E 6SL. (01 828 3400; Publicity Dept., 01 730 9600) They can help you with the exploitation and development of your invention. They have financial, technological and commercial resources and expertise.

The Chartered Institute of Patent Agents, Staple Inn Buildings, London WC1V 7PZ. (01 405 9450) They can put you in contact with a Patent Agent in your area, and advise on the subject generally.

The Design Council, 28 Haymarket, London SW1 4DG. (01 839 8000)

The Design Registry, Room 1124A, 11th Floor, State House, High Holborn, London WC1R 4TP. *For textiles:* **The Design Registry,** Baskerville House, Browncross Street, New Bailey Street, Salford M3 5FU.

Free pamphlet from either office of the Design Registry, *Protection of Industrial Designs*, June 1981, 17 pages. (There are Design Agents, but no register as such, although either a Patent Agent or a Trade Mark Agent will be able to act for you.)

The Institute of Inventors, 19 Fosse Way, London W13. (01 988 3450)

The Institute of Patentees and Inventors, Staple Inn Buildings, 335 High Holborn, London WC1V 7PZ. (01 242 7812) The institute looks after the interest of patent holders and inventors. They can provide useful advice and guidance on almost every aspect of 'intellectual' property. (More information on this society on page 107).

The Institute of Trade Mark Agents, 69 Cannon Street, London EC4N 5AB. (01 248 4444) The institute can put you in contact with a trade mark agent in your area, and advise on the subject generally.

The Patent Office, 25 Southampton Buildings, London WC1A 1AY. (01 405 8721) Open to the public 10.00–16.00, Monday–Friday. They produce a free pamphlet, *Applying for a Patent*, which was revised in August 1981. Its twenty-three pages and will set you on the right track. They also publish the weekly *Official Journal*. Another publication from the same source is *Patents, a Source of Technical Information*, which provides more details on how to investigate patents both current and applied for.

The Registrar, Stationers Hall, London, EC4M 7DD. (01 248 9279) Accepts and advises on the registration of copyrights.

The Register of Trademarks, 23 Southampton Building, London WC1A 1AY. Accepts and advises on the registration of trade marks. Free pamphlet, *Applying for a Trademark*, April 1980, twenty-four pages.

The Science Reference Library, 25 Southampton Buildings, London WC2A 1AW. The Library houses all patent details, and is open from 9.30 to 20.00, Monday to Friday, and on Saturday from 10.00 to 13.00. More details of this library are given in the section on specialist libraries.

Publications

Patents, Trade Marks, Copyright & Industrial Designs, by T. A. Blanco White and Robin Jacob, in the Concise College Texts Series, published by Sweet and Maxwell, 11 New Fetter Lane, London EC4 (01 583 9855), price £3.95.

A Practical Introduction to Copyright, by Gavin McFarlane, January 1982, published by McGraw-Hill, 34 Dover Street, London, W1X 3RA (01 493 1451), price £14.95. In July 1981 the UK Government published a Green Paper on copyright for public discussion. It is based on the recommendations of the Copyright Committee of 1977, and, if it is finally accepted, radical changes in the law are likely. This book represents, clearly and simply, the effect of today's laws and the probable effect of the new provisions. The existing Copyright Act of 1956 with all its later amendments, plus the salient points of the Green Paper, are included.

PREMISES

Buying or leasing a business premises entails a number of important and often complex laws affecting your decisions. To some extent these laws go beyond the scope of the physical premises, into areas such as opening hours and health and safety.

Planning Permission An important first step is to make sure that the premises you have in mind can be used for what you want to do. There are nearly a score of different 'use classes', and each property should have a certificate showing which has been approved. The classes include retail, offices, light industrial, general industrial, warehousing and various special classes.

Certain changes of class do not need planning permission – for example from general industrial to light industrial. Also, changes of use within a class – say, from one type of shop to another – may not need planning permission.

In November 1980 a circular was issued to local authorities by the Department of the Environment. The circular stated, amongst other things that if a business premises was put to a 'non-conforming' use, that was not in itself sufficient reason for taking enforcement action or refusing planning permission. Permission should only be refused where the business would cause a nuisance or a safety or health hazard.

Once you have taken on a premises, then the responsibilities for 'conforming' fall on your shoulders, so take advice.

Building Regulations Even if you have planning permission, you will still have to conform to building regulations. These apply to the materials, structure and building methods used, in either making or altering the premises. So if you plan any alterations you may need a specific approval.

The Lease Before taking on a lease, look carefully at the factors below.

Restrictions If you are taking on a leasehold property, then you must find out if there are any restrictions in the lease on the use of the property. Often shop leases have restrictions protecting neighbouring businesses. The lease will often stipulate that the landlords cannot 'unreasonably' withhold consent to a change in use. He may, however, insist on the premises being returned in its original shape before you leave.

Repairs Most leases require the tennant to take on either internal repairing liability or full repairing leases. Resist the latter if at all possible, particularly if the property is old. If you have to accept a full repairing lease, then it is *essential* to get a Schedule of Condition. This is an accurate record of the condition of the premises when you take it over. It is carried out by your own and the landlord's surveyor. It is one expense you may be tempted to forgo – don't.

Rent Reviews However long (or short) your lease is, it is likely that a rent review clause allowing rent reviews every three to seven years will be included. Look very carefully at the formulas used to calculate future rents.

Security of Tenure The Landlord and Tenant Act, 1954, protects occupiers of business premises. When your lease ends you can stay on at the same rent until the steps laid down in the Act are taken. These steps are fairly precise, and you would be well advised to read the Act and take legal advice.

You will get plenty of warning, as the landlord must give you six months' notice in writing, even if you pay rent weekly. The landlord cannot just ask you to leave. There are a number of statutory grounds for re-possession. The two main types of grounds are, Firstly, that you are an unsatisfactory tenant, an allegation you can put to the test in court; or secondly, that the landlord wants the premises for other purposes. In that case you must be offered alternative suitable premises. These are obviously matters for negotiation, and you should take advice as soon as possible.

Health and Safety at Work Whatever legal form your business takes (if you are a sole trader for instance, or a limited company) you will be responsible for the working conditions of all your premises. Your responsibility extends to people who work on those premises, to visitors and to the public. If you have more than five employees, you will have to prepare a statement of policy on health, and let everyone who is working for you know what that policy is. You may also be required to keep records of such events as the testing of fire alarms and accidents.

The main laws concerned are the Health and Safety at Work Act (1974), the Offices, Shops and Railway Premises Act (1963), and the Factories Act (1961). Employers' liability is based on the common law, and your responsibilities can be extensive. A catalogue listing more than 2,000 relevant publications covering health and safety legislation is available from HMSO.

The Acts cover, among other matters, fire precautions and certificates; general cleanliness and hygiene; means of access and escape; machine and equipment safety; work-space; temperature; noise; welfare; catering arrangements; security of employees' property; toilet and washing facilities; protective clothing; the appointment of safety representatives and committees; and minimum insurance cover.

Special trades Restaurants and all places serving food, hotels, pubs, off-licences, employment agencies, nursing agencies, pet shops and kennels, mini cabs, taxis, betting shops, auction sale rooms, cinemas and hair-dressers are among the special trades that have separate additional regulations or licensing requirements.

Your local authority Planning Department will be able to advise you of the regulations that apply specifically to your trade. It would be as well to confirm the position whatever you planned to do. They can also tell you if any local by-laws are in force which could affect you.

Opening Hours Sunday trading and opening hours may be the subject of local restrictions. Once again, your local authority Planning Department will be able to advise you whether or not special local rules apply.

Advertising Signs There are some restrictions on the size and form that the name or advertising hoarding of your premises can take. A look around the neighbourhood will give you an idea of what is acceptable. If in doubt, or if you are going to spend a lot of money, take advice.

Organisations

The Building Centre, 26 Store Street, London WC1E 7BT1. (01 637 1022) This has the most extensive library and information service on the whole building field, including building regulations and sources of professional advice. Their free information service (01 637 8361) will provide answers to almost any building problem. Regional centres are at the addresses below:

The Building Centre, Stonebridge House, Colston Avenue, The Centre, Bristol BS1 4TW. (0272 22953)

Northern Counties Building Information Centre, c/o NFBTE, Green Lane, Durham DH1 3JI. (0385 62611)

The Building Centre, 113/115 Portland Street, Manchester M1 6FB. (061 236 9802)

The Building Centre, 15/16 Trumpington Street, Cambridge CB2 1QD. (0223 59625)

The Building Centre, 3/4 Claremont Terrace, Glasgow G3 7PF. (041 332 7399)

The Building Centre, Grosvenor House, 18/30 Cumberland Place, Southampton sq1 2bd. (0703 27350)

The Building Research Establishment, Bucknalls Lane, Watford wd2 7jr; or Scottish Laboratory, Kelvin Road, Glasgow; or Birmingham Engineering and Building Centre, Broad Street, Birmingham b1 2db.

The Environmental Health Department will be able to advise you on particular problems related to using premises for serving or producing food or drink.

Health and Safety Executive, 1 Long Lane, London se1 4pg. (01 407 8911) Apart from supplying pamphlets and reference on the various regulations, they can put you in contact with the nearest of their twenty-one area office information services. In each of these offices there are groups of Inspectors specialising in the specific local industries and their problems.

Local authorities Each has a Planning Department, which can give information and opinions on planning applications and other matters relating to your premises; a Building Control Department, covering building regulations; an Environmental Health Department, covering health and safety at work; and an Industrial Liaison Department, giving general advice to encourage industrial development.

Royal Town Planning Institute, 26 Portland Place, London w1n 4be. (01 636 9107) A contentious or complex planning application may need the services of a planning consultant – perhaps from this institute. They produce a list of consultant firms throughout the UK. Otherwise, 'local knowledge' is the best source of a good surveyor or an architect who will be able to manage most planning and building regulation matters for you.

Publications

Land Law, by W. Swinfen Green and N. Henderson, in the Concise College Text series, published by Sweet and Maxwell, 11 New Fetter Lane, London ec4 (01583 9855), price £3.95.

Selwyn's Law of Health and Safety at Work, Butterworths, 88 Kingsway, London, wc2 (01 405 6900), price £7.95.

Planning Directory and Development Guide. The directory contains information on planning in central government in the UK, planning consultants, and organisations concerned with or related to the planning process. The information on local government, which forms the bulk of the book, includes names and addresses of chief officers in charge of planning, the names and functions of key planning staff and a summary of the development opportunities existing in each authority area, plus a list of publications relating to planning in the area. Available from Ambit Publications Ltd, 6A College Green, Glos. GL1 2LY.

TRADING LAWS

Once you start trading, whatever the legal form of your business, you will have certain obligations to your customers. These are contained in a number of legal acts.

Sale of Goods Act, 1979 This Act states that the seller has three obligations. Firstly, the goods sold must be of merchantable quality – that is, reasonably fit for their normal purpose. Secondly, those goods must also be fit for any particular purpose made known to the seller. This makes you responsible for your advice, if, for example your customer asks you whether or not a product will perform a particular job. Thirdly, the goods sold must be as described. This would include the colour or size of the goods concerned.

The Food and Drugs Act, 1955 This Act makes it a criminal offence to sell unfit food; to describe food falsely; or to mislead people about its nature, substance or quality. This regulation covers food wherever it is sold, manufactured, packed, processed or stored for sale.

Prices Act, 1974 The Prices Act enables the Government to require prices to be displayed and to control how they are displayed. This requires restaurants, pubs, cafe and petrol stations to display their prices.

Trade Description Acts, 1968 and 1972 The Acts make it a criminal offence for a trader to describe his goods falsely. These acts cover such areas as declared car mileage on second-hand cars and statement of the country of manufacture on jeans.

Unsolicited Goods and Services Act, 1971 The Act makes it an offence to send goods without a customer's order, in the hope that they will then buy them.

Weights and Measures Acts, 1963 and 1979 The Acts make it an offence not to mark the quantity (weight, volume or, in a few cases, the number) on the containers of most packaged grocery items and many other items.

Unfair Contract Terms Act, 1977 The Act prevents firms from escaping their responsibilities by using 'exclusion clauses' or disclaimers, such as statements saying 'articles left at owners' risk'. The onus is on the trader to prove that his exclusions are fair and reasonable in the circumstances. The notice itself is not enough.

Organisations

Environmental Health Departments of the local authority will be able to provide advice on all matters to do with food, drink and hygiene.

Office of Fair Trading, Breams Building, London EC4. The office provides useful booklets on most aspects of trading law from the consumer's point of view. Their booklet *Fair Deal* provides a very good, brief summary of the main laws affecting traders.

The Small Claims Court is a useful, low-cost way to collect money owed to you. Small debts of up to around £500 can be sued for relatively inexpensively, and with the minimum of formalities. Form EX50 will explain the process, and is available from your local County Court.

Trading Standards Department of the local authority can also give you advice on acceptable trading behaviour.

Publications

Hotel and Catering Law, by Davis Field, in the Concise College Texts series, published by Sweet & Maxwell, price £3.95.

How to Collect the Money That Is Owed to You, by Mel Lewis, published by McGraw-Hill, 34 Dover Street, London W1X 3RA (01 493 1451) April 1982, price £8.95. Written for managers in small- to medium-sized businesses, it contains a wealth of ideas for getting payment. It also has a guide to credit insurance and factoring, examples of contracts invoiced and collection letters, lists of useful organisations and addresses and a guide to telephone collection techniques.

Law for the Small Business, by Pat Clayton, published by Kogan Page, 120 Pentonville Road, London N1. Price £4.95. Explains all the relevant acts and their likely effect on traders.

Legal Aspects of Marketing, by John Livermore, third edition 1981, published by William Heinemann Ltd, 10 Upper Grosvenor Street, London W1X 9PA. Price £8.95.

Managing Your Business, a Complete Guide, published by Eaglemoss Publications, 87 Elysan Street, London SW3 (01 581 1371) is a loose-leaf and regularly up-dated publication, covering most aspects of running a business. It has useful sections on law related to sale of products and services.

Product Liability, by Davis, Hutchins and Madge, published by William Heinemann Ltd, 10 Upper Grosvenor Street, London W1X 9PA. Price £11.50.

Sale of Goods and Consumer Credit, by A. P. Dobson, in the Concise College Texts series, published by Sweet and Maxwell, 11 New Fetter Lane, London EC4 (01 583 9855) price £3.95.

EMPLOYING PEOPLE

Apart from the problems of finding the right people to work in your business, and making sure that the conditions under which they will have to work are satisfactory, you may have other responsibilities. Examples are given below.

Terms of Employment Within thirteen weeks of starting to work for you, you have to give people a written set of terms of employment. These terms will cover pay, holidays, sick pay and overtime commitments and pay.

Notice of Lay-offs. Once an employee has worked for you for over four weeks, they are entitled to at least one week's notice of dismissal. They are also entitled to guaranteed pay up to five days in any three months if you decide to either lay them off or to put them on short time.

Discrimination You cannot discriminate against anyone on colour or racial grounds. The same protection applies to married people. If you employ five people, including part-timers, then you cannot discriminate against them or against any applicant for a job, on the grounds of their sex. There are further laws and protections covering, amongst others, considerations, pregnancy, disabled people, minimum wages, union recognition, discipline and wrongful dismissal.

You may find it useful to join an organisation such as the Institute of Personnel Management or the Industrial Society, who can give you timely and cost-effective advice in this field. Such organisations keep absolutely up to date with all the many changes in this field of legislation, a task beyond the resources of most small firms with other, more pressing problems.

Useful Organisations

Advisory, Conciliation and Arbitration Service (ACAS), Page Street, London SW1. (01 211 3000). Although you mainly hear of ACAS in big public disputes between unions and their management, a large part of their work is concerned with preventing disputes and dispensing information. Nearly a quarter of their 12,500 advisory visits in 1981 were to firms with fewer than fifty employees.

They offer advice on recruitment and selection, payment systems and incentive schemes, manpower planning, communications and consultations, collective bargaining and so on.

They also produce free advisory booklets on job evaluation, introduction to payment systems, personnel records, labour turn-over, absence, recruitment and selection and introduction of new employees. Their Regional Offices are at:

Northern Region, Westgate House, Westgate Road, Newcastle upon Tyne NE1 1TJ. (0632 612191) Cumbria, Tyne and Wear, Cleveland, Northumberland and Durham.

Yorkshire and Humberside Region, Commerce House, St Alban's Place, Leeds LS2 8HH. (0532 431371) North Yorkshire, South Yorkshire, Humberside and West Yorkshire.

London Region, Clifton House, 83–117 Euston Road, London NW1 2RB. (01 388 5100)

South-east Region, Clifton House, 83–117 Euston Road, London NW1 2RB. (01 388 5100) Cambridgeshire, Norfolk, Suffolk, Oxfordshire, Buckinghamshire, Bedfordshire, Hertfordshire, Essex, Berkshire, Surrey, Kent, Hampshire (except Ringwood), Isle of Wight, East Sussex, West Sussex.

South-west Region, 16 Park Place, Clifton, Bristol BS8 1JP. (0272 211921) Gloucestershire, Avon, Wiltshire, Cornwall, Devon, Somerset, Dorset, Ringwood.

Midlands Region, Alpha Tower, Suffolk Street, Queensway, Birmingham B1 1TZ. (021 643 9911) Northamptonshire (except Corby), Shropshire, Staffordshire (except Burton-on-Trent), West Midlands, Hereford and Worcester, Warwickshire.

North-west Region, Boulton House, 17–21 Chorlton Street, Manchester M1 3HY. (061 228 3222) Lancashire, Cheshire, High Peak District of Derbyshire, Greater Manchester.

Midlands Region, Nottingham office, 66–72 Houndsgate, Nottingham NG1 6BA. (0602 415450) Derbyshire (except High Peak District), Nottinghamshire, Leicestershire, Corby, Lincolnshire, Burton-on-Trent.

Merseyside Office, 27 Leece Street, Liverpool L1 2TS. (051 708 6626)

Scotland, Franborough House, 123–157 Bothwell Street, Glasgow G2 7JR. (041 204 2677)

Wales, Phase 1, Ty-Glas Road, Llanishen, Cardiff CF4 5PH. (0222 762636)

Employees' Protection Insurance Services Ltd, 30 High Street, Sutton, Surrey SM1 1NF. (01 661 1491) They also undertake commercial legal proceedings insurance, provide legal fees for the protection of patents, copyright, registered designs and trade marks, and in respect of 'passing off' actions.

Industrial Participation Association, 78 Buckingham Gate, London SW1E 6PQ. (01 222 0351) The association is concerned with bringing all parties in industry together in a common effort to promote employee participation in a practical and realistic way.

The Industrial Society, Peter Runge House, 3 Carlton House Terrace, London SW1Y 5DG. (01 839 4300) The society campaigns for the involvement of people at work and argues that increased involvement means greater efficiency and productivity.

Annual membership costs £90.00 for companies with up to 250

employees, and this gives access to an extensive range of services and publications.

Their Information and Personnel Advisory Services department on ext. 249/237 will answer enquiries from members on any subject in the field of personnel management and industrial relations. Most enquiries are dealt with the same day, though complicated questions that have to be referred to their legal advisers or the medical advisory panel may take about ten days. Of particular interest to small business is the Personnel Advisory Service, which can, in effect, provide you with all the services of a professional personnel manager, from recruitment to redundancy. The fees for this service are about £1,800 per annum.

Institute of Personnel Management, IPM House, Camp Road, Wimbledon SW19 4UW. (01 946 9100) The institute has 20,000 individual members, and has extended its service to businesses through its Company Service Plan. The cost of membership for a company employing up to seventy-five people would be £69.00 per annum, an entrance fee of £17.25, plus VAT. This would give access to the institute's library, publications, conferences and seminars, and, more importantly, it would allow use of the Information and Advisory Service. This service is staffed by a small team of multi-disciplined specialists, including a legal adviser, who is a barrister at law. They can answer or find answers to, most problems in this field.

Enquiries can be made by letter, telephone or a personal visit between 09.15 and 17.00 daily, Monday to Friday.

Interestingly enough, of the 800 or so enquiries they handle each month, pay and conditions of employment account for half, followed by employment law, employee relations and then training.

Job Centres As well as providing you with employees, your local Job Centre can also advise you on most aspects of employment law, or at any rate introduce you to other local organisations which can help.

See also National Federation of Self Employed and Small Business; and Alliance of Small Firms and Self Employed People (pages 59, 62).

Publications

An A–Z of Employment and Safety Law, by Peter Chandler, covers all aspects of current employment and health safety law. Published by Kogan Page Ltd, 120 Pentonville Road, London N1, price £16.95 (528 pages, hardback).

Contract, by F. R. Davies, in the Concise College Texts series, published by Sweet and Maxwell, 11 New Fetter Lane, London EC4 (01 583 9855) price £3.95.

Employing People, Guidance for Those Setting Up in Business for the

First Time, is a free booklet from the Department of Industry, Small Firms Service. Your local office can be reached on Freephone 2444.

Labour Law, by C. D. Drake, published in the Concise College Texts series by Sweet and Maxwell, 11 New Fetter Lane, London EC4 (01 583 9855) price £3.95. It is a sort of A-level crammer which covers all the ground and case law illustrations.

The Law on Unfair Dismissal, Guidance for Small Firms, by Joan Henderson. Free from Job Centres, Employment Offices, Unemployment Benefit Offices and Department of Industry Small Firms Centres.

INSURANCE

Insurance forms a guarantee against loss. You must weigh up to what extent your business assets are exposed to risk and what effect such events could have on the business if they occurred. Insurance is an overhead, producing no benefit until a calamity occurs. It is therefore a commercial decision as to how much to carry, and it is a temptation to minimise cover. You must carry some cover, either by employment law, or as an obligation imposed by a mortgager.

You will have to establish your needs by discussing your business plans with an insurance broker. Make sure you know exactly what insurance you are buying; and, as insurance is a competitive business, get at least three quotations before making up your mind.

Employer's Liability You must carry at least £2 million cover to meet your legal liabilities for death or bodily injury incurred by any employee during the course of business. In practice, this cover is usually unlimited, with the premiums directly related to your wage bill.

Personal Accident Employer's liability only covers those accidents in which the employer is held to be legally responsible. You may feel a moral responsibility to extend that cover to anyone carrying out an especially hazardous task. You may also have to cover your own financial security, particularly if the business depends on your being fit.

Public Liability This protects employers against legal liability for death or injury to a third party on their property. These events can occur through defects in your premises, negligent acts by your employees or from liabilities arising from the product that you market.

Professional Liability Solicitors, accountants and management and computer consultants are obvious examples. Anyone involved in giving professional advice should consider their possible liability arising from wrongful advice and negligence to their client.

Business Premises, Plant and Equipment obviously need cover. There are, however, a number of ways of covering them. 'Reinstatement' provides for full replacement cost, whilst 'indemnity' meets only the current market value of your asset, which means taking depreciation off first. There are other things to consider too. Removal of debris, architect's fee, employees' effects and (potentially the most expensive of all) local authorities sometimes insist that replacement buildings must meet much higher standards than the ones they replace.

Stock From raw materials through to finished goods stock is as exposed as your buildings and plant in the event of fire or another hazard.

Consequential Loss Meeting the replacement costs of buildings, plant, equipment and stock will not compensate you for the loss of business and profit arising out of a fire or other disaster. Your overheads, employees' wages, etc., may have to continue during the period of interruption. You may incur expenses such as getting subcontracted work done.

Insurance for consequential loss is intended to restore your business's finance to the position it was in if the interruption had not occurred.

Goods in Transit Until your goods reach your customer and he accepts them, they are still at your risk. You may need to protect yourself from loss or damage in transit.

Commercial Vehicle Policy Although you may have adequate private use cover for your present vehicle, this is unlikely to be satisfactory once you start to use the vehicle for business purposes. That and any other vehicles used in the business should be covered by a commercial use policy.

Fidelity Guarantee and Other Thefts Once in business you can expect threats from within and without. A Fidelity Guarantee can be taken to protect you from fraud or dishonesty on the part of key employees. Normal theft cover can be taken to protect your business premises and its contents.

Useful Organisations

These organisations will be able to put you in contact with either a broker or an insurance company that can help you to assess your needs and level of cover.

British Insurance Association, Aldermary House, Queen Street, London EC4P 4JD. (01 248 4477)

British Insurance Brokers Association, 130 Fenchurch Street, London EC3M 5DJ. (01 623 9043)

Insurance Brokers Registration Council, 15 St Helens Place, London EC3A 6DS. (01 588 4387)

NATIONAL TAX, INSURANCE, PAYE, VAT AND PENSIONS

This is one field where good professional advice at the outset will more than pay for itself. Although considerable publicity is given to the 'Black Economy', there are also many people paying more tax than they need. However, you will get the best out of your professional adviser if you understand the basics yourself.

Tax The tax that you have to pay will depend on the legal form of the business you decide on. As a sole trader or partner you will pay tax under Schedule 'D', Case I or II. If you choose a limited company, then the company will pay corporation tax and the directors will be on Schedule 'E', under the PAYE scheme. The difference in net tax paid by a sole trader or a company can be very significant, and there are many other factors to take into account. For example, a sole trader can offset any trading losses against other income. Company losses are locked into the company. In the event of losses, a sole trader can even claw back past taxes paid – for example from PAYE in his last job. A company cannot do this.

There is also a difference in when the tax is due. As the director of a company, you pay as you earn. A sole trader or partner can pay tax up to nearly two years after earning the income, depending on his accounting year. For new businesses there are still more factors to consider and some variations on the normal rules.

This is not an area in which to take uninformed guesses.

National Insurance Contributions Once again, the legal form of your business will determine what you pay. A sole trader or partner is self-employed and pays contributions in class 2, which is a weekly sum, and in class 4, based on annual profits. A company director pays as an employee, and his company pays as an employer. So it is quite possible for a small company to pay up to four times the National Insurance contributions that it would have paid, had it been operated as a sole trader or partnership.

As a rule of thumb, if you do not expect to make more than £10,000 per annum *profit*, you would be better off not trading as a company. But the level of contributions are not the only consideration. For example, the 'employee' director has better benefits out of the National Insurance than the 'self-employed' sole trader.

Pay-as-You-Earn (PAYE) Either as an 'employee' director, or in any other form of enterprise employing people, you will be responsible for maintaining the PAYE system. This will involve you in deducting the appropriate tax from your employees' pay and sending it to the Collector of Taxes. If you do not, then you; and not the employee, will be liable for the uncollected tax.

VAT (Value Added Tax) whatever the legal form of your business, if your turn-over exceeds £6,000 in any calendar quarter, or if it exceeds £17,000 in the last four calendar quarters, then you must register for VAT. This has to be done by notifying your local VAT office, within twenty-one days of the end of the quarter in question. VAT is normally charged at 15 per cent, but some areas are zero-rated and some are exempt. There are also some special rules on exports and·imports. Before you reach this level of turn-over you would be prudent to become better informed.

Pensions Once you are working for yourself, you will have to make your own pension provision (and perhaps provision, for those working for you). Fortunately for people in profitable self-employment, there are now a large number of highly tax-efficient pension schemes. By selecting the right scheme you can get tax relief at your highest income-tax rate, and so get the Inland Revenue to contribute up to three-quarters of your pension. In addition, it is possible eventually to receive the benefit from the pension plan partly as a lump sum free of all capital-gains tax on the profits made on your contributions over the years; and partly as a pension which will be treated as earned income and so not be subject to the investment income surcharge.

It is a complex but potentially very rewarding investment, with a considerable difference in performance by the different pension plans. For example, over the period 1970–1980, the best-performing pension 'annuity' turned £500 per annum into an accumulated cash sum of £9,480 and the worst only £5,309.

You can pay up to 17½ per cent* of your net earnings into an approved pension scheme, so once again good professional advice is a must.

*This has been increased to 20 per cent for those born between 1916 and 1933, and there are also small increases for those born between 1912 and 1915.

Organisations

Association of Consulting Actuaries, 7 Rolls Building, Fetter Lane, London EC4A 1NL (01 831 7130)

Company Pensions Information Centre, 7 Old Park Lane, London W1Y 3LJ. (01 408 1933/4)

Professional Advisers see page 195 for accountants and page 220 for insurance.

Society of Pension Consultants, Ludgate House, Ludgate Circus, London EC4A 2AB. (01 353 1688)

Trade and Professional Organisations, including those independent business associations given in section 1, can often point you towards help in this field.

Publications

Business Start-Up-Package, from the Alliance of Small Firms, 42 Vine Road, East Molesey, Surrey KT8 9LF. (01 979 2293) Price, £2.00. Book II in this three-part series is on tax and National Insurance, twelve pages. Gives you a few useful clues. The others cover law generally and bookkeeping and banking. They also run an information and consultancy reference service for members.
See also National Federation of Self Employed and Small Business, which also runs an information service in this field (page 62).

Check Your Tax, by J. D. Finnigan, FCA and G. M. Kitchen, FCA, published by W. Foulsham & Co, price 95p. Covers personal tax well, but has only a small section on the self-employed and really little else of direct use to a businessman.

Employer's Guide to PAYE, leaflet P7.

Employer's Guide to National Insurance Contributions, leaflet NP15.

Grundy's Tax Havens, edited by Milton Grundy, The Bodley Head Ltd, 9 Bow Street, London W1X 3RA (01 493 1451) London. Gives details on a score of tax havens from the Bahamas to Switzerland.

Guide to Running a Small Business, The Guardian Book, edited by Clive Woodcock, published by Kogan Page Ltd, 120 Pentonville Road, London N1. Chapter 7 has nearly fifty pages of very useful advice in the taxation field. Price £4.25.

A Guide to The Taxation of Companies, by Mavis Moullin and John Sergent, published by McGraw-Hill, 34 Dover Street, London W1X 3RA (01 493 1451). Latest edition February 1982, price £35.00. A very authoritative and comprehensive book concentrating on the tax affairs of the 'average company'. Really for the professional, but if you are technically inclined it may help.

Hambro Tax Guide is produced each year and has extensive special sections on income from business and professions, partnerships, companies, VAT and a useful section on tax-saving hints. This should be available in most book shops, and is published by Macdonald General Books, Paulton House, 8 Shepherds Walk, London N1. Price £8.00.

Key to Corporation Tax, by Taxation Publishing Co Ltd, 98 Park Street, London W1Y 4BR. (01 629 7888) Price £6.00. Technical but thorough.

National Insurance Guide for the Self Employed, leaflet N1, from the Department of Health and Social Security.

Peat Marwick Mitchell & Co, 1 Puddle Dock, Blackfriars, London EC4V 3PD. Free tax booklet from the Librarian.

Pensions for the Self-Employed, by Mark Daniel, published by the *Sunday Telegraph.* First edition 1981, price £1.75. A very readable, comprehensive, yet concise guide to the subject.

Self-Employed Pensions, by the Financial Times Business Publishing Ltd, fifth edition March 1982. Price £12.50. This is the only source of detailed comparative information on pensions for the self-employed. The book analyses nearly 100 schemes, explains different types of pension plans available, and summarises the tax position. It also shows how each pension scheme has performed and makes projections on likely future results.

Starting in Business is a free pamphlet issued by the Board of Inland Revenue, and is available from your local tax inspectorate. It provides a simple and basic introduction to most aspects of tax, PAYE, National Insurance and VAT.

Tax and Insurance News Letter, published by Stonehart Publications, 13 Golden Square, London W1. Monthly, by subscription only; covers topical and highly relevant business tax and insurance problems. It will keep you up to date between budgets.

Tolley's Corporation Tax (annual) from Tolley Publishing Co., 102/104, High Street, Croydon, Surrey CRO 1ND. A very authoritative guide, concerned only with business taxation. Price £6.75.

Tolley's Value Added Tax from Tolley Publishing Co., (address as above). A new series, as yet unnamed and unpriced, coming out in spring 1983.

Value Added Tax, Scope and Coverage and *The General Guide* are two free publications from HM Customs & Excise local VAT offices.

101 Ways of Saving Tax, published by the *Sunday Telegraph*, price £2.50. Only thirty-four apply directly to a business, but they are very readable and clear guidelines. This is no substitute for Hambro's or Tolley's.

'Which' Tax Saving Guide Produced each year, gives a very good analysis of personal tax. The 1982 edition had four pages on the self-employed, which provides an insight into the subject. It only has a couple of paragraphs on partnerships and no specific coverage of corporation tax.

TRAINING FOR BUSINESS

There are now many opportunities for education and training, at every level, in the business and management field. No formal academic qualifications are required for most of the courses and costs are generally modest. In certain cases, those taking some of the longer courses may be eligible for grants.

COURSES AT COLLEGES

The types of course on offer can be divided into the following main categories:

Specialist Short Courses These are usually of one or two days' duration, and cost around £15 to £20 per day. They concentrate on giving an introduction on how to start your own business. The courses as well as providing lectures, give an opportunity for those who have recently started up in business to talk about their experiences. The demand for these courses is very high. Various estimates suggest that upwards of 5,000 people attended such courses in London alone during 1981/1982. This certainly forms the most cost-effective method of finding out very quickly a lot about what is going on in the 'new and small business world'.

This type of course is now run all over the country, with varying degrees of frequency. The London Enterprise Agency, Urbed and the Thames Enterprise Agency among them run about fifty courses each year in this field.

There are other types of one- or two-day courses. For example, after the Budget it is useful to find out how the latest changes will affect your business. A number of colleges hold conferences, with accountancy and taxation specialists, to meet this need. There are also short courses on exporting, marketing, employing people and business computer applications.

Provision on Existing Courses Many courses in colleges are modular or in discrete sections, with, say, a few weeks of one topic given in a fairly concentrated form. The subject may be marketing, finance, computer systems or business law. Although these courses are not aimed specifically at people running small businesses, the subject matter is certainly appropriate. Some colleges encourage people to join in parts of an existing full-time course, so in effect you join a class for a few weeks and learn the topic of particular interest to you.

Longer Courses Following on from the introductory, one- or two-day courses, a number of colleges run programmes lasting up to fifteen weeks. In the main, the longer courses are sponsored by the Manpower Services Commissions,* Training Services Division, through the TOPS scheme (training opportunities). Their courses, called either New Enterprise Programmes or Small Business Courses, are run at some twenty-five business schools in universities and polytechnics throughout the country.

Such courses very often consist of 3 to 4 weeks of classroom content, covering all the main aspects of running a small business. This is complemented by up to 10 further weeks, with business school staff working with the 'entrepreneurs' on the mechanics of starting up their own business. This can involve detailed work on preparing a business plan, raising finance, finding premises, applying for grants or aid, or marketing and market research. During this period the student entrepreneur can be given an allowance of around £36 per week, together with some subsistence allowance.

These schemes have been extremely successful, and the MSC is extending their provision.

There are other longer courses, on a part-time or linked weekend basis. The former may be one or two evenings each week over 10 weeks or so, covering a specific topic, such as bookkeeping or marketing.

The linked weekends tend to cover the whole field of starting up a business, with individual project work carried out between weekends. In this way participants can bring their problems back to the business school staff and get their advice and help.

Scholarships and Bursaries Mature students may be eligible for a place on a full-time (perhaps residential) course, for periods of a year or more.

Details of bursaries and courses to which they are applicable can be obtained from the Department of Education and Science (Awards 11), Honeypot Lane, Stanmore, Middx. HA7 1AZ, or the Welsh Office, Education Department, Ty Glas Road, Llanishen, Cardiff CF4 5PL.

Alternatively you could contact your nearest college and see what they have to offer. The situation is constantly changing, and many innovations in education for small business are being introduced.

Henley, the Management College, has just announced its first small business scholarships. They will be awarded for the college's

*Addresses at end of section.

major programmes in 1983: the senior course; the general management's course; and the master's degree course.

It is expected that at least three scholarships will be offered, which means that more than one may be awarded under each category. The value of the scholarships will vary, but each will be worth several thousand pounds. The senior course lasts one month, general management 10½ weeks and the master's 18 months, though this will not be on a full-time basis. Further information is available from Graham Milborrow, Programme Director, Greenlands, Henley-on-Thames, Oxon RG9 3AU. (049166 454)

Manpower Services Commission, Training Services Division

Head Office: 180 High Holborn, London WC1V 7AT. (01 836 5400)

Regional Offices
Scotland, 9 St Andrew Square, Edinburgh EH2 2QX. (031 225 8500)

Northern, Derwent House, Washington Centre, Washington New Town, Tyne & Wear NE38 7ST. (0632 466161)

Yorkshire and Humberside, Jubilee House, 33–41 Park Place, Leeds LS1 2RL (0532 446299)

North-west, Washington House, The Capital Centre, New Bailey Street, Manchester M3 5ER. (061 833 0251)

Midlands, Alpha Tower, Suffolk Street, Queensway, Birmingham B1 1TT. (021 632 4144)

Wales, 4th Floor, Companies House, Crown Way, Maindy, Cardiff CF4 3UT. (0222 388588)

South-east, Telford House, Hamilton Close, Basingstoke, Hants RG21 2UZ. (0256 29266)

South-west, 5th Floor, The Pithay, BS1 2NQ (0272 291071)

London, 180 High Holborn, London WC1V 7AT. (01 836 5400)

WHERE TO FIND A COURSE

The results of our 1982 survey of the small business education provisions are set out below. As well as showing the nature of the course run and the person to contact, you can see where advice, consultancy or relevant research may be found.

The British Institute of Management also run a major information advisory service on management education throughout the country. This includes information on starting up or running a small business. BIM, Management House, Parker Street, London WC2B 5PT. (01 405 3456)

Provision of Small Business Education

(Note: asterisk denotes regular courses; a dagger indicates that the course is held irregularly, is informal or is at the planning stage.)

	Specific short courses	Provision on existing courses	Longer courses	Advice, information and guidance given	Consultancy resources	Research activity
Acton Technical College, Dept. of Business and General Studies, Millhill Road, London W3 8UX. (01 993 2344) Contact: B. V. Marshall	*			†	*	
Airedale & Wharfedale College of Further Education, Business and General Studies Dept., Calverley Lane, Horsforth LS15 4RQ. (0532 581723) Contact: D. I. B. Hardy	*	*	*	*		
Anglian Regional Management Centre, Danbury Park, Danbury, Chelmsford, Essex CM3 4AT. (024 541 2141) Contact: Miss D. S. Vandome	*	*		*	*	*
Angus Technical College, Kephe Road, Arbroath DD1 3EA. (0241 72056) Contact: R. M. S. Tuck	*	*				
University of Aston, Management Centre, Nelson Building, Costa Green, Birmingham B4 7DU. (021 359 3011) Contact: J. E. Smith		*		†	†	
Banbridge Technical College, Castlewellan Road, Banbridge BT32 4AY (08206 22289) Contact: Denis Nightingale or Roy Monteith				†		
Basingstoke Technical College, Working Road, Basingstoke RG21 1TN. (0256 54141–2–3–4 or 0256 57491–2) Contact: T. H. Clark	*	*	*	*	*	
Special comments: Longer courses of 1 year's duration – one 1½-hour session per week – offered as independent modules from Management and Business Studies Course programme						
University of Bath, Claverton Down, Bath BA2 7AY. (0225 61244) Contact: Secretary and Registrar, N. K. Crawford					*	*
Blackburn College of Technology and Design, Dept. of Management and Business Studies, Feilden Street,	*	*	*	†	†	

Blackburn BB2 1LJ. (0254 55144) Contact: L. J. Smith
    Special comments: Dept of Management and Business
Studies is a leading member of the Lancastrian School
of Management

	Specific short courses	Prov. exist. courses	Longer courses	Adv. inf. guid. given	Consultancy resources	Research activity
Bolton Institute of Technology, Management and Business Studies Dept., Deane Road, Bolton BR3 5AB. (0204 28851 ext. 278) Contact: P. Taylor	*		†	*	*	
Bournemouth and Poole College of Further Education, North Road, Parkstone, Poole, Dorset BH14 0LS. (0202 747600) Contact: B. H. Sutton	†					
University of Birmingham, PO Box 363, Birmingham B15 2TT. (021 472 1301 ext. 3480) Contact: Mr Cavener				*		
Bradford College, Great Horton Road, Bradford, West Yorkshire BD7 1AY. (0274 34844) Contact: P. Noble	*	†	†	†	*	
University of Bristol, Industrial & Management Studies, Dept. of Extra-Mural Studies, 32 Tyndall's Park Road, Bristol BS8 1HR. (0272 24161 ext. 657) Contact: P. T. Gray, Senior Lecturer in Management Studies	*	*	*	†		*
Brunel University, Brunel Management Programme, Uxbridge, Middx. UB8 3PH. (0895 56461) Contact: Course Secretary		*			†	
Burton-upon-Trent Technical College, Lichfield Street, Burton-upon-Trent, Staffs DE14 3RL. (0233 45401) Contact: T. G. Edwards	*			*		
Cassio College, Langley Road, Watford, Herts WD1 3RH. (92 40311) Contact: K. Forrow, Senor Tutor, Retail Distribution and Services Dept.	*	*	*	*	*	*
The Polytechnic of Central London, School of Management Studies, 35 Marylebone Road, London NW1 5LS. (01 486 5811 ext. 225) Contact: Professor John Starworth, Director of Small Business Unit	*	*	*			*
Chelmer-Essex Institute of Higher Education, Victoria Road South, Chelmsford, Essex CM1 1LL. (0245 354491 ext. 260) ContactL R. W. McLary	*	*	*	*	*	†
Chichester College of Technology, Westgate Fields, Chichester, West Sussex PO19 1SB. (0243 786321) Contact: D. W. Evans, Head of Dept. of Management and Business Studies.	*	*	†	*	†	
City and East London College, The Business Opportunities Project, Dept. of Applied School Studies	*		*			

and General Education, Bunhill Row, London EC1Y 8LQ. (01 628 0864) Contact: Richard H. Chaloner

Special comments: This project is aimed at young people and is '21-hour' provision enabling students to attend for up to 3 days without loss of benefit. Students may join at any time subject to availability.

City of London Polytechnic, Short Course Unit, 84 Moorgate, London EC2M 6SQ. (01 283 1030 ext. 324) Contact: Rosemary Royds

The City University Business School, Post Experience Courses Unit, Frobishaw Crescent, Barbican London EC2Y 8HB. (01 920 0111) Contact: Mrs B. Henniker, Marketing Manager

Special comments: Advice, information and guidance provided by New Venture Ltd (contact A. J. B. Scholfield (01 488 1067 or 01 920 0111) and by Urbed (contact R. Lessem (01 379 7525 or 01 920 0111) in conjunction with City University Business School.

The College of Management, Dunchurch, Rugby, Warwicks. CV22 6QW. (0788 810656) Contact: customer liaison

Special comments: A commercial organisation owned by GEC with courses and seminars directed towards small businesses in fields of exporting, business control and development of the organisation.

College for the Distributive Trades, Dept. of Management Studies, 30 Leicester Square, London WC2H 7LE. (01 339 1547) Contact: Mr N. E. Richmond (after 6.9.82).

Cornwall Technical College, Faculty of Management, Business and Professional Studies, Redruth, Cornwall TR15 3RD. (0209 712911) Contact: W. A. N. Sully, Course Director, Small Business Unit

CoSIRA, Information Section, 141 Castle Street, Salisbury, Wilts. SP1 3TP. (0722 6255) Contact: Marilyn D. Jarvis

Coventry (Lanchester) Polytechnic, Business Management Centre, Faculty of Business, Priory Street, Coventry CV1 5FB. (0203 24166 ext. 7718) Contact: Roger Morris

Institution	Specific short courses	Prov. exist. courses	Longer courses	Adv. inf. guid. given	Consultancy resources	Research activity
City of London Polytechnic	*	*	*			†
The City University Business School	*	*		*	*	*
The College of Management			*			
College for the Distributive Trades	*	*		*	*	
Cornwall Technical College	*	*	*	*	*	
CoSIRA	*	*		*	*	*
Coventry (Lanchester) Polytechnic	*	*	*		*	

231

Special comments: Proposed provision of learning packages on a modular basis for people to use on an open learning basis.

Special comments: Enterprise North is based in Small Business Centre.

Special comments: New short course likely to start in autumn 1983.

University of Edinburgh, Dept. of Business Studies, William Robertson House, 50 George Square, Edinburgh EH8 9LY. (031 667 1011 ext. 6438) Contact: Ewan S. Gowrie, Lecturer in Marketing

Special comments: Staff teach on New Enterprise Programme or Scottish Business School.

English Multinational Business School, 3 Connaught Road, Eastbourne, East Sussex BN21 4PY. (0323 35073) Contact: P. A. Goodman

Special comments: Advice given on export documents and nationality profiles – the attitudes and likely cultural problems.

European School of Management Studies, 12 Merton Street, Oxford OX1 4NH. (0865 724545/6, 727150) Contact: K. Starting, UK Director

Special comments: 2 projects under consideration: a 'Small Business Club' for people already running their own business; a 'Small Business Development Unit', which as a component would have a European dimension.

Falkirk College of Technology, Grangemouth Road, Falkirk FK2 9AD. (0324 24981) Contact: Frank I. Suttie, Small Business Course Co-ordinator

Glenrothes and Buckhaven Technical College, Stenton Road, Glenrothes TY6 2RA (0592 772233 ext. 36) Contact: Ian Overs

Gloucestershire College of Arts and Technology, The Park Campus, The Park, Cheltenham, Glos. GL50 2RR. (0242 28021) Contact: Dorothy M. Straight

Grimsby College of Technology, Management and Business Studies Dept., Nuns Comer, Grimsby, South Humberside DN34 5BQ. (0472 79292) Contact: N. Burns (ext. 297).

Groby Community College, Ratby Road, Groby LE6 0FP. (0533 879921) Contact: Dr Graham Platts

Special comments: Investigate openings for self-employed people in the area, especially for small teams to perform 'handyman' jobs, repair services, etc.

Institution	Specific short courses	Prov. exist. courses	Longer courses	Adv. inf. guid. given	Consultancy resources	Research activity
University of Edinburgh			*	†	†	†
English Multinational Business School					†	
European School of Management Studies	*			*	*	
Falkirk College of Technology	*	*		*	*	
Glenrothes and Buckhaven Technical College	*	*	*	*	*	
Gloucestershire College of Arts and Technology	*	*		*	*	
Grimsby College of Technology	*	†	*	†	†	
Groby Community College						†

	Specific short courses	Prov. exist. courses	Longer courses	Adv. inf. guid. given	Consultancy resources	Research activity
Hackey Business Promotion Centre, 1–11 Hoxton Street, Hackney, London N1 6NL. (01 739 7606) Contact: Alan J. Gillison	*			*	*	*
Hackey College, Hackney College, Kelba House, 89–115 Mare Street, London E8. (01 985 8484) Contact: Mrs D. Trimnell	*					
Hall Green Technical College, Dept. of Business Studies and General Education, Cole Bank Road, Birmingham B28 8ES. (021 778 2311 ext. 244) Contact: Mr Ball, Short courses co-ordinator	*	*	†	†		
The Hatfield Polytechnic, School of Information Sciences, PO Box 109, College Lane, Hatfield, Herts. AL10 9AB. (30 68100 ext. 265) Contact: Mrs Kathy Levine Special comments: 3-day courses on Microcomputers in Business.		*	†	†	†	†
Henley – The Management College, Greenlands, Henley-on-Thames, Oxon. RG9 3AV. (049 166454) Contact: Graham Milborrow	*	†				
Highbury College of Technology, Dept. of Management Studies, Cosham, Portsmouth PO6 2SA. (0705 383131) Contact: D. B. Wright Special comments: Consultancy is a continued process through the Portsmouth Enterprise Scheme.	*	*		*	*	†
Highlands College, PO Box 142, St Saviour, Jersey, Channel Islands. (0534 71065) Contact: Mrs G. Renouf	*	*	*	*		
Hull College of Higher Education, Cottingham Road, Hull HU6 7RT. (0432 41451) Contact: H. Hird	*	*		*	*	*
Huntingdon Technical College, Small Business Service, California Road, Huntingdon, Cambs. (0480 52346) Contact: Mrs Sheila May	*		*	*	*	
Imperial College of Science and Technology, Dept. of Management Science, Exhibition Road, London SW7 2AZ. (01 589 5711) Contact: Dr N. Meade Special comments: Facilities for occasional students to join longer courses.	*	*		*	*	
Isle of Wight College of Arts and Technology, Newport, Isle of Wight PO80 5TA. (0983 526631 ext. 32 or 27) Contact: John Lucas	*	*		*	*	

	Specific short courses	Prov. exist. courses	Longer courses	Adv. inf. guid. given	Consultancy resources	Research activity
James Watt College, Finnart Street, Greenock PA16 8HF. (0475 24433) Contact: W. J. W. Stoddart	*	†		†		
Kendal College of Further Education, Milnthorpe Road, Kendal, Cumbria LA9 5AY (0539 24313) Contact: Malcolm Anderson		*	*	†	†	
Kidderminster College, Hoo Road, Kidderminster, Worcs. DY10 1LX. (0562 66311/2/3/4) Contact: John Moyle, Senior Lecturer Special comments: Small Firms Club.	*	*		†		
Kingston Regional Management Centre, Kingston Polytechnic, Kingston upon Thames, Surrey KT2 7LB (01 546 2181 ext 365) Contact: Dr C. R. Priestley.	*	*		*	*	*
Leicester Polytechnic, PO Box 143, Leicester LE1 9BH. (0533 551557) *See* Leicestershire Small Firms Centre	*	*		*	*	
Leicestershire Small Firms Centre, Business Advice Centre, 30 New Walk, Leicester LE1 6TF. (0533 554464)	*	*		*	*	
Lewes Technical College, Mountfield Road, Lewes, East Sussex BN7 2XH. (079 166121) Contact: J. D. Breeze		*	*	*	*	†
Lincoln College of Technology, Cathedral Street, Lincoln LN2 5HQ. (0522 30641) Contact: A. Lonsdale, Head of Dept. of Business and Management Studies	*	*		*	*	
Lisburn Technical College, 39 Castle Street, Lisburn, Co. Antrim, Northern Ireland BT27 4SU. (08462 4326) Contact: Noel Collen	†		†			
London Business School, Sussex Place, Regent's Park, London NW1 4SA. (01 262 5050) Contact: Peter Wilson	*			†	†	*
Loughborough University of Technology, Dept. of Management Studies, Loughborough, Leics. LE11 3TU. (05092 63171) Contact: Professor G. Gregory				*	*	*
Luton College of Higher Education, Faculty of Business Administration, Dept. of Management and Organisational Studies, Putteridge Bury, Hitchin Road, Luton, Beds. LU2 8LE. (0582 34111) Contact: R. J. Wooding, Small Business Unit	*	*	*	*	*	†
Manchester Polytechnic, Dept. of Management, Bracken House, Charles Street, Manchester M1 7DF. (061 2286171 ext. 2634) Contact: I. K. Debney	*	*		*	*	

	Specific short courses	Prov. exist. courses	Longer courses	Adv. inf. guid. given	Consultancy resources	Research activity
Mid-Gloucestershire Technical College, Stratford Road, Stroud, Glos. GL5 4AH. (04536 3424) Contact: Simon Cooper	*	*			†	
Mid-Kent College of Higher and Further Education, Oakwood Park, Maidstone, Kent, ME16 8AQ (0622 56531). Contact: Dr C. M. Fletcher	*	*	*	*	*	
Napier College Management Centre, 16 Spylaw Road, Edinburgh EH10. (031 447 7070) Contact: Lindsay D. S. Ramsay	†	†		†	†	†
Newbury College, Oxford Road, Newbury, Berks. RG13 1PQ. (0635 42324) Contact: Gerry Wood	*	*	*	*	*	
Northamptonshire Industrial Promotion Unit (INPUT), 65 The Avenue, Cliftonville, Northampton NN1 5BG. (0604 37401) Contact: A. G. McKay				*	*	*
North East Derbyshire College of Further Education, Dept. of Community Studies, Rectory Road, Clowne, Chesterfield, Derbys. S43 4BQ. (0246 810331) Contact: F. Marsh	†					
The Polytechnic of North London, Dept. of Management Studies, Marlborough Building, 383 Holloway Road, London N7. (01 607 2789) Contact: A. E. Lengyel	†	†	*	†		
North Nottinghamshire College of Further Education, Carlton Road, Worksop S81 7HP. (0909 473561) Contact: J. G. Wilson	*	*		*	*	*
North West Kent College of Technology, Miskin Road, Dartford DA1 2LU. (32 25471/3) Contact: Dr. T. Seddon	*	†	†	*	*	
Norwich City College of Further & Higher Education, Management Centre, Ivory House, All Saints Green, Norwich NR1 3NB. (0603 28619) Contact: Rad Spassitch	*	*	*	*	*	*
Nottingham University, Small Firms Unit, Dept. of Economics, University Park, Nottingham NG7 2RD. (0602 56101 ext. 3028) Contact: A. C. Atkin					*	
Portsmouth Polytechnic, Portsmouth Management Centre, 141 High Street, Portsmouth PO1 4HY. (0705 812611) Contact: J. F. Winterbottom	†	†	*	†		
Queen Margaret College, Cherwood Terrace,	*	†		*	*	†

Edinburgh EH12 8TS. (031 339 8111) Contacts: J. Blyth Wilson and R. Shirley

Redhill Technical College, Dept. of Business Studies and Languages, Gatton Point, Redhill, Surrey RH1 2JX. (91 64717–8) Contact: R. Fitton, Deputy Head of Dept. of Business Studies and Languages

Robert Gordon's Institute of Technology, School of Business Management Studies, Block 'C', Hilton Place, Aberdeen AB9 2TQ. (0224 42211) Contact: H. A. B. Harper

St David's University College, Lampeter, Dyfed SA48 7ED. (0570 422351 ext. 262) Contact: Dr D. A. Kirby

The St Helens College of Technology, School of Management Studies, Water Street, St Helens, Merseyside WA10 1PZ. (0744 33766 ext. 276) Contact: J. A. Wright, Principal Lecturer for Small Business Centre

University of Salford, Salford M5 4WT. (061 736 5843) Contact: B. Allison

Scottish Business School, Stock Exchange House, 69 St George's Place, Glasgow G2 1EU. (041 221 3124) Contact: Alastair Boyle

Scottish Development Agency, Small Business Division, 120 Bothwell Street, Glasgow G2 7JP. (041 248 2700) Contact: J. S. Fisher, Small Business Manager

The University of Sheffield, Crookesmoor Building, Sheffield S10 1FL. (0742 78555 ext. 6567) Contact: J. M. Norman

Slough College of Higher Education, Dept. of Business Studies and Law, Wellington Street, Slough SL1 1YG. (75 34585) Contact: J. D. Derbyshire

Southampton College of Higher Education, East Park Terrace, Southampton SO9 4WW. (0703 29381 ext. 55) Contact: Sue Williams

The University of Southampton, Dept. of Accounting and Management Economics, Southampton SO9 5NH. (0703 559122 ext. 2553) Contact: M. J. Page

Polytechnic of the South Bank, Borough Road, London SE1 0AA. (01 928 8989) Contact: Mary Mather

The South Downs College of Further Education,

Entry	Specific short courses	Prov. exist. courses	Longer courses	Adv. inf. guid. given	Consultancy resources	Research activity
Redhill Technical College	*					
Robert Gordon's Institute of Technology	*	*	*	*	*	*
St David's University College				*	*	*
The St Helens College of Technology	*	*	*	*	*	*
University of Salford	*	*		*	*	†
Scottish Business School	*		*	*	*	
Scottish Development Agency	*	*		*	*	
The University of Sheffield				*	*	
Slough College of Higher Education	*	*	†	†	†	
Southampton College of Higher Education	*		*	*	*	
The University of Southampton		*	†	†		*
Polytechnic of the South Bank		*		†	†	*
The South Downs College of Further Education	*	*				

	Specific short courses	Prov. exist. courses	Longer courses	Adv. inf. guid. given	Consultancy resources	Research activity
College Road, Purbrook Way, Havant, Hants. PO7 8AA. (070 14 57011) Contact: R. P. Jones						
South Warwickshire College of Further Education, The Willows North, Stratford-upon-Avon CV37 9QR. (0789 66245)	*	*	*			
South West London College, Centre for Higher Business Studies, Abbotswood Road, London SW16 1AN. (01 677 8141 ext. 60 or 66) Contact: P. J. Ayling Special comments: Proposed series of one-day courses covering topics of special interest, e.g. 'Self-presentation' 'Cash management' 'Costing your product', etc.	*	†	*	†	*	
South West Regional Management Centre, Coldharbour Lane, Frenchay, Bristol BS16 1QY. (0272 656261) Contact: John Howdle Special comments: Small business options offered on longer management courses.	*	*	*	†	†	*
States of Guernsey College of Further Education, Route des Coutanchez, St Peter Port, Guernsey, Channel Islands (0481 27121). Contact: M. J. Vance	*	*		*	*	*
University of Stirling, Stirling FK9 4LA. Scotland. (0786 3171) Contact: Professor Cannon or Hamilton ext. 2621) (general enquiries only); Dr R. Ball (ext. 2389) (consultancy enquiries only).	*			*	*	*
Strathclyde Business School, 130 Rotten Row, Glasgow G4 0GE. (041 552 7141) Contact: William Monahan	*	*	*	†	*	*
University of Surrey, Guildford GU2 5XH. (0483 71281) Contact: J. P. Moore						*
Telford Business Services Unit, Matthew Webb House, High Street, Dawley, Telford, Shropshire, TF4 2EX. (0952 503720) Contact: G. W. Benyon	*	*	*	*	*	*
Thames Polytechnic, School of Business Administration, Riverside House, Beresford Street, London SE18 6BH. (01 854 2030) Contact: Colin Barrow	*	*	*	*	*	*
Urban and Economic Department Ltd (URBED), 859 The Strand, London WC2R 0HP. (01 379 7525) Contact: Clare Gregory Special comments: Courses run in association with City University Business School.	*	*	*			*
Polytechnic of Wales, Pontypridd, Mid Glamorgan	*		*	*	*	

	Specific short courses	Prov. exist. courses	Longer courses	Adv. inf. guid. given	Consultancy resources	Research activity
CF37 1DL. (Pontypridd 405133) Contact: Eric Willis Special comments: Specialist advice for small business available in form of microcomputer systems.						
The University of Wales Institute of Science and Technology, Friary Building, 22 The Friary, Cardiff CF1 4JB. (0222 42522) Contact: Professor R. Mansfield				†	†	†
Walker Technical College, Management Centre, Oakengates Annex, Hartsbridge Road, Oakengates, Telford, Shropshire TF2 6BA. (0952 612505/6) Contact: G. H. Wallis	*	*	*	*	*	*
Waltham Forest College, Forest Road, London E17 4JB. (01 527 2311 ext. 225) Contact: T. H. Stead	*	*				
Wandsworth Business Resource Service, 140 Battersea Park Road, London SW11 4ND. (01 720 7053) Contact: K. G. Perks				*	*	
University of Warwick, Coventry CV4 7AL. (0203 24011) Contact: Academic Registrar	†				*	
Watford College, Dept. of Management Studies, Hempstead Road, Watford, Herts. WD1 3EZ. (92 41211–6) Contact: K. F. Young Special comments: No special facilities for new and small business, catered for with occasional special events to meet specific situations as they arise.					†	†
West Bromwich College of Commerce and Technology, Small Business Unit, Wood Green, Wednesbury, West Midlands. (021 569 4615) Contact: P. T. Wilson Special comments: About to offer a range of specialised course for small firms/units in (a) leisure and recreation; (b) The commercial sector. Run public/open meetings/exhibitions twice a year. Offer post experience certificate in Management Studies for small firms.	*	*	*	*		*
Western Education and Library Board Technical College, Omagh, Co. Tyrone, Northern Ireland BT79 7AH. (Omagh 45433/4) Contact: J. J. Devlin, Head of Dept., of Business and Secretarial Studies Special comments: Persons involved in small business can sit in on, and perhaps take end-of-year examinations in, the subjects in the full-time or day-				†		

release courses: Accounting, Business Law, Commerce, Finance.

	Specific short courses	Prov. exist. courses	Longer courses	Adv. inf. guid. given	Consultancy resources	Research activity
West Midlands Regional Management Centre, North Staffordshire Polytechnic, College Road, Stoke-on-Trent ST4 2DE. (0782 45531 and 412143) Contact: Mrs J. E. Sutherland	*	*		*	*	*
Worthing College of Technology, Broadwater Road, Worthing, West Sussex BN14 8HJ (0903 31445 and 64424) Contact: D. N. Haynes						
Yorkshire and Humberside Regional Management Centre, Management House, 32 Collegiate Crescent, Sheffield S10 2BJ. (0742 667051/683158) Contact: Dr P. Prynne, Manager, Small Business Development Unit	*	*	*		*	
Wigan College of Technology, The Management Centre, Ashfield House, Wigan Road, Standish WN6 0EQ. (0942 494911 ext. 2881289) Contact: J. M. Swift	*	*	*	*	*	*

DIY TRAINING

There are now a number of home study kits and books that can help you learn the basics of running a business, if for one reason or another it is not possible for you to attend a college-based course. Home study kits include:

The Business Club is a BBC–TV series, that shows how other small businesses have faced and dealt with a range of problems. This gives a 'live' insight into the proprietors' thoughts as they face each problem and put solutions into effect. For details of transmissions of the *The Business Club* series in 1983–4 write to Education Liaison,BBC, London W1A 1AA.

The Department of Trade plan to launch a Home Study Kit for small business, together with a back-up tutorial network. This may start up in 1983, and you should contact your nearest DT office. Section 1 has the addresses and telephone numbers.

Running Your Own Business, a correspondence course launched in 1982. The programme covers starting off; setting up your business; selling; money matters and staff. It costs £95.00, and further details are available from Golden Square Services Ltd, Freepost, Stone Cross, Sussex BN24 5BR.

The Small Business Kit (second edition, 1982), National Extension College, 18 Brooklands Avenue, Cambridge (0223 316644) Price £5.95. This takes the form of a series of check-lists and commentaries, taking you through the various stages of starting up a business.

Starting and Running a Business, A six-cassette system was launched in March 1982 by Lindum Management Services, Lindum House, 6a Harwick Grove, Nottingham N26 5HL. The cost is £26 for the series, and the subjects include:

Cassette 1, Getting Started the Right Way, The Business Idea/Information Sources;
Cassette 2, Marketing/Market Research, Sales, Advertising and Promotion;
Cassette 3, Finance/Financial Control/Taxation/Legislation/Insurance;
Cassette 4, Retailing Business/Factors Affecting Business;
Cassette 5, Manufacturing Business/Factors Affecting Business;
Cassette 6, Service Business/Factors Affecting Success.

Books and Journals This is a selection of useful reading that will give you a good appreciation of the subject. Other, more specialist reading is given in other sections.

The Complete Guide to Managing Your Business, available from Managing Your Own Business Ltd, Vine House, Portsmouth Road, Cobham, Surrey. (Cobham 7008) The price is £20.00. for the manual, and £24.50 for the up-dating service.

Creating Your Own Work, by Micheline Mason, published by Gresham Books, The Gresham Press, Old Woking, Surrey GU22 9LH; price £1.25.

Croner's Reference Book for the Self-Employed and Small Business and *Croner's Reference Book for Employers,* Croner Publications Ltd, 16–50 Coombe Road, New Malden, Surrey KT3 4QL. Price £16.40. and £19.20 respectively.

The Daily Telegraph Guide – Working for Yourself, published by Kogan Page Ltd, 120 Pentonville Road, London N1 9JN. (01 278 3393) Price, £4.95 including p&p (paperback).

Going Solo (1981 edition) by William Perry and Derek Jones. BBC Publications, price £1.95.

The Guardian Guide to Running a Small Business (second edition 1981) Edited by Clive Woodcock, published by Kogan Page Ltd, 120 Pentonville Road, London N1 9JN. (01 278 3393) £4.95 including p&p.

In Business is a monthly brief for managing your own business. It is edited by John Stanworth and published by Croner, 16–50 Coombe Road, New Malden, Surrey KT3 4QL. Subscription price is £30.00. per annum. It is a very good way to keep up to date on courses, tax changes, employment law and other changes.

London Business School Small Business Bibliography lists and indexes approximately 2,600 current books and articles on small business management. Published 1980, up-dated at 9-monthly intervals. Price £47.00.

Small Business Check-list Series (1982) is a series of check-lists covering the range of likely needs of anyone thinking of starting up on their own. Thames Polytechnic School of Business Administration, Riverside House, London SE18. (01 854 2030) Price £1.50.

The Practice of Entrepreneurship, by Meredith, Nelson & Neck, published in 1982 by the ILO, Ch-1211 Geneva 22, Switzerland. Price 20 Swiss Francs. The first third of the books 196 pages are devoted to analysing the personal characteristics of Entrepreneurs, and as such provide enlightening reading.

Starting up a New Business, a free publication (2nd Edition 1982) from the Small Firms Division of Department of Industry, Abell House, John Islip Street, London SW1 4LN.

THE NATIONAL TRAINING INDEX

The National Training Index, founded in 1968, provides comprehensive information and advice on business training courses, correspondence courses, training films and training packages. The Index provides

- Detailed information (dates, duration, location, cost and syllabus summaries) on more than 12,000 business courses in the UK;
- Comprehensive listings of in-company training schemes, course organisers, correspondence courses, training films and packages;
- A thorough but easy-to-use classification system which lists all courses and other training aids under 124 different subject headings;
- A quarterly information up-date and newsletter;
- A unique and confidential assessment of the quality of courses and training films listed in the Index, based on constant reports (more than 10,000 a year) sent in by members;
- The Lecturers' Index maintains cards on 9,600 lecturers who have spoken at training courses, external and internal, during the past decade. Advice can also be given to members planning to run their own in-company training programmes on suitable external speakers.
- The Conference Location Guide maintains files on hotels and conference centres with facilities for courses and conferences. Members who let them know the location, size and audiovisual requirements of any external course planned, will be supplied promptly with the names and address of suitable venues.

Contact Stuart Macnair, Manager, National Training Index, Prince's Street, London W1R 7RB. (01 629 7262)

Membership costs £350, which is probably the cost of sending one person on one of the shorter courses in the Index.

The service may be an attractive proposition to a small company which is sending people on external courses for the first time, or considering running its first internal business course.

GLOSSARY OF KEY BUSINESS TERMS

This glossary gives a meaning to words that have either been used in the book (unless explained in the context of their use), or that you are likely to meet early on in your business life.

Access time Time between asking a computer for information, and the information being available.

Account(s) Usually annual financial records of a business.

Accrual An accounting concept that insists that income and expenses for the accounting period be included, whether for cash or credit.

Added value The difference between sales revenue and material costs. *See also* Value added.

Annual report *See* Audit

Articles of association Usually a standard and comprehensive set of rules drawn up when a company is formed to show the purpose of the business.

Asset Something owned by the business which has a measurable cost.

Audit A process carried out by an accountant (auditor) on all companies each year, to check the accuracy of financial records. The auditor cannot be the company's own accountant. The result is the annual report.

Authorised capital The share capital of a company authorised by law. It does not have to be taken up. For example, a £1,000 company need only 'issue' 2 £1 shares. It can issue a further 998 £1 shares without recourse to law. After that sum it has to ask the permission of its shareholders.

Balance sheet A statement of assets owned by a business and the way in which they are financed taken from both liabilities and owner's equity. This report does not indicate the market value of the business.

Bankruptcy Imposed by a court when someone cannot meet his bills. The bankrupt's property is managed by a court-appointed trustee, who must use it to pay off the creditors as fairly as possible.

Basic Beginners' All-purpose Symbolic Instruction Code. The most popular microcomputer language.

BIT A binary digit, usually represented by 'O' or '1', or 'off' and 'on'.

Black economy Usually refers to businesses run by the self-employed who illegally avoid tax and National Insurance. There is therefore no official record, and they are collectively referred to as the Black Economy.

Blue chip In gambling, the high chips are usually blue. In business, this refers to high-status companies and their shares. They are usually large companies with a long successful trading history.

Bookkeeping The recording of all business transactions in 'journals' in order to provide data for accounting reports.

Book value Usually the figure at which an asset appears in the accounts. This is not necessarily the market value.

Break-even-point The volume of production at which revenues exactly match costs. After this point profit is made.

Byte A sequence of eight 'bits', used to represent one character of information. A letter, digit, symbol or punctuation mark.

Capital It has several meanings, but unprefixed it usually means all the assets of the business.

Cash The 'money' assets of a business, which include both cash in hand and cash at the bank.

Cash flow The difference between total cash coming in and going out of a business over a period of time.

Computer programme Instructions telling a computer to carry out a specific task.

Cost of goods sold The cost of goods actually sold in any period. It excludes the cost of the goods left unsold, and all overheads except manufacturing.

Current asset Assets normally realised in cash or used up in operations during the year. It includes such items as debtors and stock.

Current liability A liability due for payment in one trading period, usually a year.

Debenture Long-term loan with specific terms on interest, capital repayment and security.

Depreciation A way of measuring the cost of using a fixed asset. A set portion of the asset's cost is treated as an expense each period of its working life.

Direct costs Expenses, such as labour and materials, which vary 'directly' according to the number of items manufactured. Also called variable costs.

Diskette A flexible disc used to store computer data, often called a 'floppy disc'.

Entrepreneur Someone who is skilled at finding new products, making and marketing them, and arranging finance.

Equity The owner's claims against the business, sometimes called the shareholder's funds. This appears as a liability because it belongs to the shareholders and not to the business itself. It is represented by the share capital plus the cumulative retained profits over

245

the business's life. The reward for equity investment is usually a dividend paid on profits made.

Financial ratio The relationship between two money quantities, used to analyse business results.

Financial year A year's trading between dates agreed with the Inland Revenue. Not necessarily the fiscal year, which starts on 5 April.

Firmware Computer instructions stored in a read-only memory (*see* ROM).

Fixed assets Assets such as land, building, equipment, cars, etc., acquired for long-term use in the business and not for stock in trade. Initially recorded in the balance sheet at cost.

Fixed cost Expenses that do not vary directly with the number of items produced. For example, a car has certain fixed costs, such as tax and insurance, whether it is driven or not.

Floppy disc *See* Diskette.

Forecast A statement of what is likely to happen in the future, based on careful judgement and analysis.

Funds Financial resources, not necessarily cash.

Gearing The ratio of a business's borrowings to its equity. For example, 1:1 ratio would exist where a bank offered to match your investment £1 for £1.

Going concern Simply an accounting concept, it assumes in all financial reports that the business will continue to trade indefinitely into the future unless there is specific evidence to the contrary – i.e. it has declared an intention to liquidate. It is not an indication of the current state of health of the business.

Goodwill Value of the name, reputation or intangible assets of a business. It is recorded in the accounts only when it is purchased. Its nature makes it a contentious subject.

Gross Total before deductions. For example, gross profit is the difference between sales income and cost of goods sold. The selling and administrative expenses have yet to be deducted. Then it becomes the net profit.

Hardware The physical parts of a computer.

Income statement *See* Profit and loss account.

Insolvency A situation in which a person or business cannot meet the bills. Differs from bankruptcy, as the insolvent may have assets that can be realised to meet those bills.

Interface Electronic device that links computer hardware together. For example, a printer or VDU to the computer itself.

Know-how-agreement This is a promise to disclose information to a third party. If the disclosure is made for them to evaluate the usefulness of the know-how, the agreement is called a secrecy agreement. If the disclosure is made to allow commercial production, it is called a know-how licence.

Learning curve The improvement in the performance of a task as it is repeated and as more is learned about it.

Liabilities The claims against a business, such as loans and equity.

Liquidation It is the legal process of closing down a business and selling off its assets to meet outstanding debts.

Loan capital Finance lent to a business for a specific period of time at either a fixed or varied rate of interest. This interest must be paid irrespective of the performance of the business.

Marginal cost The extra cost incurred in making one more unit of production.

Marketing mix The combination of methods used by a business to market its products. For example, it can vary its price; the type and quantity of advertising; the distribution channels can be altered; finally, the product itself can either be enhanced or reduced in quality.

Market segment A group of buyers who can be identified as being especially interested in a particular variant of the product. For example, a cheap day return ticket for a train is a variant of a rail fare, especially attractive to people who do not have to get to their destination early perhaps to work.

Market share The ratio of a firm's sales of a product, in a specified market, during a period, to the total sales of that product in the same period in the same market.

Microcomputer A small computer using a microprocessor as its central processing unit.

Microfiche A sheet of photographic film on which a number of microcopy images have been recorded. You need a special viewer to look at the recorded information, which is very efficiently stored.

Microprocessor Electronic circuitry etched onto a silicon chip that can be used to manipulate information.

Modem A device that allows computers (and ancillary equipment) to communicate over telephone wires. The portable version is called an accoustic coupler.

Non-disclosure agreement An agreement which allows you to reveal secret commercial information – for example, about an invention – to a third party, and which prevents them from making use of that information without your agreement.

Opportunity cost The value of a course of action open to you but not taken. For example, keeping cash in an ordinary share account at a building society will attract about 2 per cent less interest than a five-year-term share at the same society. So the opportunity cost of choosing not to tie up your money is 2 per cent.

Overhead This is an expense which cannot be conveniently associated with a unit of production. Administration or selling expenses are usually overheads.

Overtrading Expanding sales and production without enough financial resources – in particular, working capital. The first signs are usually cashflow problems.

Piggy-backing Usually associated with firms that market other firms' products as well as their own, but the term can be used to describe any 'free riding' activity.

Profit The excess of sales revenue over sales cost and expenses during an accounting period. It does not necessarily mean an increase in cash.

Profit and loss account A statement of sales, costs, expenses and profit (or loss) over an accounting period monthly, quarterly or annually. Also known as the income statement.

RAM Random-access Memory is the space used for storing computer data as programs. It can be changed as new programs or data are called up.

Reserves The name given to the accumulated and undistributed profits of the business. They belong to the ordinary shareholders. They are not necessarily available in cash, but are usually tied up in other business assets.

Revenue Usually from sales. Revenue is recognised in accounting terms when goods have been dispatched (or services rendered) and the invoice sent. This means that revenue pounds are not necessarily cash pounds. A source of much confusion and frequent cash-flow problems.

ROM Read-only memory.

Schedule 'D' Cases I and II are the Inland Revenue rules that govern tax allowances for self-employed people.

Schedule 'E' Allowances for employed people.

Seasonality A regular event, usually one that causes sales to increase or decrease in an annual cycle. For example, the weather caused by the seasons or events associated with the seasons: Christmas, spring sales, summer holidays, etc.

Secured creditor Someone lending money to a business whose debt is secured by linking a default in its repayment to a fixed asset, such as a freehold building.

Share capital The capital of the business subscribed for by the owners or shareholders (*see* Equity).

Software A computer term usually associated with programs and related documentation.

Strategy A general method of policy for achieving specified objectives. It describes the essential resources and their amounts, which are to be committed to achieving those objectives (*see* Tactics).

Synergy A co-operative or combined activity which is more effective or valuable than the sum of their independent activities.

Tactics The method by which resources allocated to a strategic objective are used.

True and fair An accounting concept that states that the business financial reports have been prepared using generally accepted accounting principles.

Turn key Usually refers to a client-commissioned system, accepted only when you can 'turn on a key' and are satisfied with the results, or output.

Value In accounting it has several meanings. For example, the 'value' of a fixed asset is its cost less its cumulative depreciation. A current asset, such as stock, is usually valued at cost or market value, whichever is the lower.

Value added The difference between sales revenue that a firm gets from selling its products (or services), and the cost to it of the materials used in making those products.

Variable cost *See* Direct cost.

Variance The difference between actual performance and the forecast (or budget or standard).

Working capital Current assets less current liabilities, which represents the capital used in the day-to-day running of the business.

Working life The economically useful life of a fixed asset. Not necessarily its whole life. For example, technological development may render it obsolete very quickly.

Work in progress Goods in the process of being produced, which are valued at the lower of manufacturing costs or market value.

GAZETEER

Geographic listing of local organisations referred to in the text.

Location and Page Reference	Small Firms Centre	CoSira	Action Resource Centre	BSC (Industry) Centre	Enterprise Agency	Enterprise Zone	Co-operative Agency	Science Park	Micro-Centre	Business Library	Small Business Courses
Aberdeen, 237											■
Aldershot, 21					■						
Andover, 232											■
Angus, 229											■
Ashford, 21					■						
Banbridge, 229											■
Bangor, 72							■				
Barnsley, 16, 21		■			■						
Barnstaple, 21					■						
Basingstoke, 22, 229					■						■
Bath, 22, 229					■						■
Bedford, 14, 27, 232		■			■						■
Belfast, 13, 57, 115	■	■				■			■		
Bingham, 15		■									
Birkenhead, 22					■						
Birmingham, 13, 17, 22, 23, 100, 115, 139, 229, 230, 234	■		■		■			■	■	■	
Blackburn, 229											■
Bolton, 230											■
Bournemouth, 230											■
Bradford, 72, 230							■				
Braintree, 15, 23		■			■						
Bridgewater, 23					■						
Bristol, 13, 23, 24, 72, 73, 115, 139, 230, 238	■				■		■		■	■	■
Broxbourne, 232											■
Cambourne, 26					■						
Cambridge, 13, 14, 101, 139	■	■							■	■	

Location and Page Reference	Small Firms Centre	CoSira	Action Resource Centre	BSC (Industry) Centre	Enterprise Agency	Enterprise Zone	Co-operative Agency	Science Park	Micro-Centre	Business Library	Small Business Courses
Cardiff, 13, 18, 73, 137, 239	■			■			■			■	■
Carrickfergus, 26					■						
Chatham, 24					■						
Chelmsford, 229, 230											■
Cheltenham, 139, 233										■	■
Chesterfield, 236											■
Chichester, 230											■
Cleveland, 18, 29, 72				■	■		■				
Clydebank, 57						■					
Clwyd, 18				■							
Consett, 25					■						
Corby, 18, 25, 57				■	■		■				
Coventry, 26, 231					■						■
Darlington, 15, 27			■		■						
Dartford, 236											■
Derby, 15			■								
Doncaster, 232											■
Dorchester, 15			■								
Dudley, 57, 232						■					■
Dundee, 232											■
Eastbourne, 233											■
Edinburgh, 13, 17, 104, 233, 236, 237	■	■	■					■			■
Exeter, 15, 72, 139		■						■		■	
Falkirk, 233											■
Gateshead, 57, 104						■		■			
Glasgow, 13, 17, 18, 28, 73, 115, 139, 237, 238	■		■	■	■		■		■	■	■
Glenrothes, 233											■
Goole, 15		■									
Gravesend, 28						■					
Greenock, 235											■
Grimsby, 233											■
Groby, 233											■
Guildford, 15, 238		■									
Gwent, 16, 18, 72			■	■			■				
Halifax, 28					■						
Harlow, 28					■						
Harrogate, 17			■								
Hartlepool, 57						■					
Hatfield, 234											■

Location and Page Reference	Small Firms Centre	CoSira	Action Resource Centre	BSC (Industry) Centre	Enterprise Agency	Enterprise Zone	Co-operative Agency	Science Park	Micro-Centre	Business Library	Small Business Courses
Henley-on-Thames, 234											■
Honiton, 27					■						
Horsforth, 229											■
Huddersfield, 72							■				
Hull, 72, 101, 234							■	■			■
Huntingdon, 234											■
Hyde, 17			■								
Ipswich, 15, 139		■								■	
Jersey, 234											■
Kendall, 235											■
Kidderminster, 235											■
Kilburnie, 18				■							
Lampeter, 237											■
Lancaster, 30					■						
Leeds, 13, 30, 73, 140	■				■		■			■	
Leicester, 16, 30, 31, 36, 255			■		■						■
Lewes, 15, 235		■									■
Lincoln, 235											■
Lisburn, 235											■
Liverpool, 13, 16, 57, 72, 102, 115, 140	■		■		■		■	■	■	■	
Livingston, 232											■
Loughborough, 235											■
London, 13, 16, 17, 18, 32, 33, 34, 57, 71, 72, 73, 103, 105, 115, 140, 229–240	■		■	■	■	■	■	■	■	■	■
Luton, 34, 140, 235					■					■	■
Lowestoft, 34					■						
Maidstone, 15, 35, 236		■			■						■
Malvern, 15		■									
Manchester, 13, 35, 36, 73, 103, 115, 140, 235	■				■		■	■	■	■	■
Middlesborough, 36					■						
Milton Keynes, 72							■				
Motherwell, 18				■							
Morpeth, 15		■									
Newbury, 236											■
Newcastle-upon-Tyne, 13, 16, 57, 73, 115, 140	■		■				■		■	■	
Newport, I.O.W., 15, 29, 234		■			■						■

Location and Page Reference	Small Firms Centre	CoSira	Action Resource Centre	BSC (Industry) Centre	Enterprise Agency	Enterprise Zone	Co-operative Agency	Science Park	Micro-Centre	Business Library	Small Business Courses
Newton, Powys, 232											■
Northampton, 15,37,236		■			■						■
Northwich, 37					■						
Norwich, 15, 38, 236		■			■						■
Nottingham, 13, 16, 138, 140, 236	■		■		■					■	■
Omagh, 239					■						■
Oxford, 38, 140, 233					■					■	■
Par, 25					■						
Penrith,14		■									
Peterborough, 39					■						
Petersfield, 140										■	
Plymouth, 39					■						
Pontypridd, 13, 238	■	■									■
Poole, 232											■
Porstmouth, 39, 234, 236					■						■
Preston, 15		■									
Reading, 40					■						
Redhill, 237											■
Redruth, 231											■
Rochdale, 40					■						
Rossendale, 29					■						
Rugby, 231											■
Runcorn, 40					■						■
St. Helens, 41, 237					■						■
St. Petersport, 238											■
Salford, 102, 237								■			■
Salisbury, 16, 231		■									■
Scunthorpe, 18, 40				■	■						
Sheffield, 16, 73, 237, 240			■		■		■				■
Sittingbourne, 41					■						
Sleaford, 15		■									
Slough, 237											■
Southampton, 41, 140, 237					■					■	■
Southport, 41					■						
Stafford, 42, 230					■						■
Standish, 240											■
Stirling, 42, 238					■						■
Stoke-on-Trent, 42, 240					■						■
Stratford-upon-Avon, 238											■
Stroud, 236											■

Location and Page Reference	Small Firms Centre	CoSira	Action Resource Centre	BSC (Industry) Centre	Enterprise Agency	Enterprise Zone	Co-operative Agency	Science Park	Micro-Centre	Business Library	Small Business Courses
Sunderland, 43					■						
Swansea, 57, 73						■	■				
Swindon, 43					■						
Taunton, 15, 102	■							■			
Telford, 43, 73, 238, 239					■		■				■
Thornaby-on-Tees, 37					■						
Trafford Park, 57							■				
Truro, 14	■										
Uxbridge, 101, 230								■			■
Wakefield, 44, 57					■	■					
Wallasley, 105								■			
Wallingford, 15	■										
Walsall, 44					■						
Warwick, 16, 105, 143, 239	■							■		■	■
Watford, 230, 239											■
Warrington, 73, 101							■	■			
Washington, 44					■						
Wednesbury, 239											■
Wellington, Salop, 14		■									
Winchester, 15		■									
Wolverhampton, 45					■						
Worcester, 45					■						
Workington, 18, 45				■	■						
Worksop, 236											■
Worthing, 240											■